# THE HUMAN FACE OF INDUSTRIAL CONFLICT IN POST-WAR JAPAN

Japanese Studies
General Editor: Yoshio Sugimoto

Images of Japanese Society: *Ross E. Mouer and Yoshio Sugimoto*
An Intellectual History of Wartime Japan:
*Shunsuke Tsurumi*
A Cultural History of Post-war Japan:
*Shunsuke Tsurumi*
Beyond Computopia: *Tessa Morris-Suzuki*
Constructs for Understanding Japan:
*Yoshio Sugimoto and Ross E. Mouer*
Japanese Models of Conflict Resolution:
*S. N. Eisenstadt and Eyal Ben-Ari*
Changing Japanese Suburbia: *Eyal Ben-Ari*
The Rise of the Japanese Corporate System:
*Koji Matsumoto*
Science, Technology and Society in Post-war Japan:
*Shigeru Nakayama*
Group Psychology of the Japanese in Wartime:
*Toshio Iritani*
Enterprise Unionism in Japan:
*Hirosuke Kawanishi*
Social Psychology of Modern Japan:
*Munesuke Mita*
The Origin of Ethnography in Japan:
*Minoru Kawada*
Social Stratification in Contemporary Japan:
*Kenji Kosaka*
Sociology and Society of Japan:
*Nozomu Kawamura*
Diversity in Japanese Culture and Language:
*John C. Maher and Gaynor Macdonald*
Difference in Modernity: Social Theory and Contemporary Japanese
Society: *John Clammer*
Kanji Politics: *Nanette Gottlieb*
Migrant Workers in Japan: *Hiroshi Komai*
Japanese Encounters with Postmodernity: *Johann P. Arnason and Yoshio Sugimoto*
Hibakusha Cinema: Hiroshima, Nagasaki and the Nuclear Image in Japanese Film:
*Mick Broderick*
Foreign Workers and Law Enforcement in Japan: *Wolfgang Herbert*
Social Theory and Japanese Experience: *Joham P. Arnason*
The Human Face of Industrial Conflict in Post-war Japan:
*Hirosuke Kawanishi*

# THE HUMAN FACE OF INDUSTRIAL CONFLICT IN POST-WAR JAPAN

edited by

Hirosuke Kawanishi

Routledge
Taylor & Francis Group
LONDON AND NEW YORK

First published 1999 by Kegan Paul International

2 Park Square, Milton Park, Abingdon, Oxon OX14 4RN
711 Third Avenue, New York, NY 10017, USA

*Routledge is an imprint of the Taylor & Francis Group, an informa business*

First issued in paperback 2016



ISBN 978-0-7103-0563-3 (hbk)
ISBN 978-1-138-97209-4 (pbk)

**British Library Cataloguing in Publication Data**

The human face of industrial conflict in post-war Japan.–
(Japanese studies series)
1. Labor disputes - Japan - History - 20th century
2. Industrial relations - Japan History - 20th century
I. Kawanishi, Hirosuke, 1942–
331.8'92952'09045

**Library of Congress Cataloging-in-Publication Data**

Sengo Nihon no sōgi to ningen. English
The human face of industrial conflict in post-war Japan/edited by Hirosuke Kawanishi.
p. 287 cm. 23.4 (Japanese studies)
Includes bibliographical references and index.
ISBN (invalid) 0–7103–0563–X (alk. paper)
1. Labor disputes—Japan—History—Case studies. 2. Trade-unions—Japan—History. I. Kawanishi, Hirosuke, 1942– II. Title.
III. Series.
HD5427.A6S4413 1997
331.892'952——dc21 97–25684
CIP

# Contents

# Preface

This volume first appeared in Japanese as *Sengo Nihon no Sōgi to Ningen* (1986). Published by Nihon Hyōronsha in Tokyo it included the reflections of nine union leaders who had taken their unions through some of Japan's most important post-war industrial disputes. In 1983 each of the leaders came to my student seminar at Chiba University near Tokyo.

The talks were recorded and then transcribed with two aims in mind. One was to provide information on the events which led to the formation of Japan's industrial relations as we know them today. During the 1950s and early 1960s a number of Japan's key labour unions lost a succession of campaigns to establish and to defend what they saw as the natural rights of their members. Many of the unions experienced schisms, and the end result was a fundamental shift in the balance of power between labour and management.

The second aim was to provide a public record of the processes through which the struggles were waged. In recent years it has been popular for writers to glorify the achievements of Japanese-style management without any reference to the way in which the present system of industrial relations was forged out of struggles in the workplace. The leaders who spoke at my seminars provided a very important corrective to the glossy picture which is often painted of work relations in Japan's large firms.

This volume may be read as a companion to the other volume I have in Kegan Paul International's Japanese Studies Series, *Enterprise Unionism in Japan* (translated by Ross Mouer and published in 1992). Whereas the earlier volume focused on a number of case studies highlighting the way enterprise unions actually functioned in many Japanese firms in the 1970s and early 1980s, this volume provides an historical account of how unionism evolved in Japan during the 1950s and 1960s.

Following Japan's defeat in the Second World War in 1945, it was common to see work relations in Japan as representing a set of interpersonal interactions which had been directly transplanted from Japan's feudal past. Those interactions were viewed critically along with the Emperor system and the militarism which had taken Japan into the war. The emphasis between 1945 and 1970 was on fundamentally altering those institutions and on democratising Japanese society.

In the 1970s Japan came to be seen as one of the advanced capitalist economies. As other capitalist societies came to experience prolonged stagnation following the oil shocks of the 1970s, Japan seemed to sail through the storms without too much trauma. It emerged more competitive than ever, and its industrial relations were lavishly praised for providing the flexibility necessary for firms to adjust to the new cost structures. Much of that flexibility was attributed to the systems of lifetime employment, to seniority wage structures and to enterprise unionism. These were seen as providing the institutional basis for cooperative or collaborative relations between management and workers in Japan.

In the 1980s these practices came to be widely regarded as a model for steering economic reform both in the highly advanced capitalist economies and in the developing world. Although some doubts began to appear in the early 1990s, Japan continues to command the most competitive economy in the world; the value of the yen has continued to rise and Japan now records the highest levels of per capita income. In this context, the same basic features of Japanese-style management have come to be reformulated in various ways. Today Japanese-style management is synonymous with consensual and responsive work practices but with high levels of corporate identity in the literature on industrial relations and management.

Most discussions of the origins of Japanese-style management focus either on cultural factors or on internal labour markets. Paternalism is often seen as linking Japanese notions of the family to an ingrained Japanese orientation to working in groups. On the other hand, those who emphasise the importance of internal labour markets see the formation of Japan's industrial work practices as a more universal trend characterising advanced capitalism. They point to tenured employment, career structures and a company-oriented form of business unionism.

In opposition to those types of explanations, I have emphasised the importance of understanding the structural contradictions which define the relationship between workers and their employers. While accepting the various influences which culture may have on how work is carried out and on how employees may think about those processes, I have taken the position that the basic determinant of work relations will be the balance of power between organised labour and management. This approach rests first on the assumption that labour and management have different interests to serve, and that a basic contradiction is built into their relationship. From this perspective, systems of industrial relations develop as means of managing that contradiction. Each country's system emerges as various schemes are introduced over time to accommodate the interests of management and labour. Each country's industrial relations emerge out of its historical, cultural and social conditions, but are driven by the power relations between labour and management. Accordingly, industrial relations will be the outcome of the ways in which labour and management go about resolving the contradictions which exist between them. Today's solutions become tomorrow's relations. In putting forward a theory of structural contradictions, attention is focused on (a) the structural contradictions themselves, (b) the power relations at the time resolutions occur and (c) the dynamic of constant change.

The major shortcoming of those models – whether they be culturalist models or schema based on the notion of internal labour markets – is that they often seek generalisations which downplay important particularities of the historical context. However, conflict sustains change. As the historical setting and the power relations change, so too do Japan's industrial relations. Without such a perspective it is difficult to get away from the static models which have in the past characterised discussions of industrial relations in Japan. The basic logic for viewing Japan's industrial relations in this manner can be found in the chapters of this book. The testimonies of the labour leaders who have contributed to this volume help us to fill in the history of how Japan's present system of industrial relations came to be. They provide a compelling account of an important chapter in Japan's history.

In the years immediately after the war, the union movement in Japan was quite strong, and unions generally had the upper hand when dealing with management. Their power was checked only by the occupation authorities. They allowed the police to clamp down on production control. They also prohibited the 1 February general strike at the eleventh hour. It was a period when many arrangements favourable to socialist labour – such as the *Densan-gata* wage system – were institutionalised. As the world entered the Cold War, however, the government began to cooperate with the occupation authorities to bolster the hand of management. Management soon launched a powerful counter-offensive and in a number of ways encouraged schisms in the union movement. Management was successful in its tactics, and it was soon taking the initiative in establishing cooperative relations with conservative factions in the union movement – the 'number two unions'. It was such cooperation which made the period of high economic growth possible. Government and management were able to co-opt the number two unions and thereby achieve a kind of nationalism built around notions which focused attention on maximising the size of 'the pie' (i.e. the national economy). The essays in this volume help to clarify the processes by which the restructuring took place.

The labour leaders seminar was also established as a means of stimulating the students' interest in the history of Japan's industrial relations. The gradual decline of student interest in such critical history has been conspicuous in Japan. Moreover, that decline cannot be blamed on the students alone. Accordingly, it is necessary for the universities and their academic staff to take the lead in developing new approaches to teaching. With such thoughts in mind, I endeavoured in 1983 to establish a formally approved series of lectures. The plan was to shape the lectures around a fundamental and basic social issue which was closely tied to the post-war history of Japan. Students in the 1980s had little interest in labour issues and in the post-war history of Japan.

Students coming to my seminar in 1983 had been born in the mid-1960s. They grew up in an affluent Japan. Many grew up thinking Japan had always been a wealthy country. Few had any sense of history or knowledge about how that affluence had been produced. Most university students in the mid-1980s had been absorbed in passing exams until they were finally able to graduate from high school and to enter a university. The students come from a generation which celebrated the present with scant regard for the past.

Unfortunately students have little interest in unions. At best unions exist in a world beyond that of the students; few have any direct experience of unions and the labour movement. At worst, unions are seen as a negative force within society. This probably reflects a general decline in the public image of the role of unions in Japanese society. Judged simply from the viewpoint of the students in my seminar, it would seem that these negative images have in part been created by the media's campaign of sensationalist speculation about the extent to which a few unions had been responsible for the financial difficulties of the Japan National Railways and the national debt.

Particularly disturbing is the conspicuous decline in the number of students who see anything positive in the union movement. I think that many involved in educating our youth would confirm that most students now see the entire union movement in a negative light. For those who feel that unions have an important role to play in maintaining Japan's post-war democracy, the marginalisation of the union movement is indeed a serious concern and a source of sadness. With this background in mind, I invited the labour leaders to my seminar in 1983. By allowing students to hear directly the accounts of those involved in some of Japan's most influential post-war disputes, I sought to encourage them to develop a critical perspective for knowing their own society.

When one begins to think about restructuring the way in which education is delivered by Japanese universities, one must begin by carefully considering the views of the students themselves. It is unlikely that students will respond much to traditional lecturing. For this reason I thought I would invite a number of guest speakers. I believed that students could be stimulated to learn more by meeting a number of historical figures whom they would normally know only indirectly through the literature on Japan's post-war history. The talks of the unionists were supplemented by various audio-visual aids – documentary films, slides, photographs and various recordings. It was felt that the impact of such audio-visual material on the younger generations, which had been raised on the electronic media, would be considerable. Finally, the seminar presentations were followed by a social function which allowed students the opportunity to interact on a one-to-one basis with each of the guest speakers. The goal was to allow students to take part in creating their own history. Related to this were two other aims. One was the desire to open the university to the public. The other was to record for posterity an official oral history of these leaders who were well into their seventies by the mid-1980s. Unless someone recorded their views, they would soon be lost forever.

The accounts found in this volume focus on the period from the end of the war until about 1960. The students coming to universities in the mid-1980s had all been born after 1960; they were born during the period of high economic growth and had not experienced the turbulent years which prepared the way for that growth. Most scholars writing about the post-war period would agree that those were the years during which 'Japanese-style management' as we know it today developed. It was also a period in which nearly all of the major popular disturbances were disputes between labour and management.

Once the idea had jelled, there was the difficult task of deciding who to invite to the seminar. The first step was to list the major disputes, and then to locate the key actors. In the process, it soon became obvious that nearly all those on management's side had died. This reflected the fact that most had already been in their fifties or sixties when the disputes occurred. On the other side of these disputes were the labour leaders. Nearly 70 per cent of the labour leaders in the key disputes had also passed on. Accordingly, only a limited number of labour leaders could be invited to participate in this project. Working against the clock, we often wondered whether the project would be viable.

The selection of participants was frustrated by the small number of labour unions from which informants could be drawn. Already accepting that Japan's labour leaders would present us with a view quite different from that of their management counterparts, we were also sensitive to the fact that Japan's post-war labour movement has been characterised by a number of ideological cleavages. This meant that great care was needed to ensure that the final selection resulted in an ideologically balanced sample of union views. The result was that we had to agonise over each invitation.

The approach that was adopted for this seminar was of inviting a labour leader along with a scholar with expertise in the field. Given the ideological sensibilities of the labour leaders, considerable care was also required in the selection of the academic researchers. The aim was to invite a scholar who could provide the background necessary for the students to understand the speaker whilst also stimulating the speaker to 'open up'. To be successful, the scholars would also need to be beyond reproach in the academic community: otherwise, the unionists' accounts would be much less convincing as historical evidence.

The result was a spectacular line-up of expertise and experience. Any expression of appreciation to those who participated would be inadequate. In addition to their time and their knowledge, the various guests imparted their enthusiasm and their sense of purpose to the students who attended my seminar that year.

Given the limitations of space allowed by a publication of this sort, I have had to leave out the questions and answers and other discussion initiated by the students. I have also not been able to append the interpretive essays later prepared by the students. The result has been a volume which concentrates more on providing a record of views useful to the research community interested in the post-war history of Japan.

The original volume was fortunate to have received good reviews both in a large number of newspapers and popular magazines and in the academic journals. As a result the volume was able to enjoy more than one printing. Shortly after its publication in Japanese a German translation appeared from a group of students organised for the purpose by Professor Wolfgang Seifert, University of Heidelberg (H. Kawanishi, *Japan in Umbruch*, Köln, Bund-Verlag, 1989). The good reviews given the volume in German motivated one of the students, Mr Christoph Törring, to translate the volume into English. It can thus be read as a companion volume with my *Enterprise Unionism in Japan* (translated by Ross Mouer) published by Kegan Paul International in 1992. In addition to Mr Törring I must thank Professor Ross Mouer (currently Head of the Department of Japanese Studies at Monash University in Australia) and others who have helped in preparing the final version of the English-language text. Without the cooperation of these individuals this volume would not have been possible.

Hirosuke Kawanishi

# 1 Theoretical and Historical Introduction

*Hirosuke Kawanishi*

## What are Labour Disputes?

Labour disputes are a vehicle of social change within an industrialised society or the microcosm of the enterprise. Through them contradictions of capital–labour relations (industrial relations) are brought to light by the independent action of those who established these relations, and the social interrelationship is suddenly transformed.

Labour disputes thus are a result of pre-existing social interrelationships and, as a recurring phenomenon in the history of social relations, serve as a means of solving social contradictions and in turn shape new social interrelationships. Consequently, labour disputes are nothing extraordinary, but are normal and recurring events within the history of capital–labour relations. As the emotions and the behaviour of both sides in a conflict cannot always be confined to institutionalised channels, labour disputes are inevitable as a non-institutionalised way of solving contradictions.

In order to grasp the characteristic features of each labour dispute, its principal actors, points of conflict, course of events, outcome and other factors must be analysed. Because unions are by no means the only party initiating industrial disputes, it is very important to look at the actors involved. The term 'labour disputes' covers measures taken by both sides involved in capital–labour relations (or the relations between employers and employees); on the part of management these include singling out individuals for dismissal, lock-outs, refusing to bargain collectively with a union and so forth, while on the part of the workers they include strikes, sabotage, insubordination, sit-ins, etc. The analysis of labour disputes therefore must begin by asking who are those engaged in disputative action and what are their objectives. For reasons of space, we confine ourselves to observing the actors and the results.

Classifying the labour disputes which have occurred in Japan since 1945 according to their initiators and in terms of the general objectives of those initiators, the following four types of labour disputes can be identified:

Type 1 In a situation where no side in capital–labour relations has an effective leadership, the employees (unions, struggle committees and other workers' organisations) come up with demands for higher wages or try to restrict a previously recognised right of management (labour-offensive type).

Type 2 In another type of conflict, management resorts to aggressive measures such as massive lay-offs (management-offensive type).

Type 3 In an attempt to regain its prerogatives previously lost to the union, management tries to enforce the dismissal of union leaders (management counter-offensive type).

Type 4 Growing worker dissatisfaction with management domination of capital–labour relations leads to a labour dispute (labour counter-offensive type).

The general tendency of post-war labour disputes appears to be one in which, with few exceptions, it was management which took the initiative and succeeded in achieving its objectives. Classifying disputes according to the typology above, the main type appears to have been the management counter-offensive. It becomes clear that in the majority of labour conflicts in post-war Japan, management strategies for solving existing contradictions prevailed.

Analysis of post-war industrial disputes further reveals that conflicts of the labour-offensive and the management-offensive type occurred only in the period from 1945 until the end of 1946; thereafter, the management counter-offensive type was dominant, and in all cases management won a decisive victory. A further characteristic of this type of dispute was that it nearly always led to a split within the union, i.e. to the establishment of a second union within the company. Only since 1970 have some disputes been of the labour counter-offensive type.

Table 1 Twenty-three major labour disputes in the post-war period by outcome and by the locus of the initiative: 1945–80

| Party instigating the dispute | Aim | Outcome | |
|---|---|---|---|
| | | Won by the labour union | Won by management |
| The labour union | Attack | first Yomiuri dispute (SK) (1945)<br>Tōshiba dispute (SK) (1946)<br>October struggle in Electric Power (Densan) (SK) (1946) | 1 February general strike (SK) (1947) |
| | Counter-attack | Ōmi Kenshi dispute (Z) (1954)<br>Anti-rationalisation struggle in the JNR (S) (1971)<br>Japan Seamen's Union struggle for human dignity (D) (1972)<br>Saseho Shipbuilding dispute (D) (1979–80) | Strike for the Right to Strike (S) (1975) by workers in the public sector |
| | Attack | Struggle against firings in the JNR (SK) (1946)<br>Seaman's struggle against firings (SK) (1946) | |
| Management | | | *Second Yomiuri dispute (SK) (1946)<br>*Tōhō dispute (SK) (1948)<br>*Tōshiba dispute (SK) (1949)<br>*dispute over personnel adjustments in the JNR (SK) (1949)<br>*Coal (Tanrō)/Electric Power dispute (Densan) (S) (1952) |
| | Counter-attack | *Nissan dispute (S) (1953)<br>Amagasaki Steel dispute (S) (1954) | Nihon Seikō Muroran dispute (S) (1954)<br>*JNR Niigata dispute (S) (1957)<br>Steel Workers' Federation dispute (S) (1957)<br>*Mitsui Miike Mine dispute (S) (1960)<br>*Zeneraru Oil Refinery dispute (C) (1970) |

*Notes*: * = dispute resulting in a split in the union
SK = Sanbetsu Kaigi
S = Sōhyō
Z = Zenrō Kaigi
D = Dōmei
C = Chūritsu Rōren
JNR = Japan National Railways

Source: Hirosuke Kawanishi, *Enterprise Unionism in Japan*, London, Kegan Paul International, 1992, pp. 69–70.

Table 2 Five periods of disputation in post-war Japan

| Period (years) | Major balances of power | Major events | Major industrial disputes | Type of industrial relations |
|---|---|---|---|---|
| I<br>1945–7 | (1) GHQ<br>unions >> mgmt<br>(2) Sanbetsu Kaigi >> Sōdōmei | End of the war 15.8.45<br>Sōdōmei established 1.8.46<br>Sanbetsu Kaigi established 19.8.46<br>General strike planned for 1 February 1947 | Yomiuri 1945–6<br>Tōshiba 1945–6<br>Seamen, JNR, Densan (electric power workers) | Consolidation of union-led industrial relations |
| 1947–50 | (1) GHQ<br>unions > mgmt<br>(2) Sanbetsu Kaigi > Sōdōmei + Sanbetsu Mindō | | *Tōhō 1948<br>*Tōshiba 1949<br>*JNR 1948 | |
| II<br>1950–5 | (1) Government<br>unions > mgmt<br>(2) Sōhyō >> Sōdōmei + Zenrō Kaigi | Beginning of Korean War 25.6.50<br>Sōhyō formed 11.7.50<br>Sōdōmei reconstituted 1.6.51<br>San Francisco Peace Treaty 8.9.52<br>Red purge 24.7.50<br>Zenrō Kaigi established 22.4.54 | Tanrō, *Densan 1952<br>*Nissan 1953, Tekkorōren 1953–6<br>Amagasaki Steel 1954 Ōmi<br>Ōmi Kenshi 1954<br>Nihon Seikō Muroran 1954 | Reordering of union-led industrial relations |
| III<br>1955–60 | (1) Government<br>unions — mgmt | Announcement of 8 industrial unions' joint struggle (*shuntō*) 22.1.55<br>Japan Productivity Centre established 14.2.55<br>'1955 political arrangement': JSP's first national convention 13.10.55 LDP's first national convention 15.10.55 | | Reordering of union-led industrial relations |
| | (2) Sōhyō > Zenrō | | *JNR Niigata struggle 1957<br>Tekkōrōren's 11-wave strike 1957 | |

| | | | | |
|---|---|---|---|---|
| IV<br>1961–73 | (1) Government<br>/ \\<br>unions < mgmt<br>(2)Sōhyō = Dōmei + IMF-JC | AMPO and Miike 1960<br>Dōmei formed 26.4.62<br>IMF-JC formed 1964 | Struggle against the police law 1958<br>Struggle against teacher evaluations 1958<br>*Ōji Paper 1958<br>*Mitsui-Miike Mine 1960<br>Kokurō's struggle against removing assistant drivers 1969<br>Zen-gunrō, *Zeneraru Oil Refining 1970<br>Kokurō against rationalisation 1971<br>Seamen (to recover humanity) 1972 | Consolidation of the newly established industrial relations |
| V<br>1973–86 | (1) Government<br>⋰ \\<br>union << mgmt<br>(2) Sōhyō < IMF-JC + Dōmei | Oil shock 1973<br>Seisaku Suishin Rōsō Kaigi formed 1976<br>Zenminrōkyō formed 14.12.82 | Kōrōkyō 'right-to-strike strike' 1975<br>Saseho Shipbuilding 1979–80 | Consolidation of management-led industrial relations |
| VI<br>1987– | Government<br>⋰ \\\<br>union <<< mgmt<br>Zenrōren, Zenrōkyō << Zenminr Rōren | Japan National Railways dissolved and privatised (1.4.87)<br>Zenmin Rōren formed (20.11.87)<br>Rengō and Zenrōren formed (21.11.1989)<br>Zenrōkyō formed (9.12.89) | | |

*Notes:* (1) * union split occurred
- weak interaction
= close interactions
≡ symbiotic relationship

(2) Power relations are expressed as follows:
A = B  A and B are equally powerful
A > B  A is somewhat more powerful than B
A >> B  A is considerably more powerful than B
A >>> B  A is able to dictate fairly freely to B

*Source:* Hirosuke Kawanishi, *Enterprise Unionism in Japan*, London, Kegan Paul International, 1992, pp. 89–90.

Disputes may be classified according to the national union umbrella organisations involved (the so-called 'national centres'). Those led by Sanbetsu Kaigi (the All-Japan Congress of Industrial Unions, AJCIU, founded on 19 August 1946) were the first of the labour-offensive type, while at a later stage the management counter-offensive type prevailed. This is a clear reflection of the process in which the unions' power of restricting the prerogatives of management was soon curbed and those prerogatives were again lost to management. Although unions under the leadership of Sanbetsu Kaigi at the beginning of the period of post-war unrest had gone on the offensive and restricted previously recognised rights of the management, the decisive efforts of management to regain its freedom of action could later win them back. (Following its fifth plenary conference in November 1949, the activities of Sanbetsu Kaigi were almost completely suspended; on 15 February 1958 Sanbetsu Kaigi was finally dissolved.) Labour disputes led by Sōhyō (the General Council of Trade Unions of Japan, GCTUJ) were mostly of the management counter-offensive type and ended with a victory by management. Although labour had regained some of its vitality in the wake of the establishment of Sōhyō (it was established on 11 July 1950), it then progressively suffered loss of its power in a series of attacks by management. Labour disputes under the leadership of Dōmei (the Japanese Confederation of Labour, JCL) and its predecessor Zenrō Kaigi (the All-Japan Labour Union Congress, AJLUC) generally belonged to the labour counter-offensive type and resulted in a victory for the workers (Zenrō Kaigi was established on 22 April 1954, Dōmei on 26 April 1962). These labour disputes indicate that where capital–labour relations are dominated by management, employees usually rise up only when their dissatisfaction has reached an extremely high level. (The last type of labour dispute often occurred in small and medium-sized companies.)

## The First Period: From 1945 until 1949 – The Period of Post-war Upheaval

In Japan, the five years after the war were a period of upheaval, a time of social unrest and disagreement as to who should take the leadership in the process of reconstruction. Japan's unprecedented defeat had left the capitalist system in a state of shock, and the first five post-war years saw a series of conflicts over how the system should be reorganised.

The first post-war labour disputes occurred in the Yomiuri Newspaper Company (beginning in October 1945). The strike, which ended in a complete victory for the workers, focused on the following demands: 'Those responsible for the war must be held to account, the hunger crisis must be overcome, and the company must be democratised.' As a result of the Yomiuri workers' victory, two of their tactics – appropriating management's prerogative by taking over production control (self-management of the workers through control of editorial policy) and establishing a management consultative group – spread throughout the country. One link in this chain of disputes was the Tōshiba strike of 1946. In this dispute, as well as establishing a management consultative group and acquiring a sweeping say in management matters and the regulation of working conditions, the workers were even able to push through a clause requiring the union's approval in cases of dismissal or personnel transfer, thus considerably weakening the management's authority.

Struggles for production control were then waged in factories throughout the country; scandals concerning hoarders of goods led to violent street demonstrations; people gathered to demand food; a 'Food May Day' was planned and mass demonstrations took place. Political movements called for a 'democratic people's government' and a revolutionary situation began to take shape which rocked the capitalist system to its very foundations.

At this juncture, the General Headquarters (GHQ) of the Allied Forces occupying Japan, and the Japanese government, initiated a policy of suppressing the union movement in order to reconstruct capitalism in Japan. The Supreme Commander of the American Occupation Forces, General MacArthur, issued a decree prohibiting demonstrations, and on 20 May 1946 he ordered the government to draft legislation for the settlement of labour disputes (the Minister of Welfare complied with this request on 31 May). The government issued a declaration on the maintenance of social order on 13 June 1946 which established measures for curbing mass demonstrations and which stated that production control would be considered illegal. In reaction to the Yomiuri workers who intended to create an 'organ of the people' (which they called '*Democratic Yomiuri*' or '*People's Yomiuri*') and who were promoting a people's democracy in opposition to

GHQ's imposition of democratisation from above, six union officials were dismissed as a further measure of suppression (the Second Yomiuri Conflict of June 1946).

In order to resist these reactionary developments, the twenty-one industrial federations affiliated with Sanbetsu Kaigi decided to launch a joint struggle (the October Struggle of Sanbetsu Kaigi). The struggle against the dismissal of 75,000 workers of the National Railways and 43,000 seamen were skirmishes in this much larger battle. In both cases the employees managed to achieve their goals through industry-wide strikes (in September 1946). However, Tōshiba Rōren (the Tōshiba Union Federation, TUF) which had been expected to play a central role, gradually lost ground; the Yomiuri struggle committee suffered a devastating defeat and strikes of other organisations were also unsuccessful. But Densan, (Industrial Union of Electrical Power Workers; IUEPW), which had become the main force within the labour movement during the second half of this period, managed to establish the so-called 'Densan-gata wage system', so labour at last achieved one victory (October Struggle of Densan in 1946).

As the balance of power again shifted towards labour, the unions of the public sector, led by the employees of the National Railways, began a fight for higher wages and other goals aimed at securing the workers' livelihood. Soon afterwards, the unions began preparing for a general strike on 1 February 1947 with the goal of establishing a 'democratic people's government'. However, GHQ, against the background of the emerging Cold War, implemented a policy designed to transform Japan into a 'fortress against Communism in Asia' (speech of the US Secretary of the Army Kenneth C. Royal on 6 January 1947), increasing its pressure on the labour movement. This policy led to disputes of the management counter-offensive type such as the Tōhō dispute of 1948, the Tōshiba disputes of 1949, and the strike of National Railway employees in protest against the law on personnel levels in 1949. In all of these conflicts, labour suffered clear defeats. With the beginning of the Korean War in 1950, anti-communist purges were conducted which also affected workers in industry, and in these the labour movement led by Sanbetsu Kaigi was almost totally destroyed. This marked the end of the period of post-war upheaval and the beginning of the period of economic recovery.

## The Second Period: From 1950 until 1954 – The Period of Economic Recovery

A period of economic recovery is one in which, after an initial phase of unrest, the balance of power between the main social forces has been stabilised and the preconditions for a policy of economic reconstruction have been established. Given stabilisation of the socio-political system, a reorganisation of the social system can be implemented. In Japan this happened during a five-year period beginning with the Korean War in 1950 and the San Francisco Peace Treaty of 1951. Against the background of the Cold War between the Soviet Union and the United States, a course was set which aimed at transforming Japan into the Asian bridgehead of the Western camp under the protection of the United States, and economic recovery of the country was pursued on this premise.

During this phase the Japanese political scene was still somewhat confused. The conservative forces were divided into the Liberal Party and the Democratic Party, while the Socialist Party split into a left-wing and a right-wing faction after a heated debate on the Peace Treaty. Until its sixth national conference in 1955 at which a settlement of the internal dispute was finally reached, the Communist Party was also divided.

Thus management was the only force capable of taking the initiative in socio-political matters during this period, and it regained much of its power. Having successfully recovered its entrepreneurial prerogative in key industries after the period of upheaval, management also had the financial resources necessary for implementing economic recovery, due to a boom in demand created by special procurements in connection with the Korean War. In order to make the Japanese economy independent from outside support, it promoted in particular the recovery of the chemical and heavy industries and concentrated on the rebuilding of large enterprises. Accordingly management sought to gain a predominant position in capital–labour relations, first in the electric power sector and then in the steel and other core industries.

In the labour movement, Sōhyō, which was dominated by the 'Democratisation League', replaced Sanbetsu Kaigi as the leading force. By concentrating on a 'fight for the preservation of peace' and on demands for higher wages, Sōhyō managed to recapture some of the earlier momentum of the labour movement, and the organisation which at first had been regarded as 'tame' was soon said to have grown 'from a chicken to a gander'.

The attacks by management focused on Tanrō (Federation of Coal Miners' Unions, FCMU) and the union of the electric power industry (Densan) which were the main forces behind Sōhyō's turn to the left and which, with their joint control over the electric power supply, held a key position with regard to economic recovery. (Strikes of Tanrō and Densan occurred in 1952.) Tanrō was confronted with measures designed to put a curb on wages in order to finance rationalisation, while management tried to smash the electrical power unions which had made good progress in their attempt to establish themselves as an industrial union federation. Management had grasped that an important factor contributing to the strength of the post-war Japanese labour movement would be its organisation according to the industrial union principle, and realised that it must destroy the main promoter of this course, the union federation of the electric power industry, in order to establish enterprise unions and gain a position of supremacy in capital–labour relations. Both unions were forced into a rearguard action which ended in defeat after a 63-day strike by the miners and an 86-day strike by the electric power workers.

During the Nissan Labour Dispute of 1953, management sought to attain the same goals as in the fight against the union federation of the electric power workers. Workers in the automobile industry who were organised in Zenji (the Industrial Union of Japanese Automobile Workers', IUJAW), a so-called industrial union with subdivisions, were proud of their strong bargaining position and boldly demanded an industry-wide wage system of six different categories independent of the firm to which a worker belonged, but which reflected the length of employment with the same company. (The six groupings were unskilled, semi-skilled, first-grade skilled, middle-grade skilled, upper-division skilled, and senior skilled.) In order to smash this organisation, which came very close to being an industrial union, and to regain its prerogative, management went on the offensive. The ensuing conflict led to a split in the union, and in the following year, after the Nissan subdivision had lost its fight, Zenji was dissolved. The defeats in both the Nissan and the Densan conflicts marked the end of a period in which the Japanese labour movement had, at least to some extent, been able to implement the principle of industrial unionism. From then on the trend moved towards the establishment of enterprise or company unions.

In the next stage management targeted the steel industry, where it provoked the so-called 'iron and steel strikes' of 1953, 1955 and 1956, with strikes occurring also in 1954 at Amagasaki Steel and Nihon Seikō Muroran plant. These were disputes of the by then well-known management counter-offensive type, but Sōhyō chose to react with a completely new strategy. In Sōhyō's view, the enterprise unions established after the defeat in the Nissan and the Densan conflicts showed some serious weaknesses. Under the leadership of its Secretary-General Minoru Takano, Sōhyō intended to overcome these problems by organising support among the local population for the striking workers (this strategy was called the 'Takano Line'). The families of the strikers, and local communities, were to be active participants in the strike.

The disputes lasted for 53 and 193 days but again ended in a defeat for the union. From then on management was able to prepare the key industries for the period of high economic growth almost without interference from labour.

A quite extraordinary labour dispute during this period occurred in 1954 at the Ōmi-Kenshi Silk Mills. Since its establishment, Sōhyō had suffered from in-fighting between a left-wing and a right-wing faction and, after the defeats of Tanrō and Densan, the conservative grouping accused Sōhyō of taking a line too oriented to political goals. It published a joint declaration signed by Zensen Domei (the Japanese Federation of Textile Workers' Unions, JFTWU), Kaiin Kumiai (the All-Japan Seamen's Union, AJSU), Nipparō (Employees Union of the Japanese Broadcasting Association, EUJBA) and Zen'eien (the Federation of Cinema and Theatre Workers' Unions, FCTWU) (the Declaration of the Four Industrial Federations) and then left Sōhyō to found Zenrō Kaigi, the All-Japan Labour Union Congress (AJLUC), on 22 April 1954. Minoru Takita became its first chairman. Immediately after its establishment, the Ōmi-Kenshi Silk Mills dispute was the first labour conflict this new movement encountered. It was termed a fight for human rights and against feudal personnel practices, and because the union received strong public support, it was able to achieve its goals after a strike of 106 days. This success paved the way for reform of personnel practices in small and medium-sized companies whose situations were similar to that at Ōmi-Kenshi, leading to an improvement in working conditions. It can be regarded as an early case of a labour dispute of the labour counter-offensive type.

## The Third Period: From 1955 until 1959 – The Early Years of High Economic Growth

A period of high economic growth is one in which growth of the economy becomes the paramount social objective and it is widely accepted that economic growth will lead to prosperity at all levels of society. In Japan from 1955 onwards, capital investment and technical innovations financed by a trade surplus, gained during the period of economic recovery, mostly went to key industries such as steel, automobiles and shipbuilding. This marked the beginning of a period of high economic growth.

At the political level, in 1955 the conservative forces united and formed the Liberal Democratic Party (LDP), while the two factions of the Socialist Party on the left settled their differences. Thus the so-called '1955 arrangement' characterised by a two-party system under the leadership of the LDP was institutionalised. The most important labour disputes during this period were the so-called spring wage offensives or *shuntō*. Sōhyō replaced the former 'Takano Line' which had emphasised regional disputes with the 'Ōta-Iwai Line' which favoured joint struggles of the industrial federations in key industries. The formula of spring wage offensives in which the unions, in return for higher wages for the employees (from the base up, i.e. an increase of average wage levels), offered their cooperation in raising productivity, became the generally accepted union strategy.

This strategy turned out to be successful because the economy grew steadily during this period and accordingly the living standards of the workers rose to a certain degree. Post-war Japanese society was transformed into a society oriented to growth. This development also left its marks on post-war Japanese democracy, being reflected in the struggles against the revision of the police law intended to expand police power, the introduction of an evaluation system for teachers and AMPO (US–Japan Mutual Security Treaty). The last struggle in particular, which coincided with a strike in the Mitsui–Miike coal mines, developed into the biggest mass movement post-war Japan has ever seen.

Although the spring wage offensives were labour disputes based on the principle of cooperation between labour and capital, a number of fierce struggles occurred. Because Tekkōrōren (the Japan Federation of Steel Workers' Unions, JFSWU) was a very powerful industrial federation whose members included employees of Fuji Steel and Nihon Kōkan, this industry became the prime target of rationalisation measures implemented by management. In 1957, after having formed a struggle committee, Tekkōrōren, which was at the centre of that year's spring wage offensive, engaged in eleven waves of strikes lasting from 24 to 48 hours, demanding a wage-hike and higher retirement pay, and maintaining that responsibility for calling strikes lay with the federation. Nevertheless, managers of the steel industry, who spoke of their industry as 'the most important business of the nation' and regarded themselves as 'the champions of Japanese management', made a determined effort to weaken Tekkōrōren and refused to increase wages. After its defeat in this dispute, Tekkōrōren henceforth adopted the principle of cooperation between capital and labour. In subsequent spring offensives it became the accepted practice for the managements of five major companies of this industry to respond to the union's wage demands with a joint answer (*ippatsu kaitō*). The 'one-shot answer' formula became the norm not only for the steel industry which best reflected the overall power balance between management and labour, but also in other industries, where the 'joint answer', i.e. the wage increase offered by the steel companies, was then supplemented by additional allowances depending upon the economic performance of particular industries and enterprises.

While unions in the private sector all had suffered defeats and switched to a course of cooperation between capital and labour, public sector unions, in particular Kokurō (the National Railway Workers' Union, NRWU) had retained much of their fighting power. But in the 'Niigata National Railways Struggle' of 1957 even Kokurō experienced a devastating defeat. As Kōrōkyō (The Union Council of Public and State-Owned Enterprises) had failed to gain wage increases for four consecutive years, in the spring wage offensive of 1957 it organised four waves of strikes and finally managed to push through its demands for higher wages and salaries. However, the relevant authorities took massive disciplinary action against a number of Kōrōkyō's leaders in accordance with the law covering labour relations in public enterprises which prohibited strikes, whereupon Kōrōkyō responded again with a strike. The Niigata regional branch of Kokurō which for some time had actively promoted so-called shop-floor struggles, became the main focus of events. As the ensuing shop-floor struggle paralysed train services, armed police were sent in and the struggle which then broke out drew nationwide attention. Subsequently four leading members of the regional union organisation were fired and 46,734 Kokurō members faced disciplinary action. The union had not managed to achieve its goals, and the defeat led to a split in Kokurō. Henceforth Kokurō had to compete with a second union – Tetsurō – and management from then on employed a strategy of handing out severe disciplinary punishment after each strike, so the labour movement in the public sector in general lost its driving force.

During this period in which the unions one after another experienced failure and the labour movement continued to fragment, the Mitsui-Miike union remained the most powerful. Already firmly following the course of capital–labour cooperation, its so-called '113-Day Fight Without Heroes' gave the labour movement a fresh impetus. By leading shop-floor disputes aimed at achieving enhanced workplace safety, a new system of severance payments, production control and other goals, it was able to maintain some elements of workers' self-management relating to wages and working conditions, and was generally believed to be the most formidable Japanese labour union. However, as these elements of self-management meant a corresponding reduction of the management's authority, management, fearful that such practices might again spread, fired about 2,000 workers, among them 300 union activists. This was an unprecedented attack. It can indeed be claimed that this dispute of the management counter-offensive type was a sort of ultimate showdown. Although the conflict was linked with the struggle against the mutual security treaty between Japan and the United States and developed into the biggest strike Japan had ever seen, it failed after 282 days, following a split in the union and the establishment of a second union.

Because of the failure of this strike, the strategy of shop-floor disputes in private industry was abandoned and no further big disputes occurred. In industry generally, industrial relations from then on remained firmly under management control.

## The Fourth Period: From 1960 until 1972 – The Later Years of High Economic Growth

During this period the notion that economic prosperity must be the highest objective of society was taken for granted by almost all levels of society. Within the private sector labour movement, the Japan Council of Metalworkers' Unions (IMF-JC), Dōmei and other trade union organisations had adopted a policy of cooperation in raising productivity as their main political goal. Although the share of wage-dependent labour in the total national income was on the decline, wages continued to rise due to economic growth (a situation which was characterised by the saying: 'A full lake keeps all boats afloat'). Within the labour movement the number of those who believed that even without the unions' assistance higher wages could be obtained and who were apathetic to the union movement grew steadily.

Young workers in particular turned their backs on the unions. But although the number of disputes declined, unions in major private enterprises were able to maintain much of their influence by participating in the management consultative system. As Sōhyō, Dōmei and other national umbrella organisations enhanced their ability to formulate policy guidelines, their intentions were to some extent also reflected in government programmes. Moreover, unions strengthened their cooperation with international trade union bodies and were able to contribute to the international labour movement. These achievements must not be under-rated.

The only major labour dispute in this period was the 'Fight against Raising Productivity' at the National Railways in 1971. The administration of the National Railways pushed ahead with its efforts to raise productivity and adopted a strategy of discriminating against the railway workers' union, Kokurō, and Dōrō, the union of engine drivers, while at the same time supporting the second union Tetsurō. Being thus driven into an organisational crisis, both of the former opted for battle according to the slogan 'Better to stand and fight than sit and await death', and managed to force the administration to apologise publicly and to stop the productivity programme. This gave fresh impetus not only to the National Railways union, but to the public sector unions generally.

During this period it was Kaiin Kumiai in particular which

caught the attention of the public. The union of seamen has a tradition which goes back to pre-war times, and as one of the most influential unions affiliated with Dōmei it had a long-standing record of promoting cooperation with regard to raising productivity and furthering rationalisation. However, as a result of this policy the strain on crews and their families increased and dissatisfaction with the union spread among its rank and file members who sought to bring their complaints to the attention of their union's leadership. In 1972, the union reacted to its members' demands by calling a 'Struggle to Recover Humanity', a 92-day strike which was crowned with success. The dispute gave the Japanese union movement new energy and was closely observed by the public.

## The Fifth Period: From 1972 to the mid-1980s – The Period of Slower Economic Growth

During the period of slower economic growth it became necessary to find a new balance not only in economic areas, but in all areas of society. When this period began with the 1973 oil crisis, broad sections of society started to reconsider a way of life which made economic prosperity its highest value and to grasp the significance of respect for human dignity as one of the bases of social relations. Nonetheless, workers turned their backs on the unions in increasing numbers and the paralysis of the labour movement continued. Moreover, the proportion of employees among those working in key industries steadily declined. As a consequence, the influence of enterprise and company unions whose membership was limited to regular employees dropped even further. The share of union members among the total workforce sank below the 30 per cent mark.

In this situation, major labour disputes hardly occurred. The only one worthy of mention was the 'Strike for the Right to Strike' by Kōrōkyō in 1975, in which Kokurō, Dōrō and Zentei (the Japan Postal Workers' Union, JPWU) played the leading role. Because of the prohibition of strikes by Kōrō Hō the Law on Labour Relations in Public Enterprises) and Kōmuin Hō (the Law on Public Servants), 1,050,000 union members faced disciplinary action, and 1,016 of them were fired. The unions launched an eight-day strike with the aim of recovering their right to strike. However, not only did they fail to achieve their goals, but public employees also came under heavy criticism for taking advantage of their secure positions as employees of the state. The public sector unions were again targeted for criticism when plans for administrative reform were set in motion. Kokurō in particular was attacked because it was claimed that, after the victory in the fight against the raising of productivity, railway workers had taken a slack attitude towards their work. The mass media unfairly portrayed the union as being responsible for the huge budget deficit of the National Railways. Plans were announced to split the National Railways into several independent private enterprises. Today even the public sector unions which managed to retain some of their vitality are threatened with paralysis. The labour movement in general appears to have a very difficult time ahead of it.

The private sector unions, however, under the leadership of the 'Union Council for the Promotion of Political Measures' and the IMF-JC, made some progress on their way towards a united trade union front which includes the four national umbrella organisations, one of their achievements being the establishment of Zenmin Rōkyō (the Japanese Private Sector Trade Union Council) in 1982. Zenmin Rōkyō changed into Zenmin Rōren in 1987. Moreover, the new national centre Rengō was founded by Zenmin Rōren, Sōhyō and others in 1989. There are diverging opinions on how to assess the significance of this new organisation Rengō, and attention will focus on the question of whether the council in future will be the beginning of a new type of Japanese labour movement characterised by an enhanced capability to influence government policies through its bargaining power.

# 2 The Yomiuri Labour Disputes, 1945–46

*Tasuke Masuyama*

**Tasuke Masuyama**

1913 Born in Tokyo on 20 August
1931 Graduated from Tokyo Kaisei Middle School
1935 Graduated from Seijō High School
1939 Graduated from the Faculty of Economics, Kyoto Imperial University; joined the *Yomiuri* newspaper (editor for economic affairs)
1940 Drafted for military service
1945 Demobilised
1947 Resigned from the *Yomiuri* newspaper
1947 Executive member of the board of the Japanese Cultural Association for Democracy (elected by the Japanese Association of Journalists in January)
1959 Head of the planning department of the Murakami Institute for Colour Technology
1972 Head of planning of the Star printing company
1975 Representative of the journal *Ichidō* (All Together)
1977 Executive director of the company publishing *Shinchihei* (New Horizon) and chief editor of this journal

## Trade union functions

1945 Secretary of the Union of Employees of the Yomiuri Newspaper Publishing Company
1946 Member of the Permanent Council of the Yomiuri subdivision within the Union of Newspaper, News Agency and Broadcasting Service Employees (in April), Member of the Supreme Struggle Committee of the Yomiuri strikers (in June), Vice Chairman of the Executive Committee of the newspaper division (in July)

Publications

*Yomiuri sōgi 1945/46* (The Yomiuri Labour Dispute 1945/46), Aki Shobō, 1976
*Sanbetsu Kaigi jūgatsu tōsō* (The October Struggle of Sanbetsu Kaigi), Gogatsusha, 1978
*Kenshō: Senryōki no Rōdoundo* (The Labour Movements during the period of occupied Japan), Renga-Shobo, 1993

## I Editor's Overview

The first labour conflict in post-war Japan was initiated by the employees of the *Yomiuri* newspaper. In October 1945, the employees of this newspaper publishing company called the managers, and in particular the company's managing director Matsutarō Shōriki, to account for their wartime activities, presenting a list of five demands. These included the demands that the managers, and in particular Matsutarō Shōriki, be called to account for their responsibility for the war; that the internal structures of the publishing company be democratised, and that the treatment of the employees be improved. Thus began a struggle for production control, during which the employees took control of editing, printing and distributing their paper (the First Yomiuri Conflict). This struggle was so successful that by the end of 1945 the union was able to start an independent newspaper, the *Democratic Yomiuri*. Having established a management consultative group within the company, the workers participated in the decision-making process, and responsibility for editorial policy was taken away from the paper's owners. A declaration was published which stated: 'This paper is to become a friend of the population, a voice of the people.' In the history of commercial newspapers, this marked a new era. As the struggle for production control initiated by the employees became a tactic widely used in other companies as well, this conflict gave rise to an important trend within the labour movement after 1945.

However, after the American delegate to the Allied Council, George Acheson, issued a declaration of anti-communist principles on 29 May 1946, General Headquarters (GHQ), having taken a sharp turn to the right in its implementation of the occupation policy, accused the *Democratic Yomiuri* of having breached the press code promulgated by the occupation administration. Taking this accusation as its pretext, management conducted a purge among union leaders (the red purge), thus trying to regain authority over editorial policy. In the events that followed, the Yomiuri conflict developed into an all-out fight between management and workers (the Second Yomiuri Conflict). The union offered resistance to direct armed intervention by the occupation forces and police, organised a walkout and, after a lock-out on 16 July 1946, founded a struggle committee. The fight for control of editorial policy and opposition to unfair management practices continued. The union became one of the main participants in the 'October Struggle of Sanbetsu Kaigi', declaring a general strike of all newspaper, news agency and broadcasting service employees, thereby aiming at a decisive victory. Its plans were thwarted when unions of the other big newspaper publishers such as *Asahi* left the strike front. The struggle ended after 128 days (on 16 October 1946) when union leaders voluntarily withdrew from the company. The union, which had split into two factions, reunited as had been envisaged by the union leaders when they retired from the company.

## The First Yomiuri Dispute (1945)

The objects of the First Yomiuri Conflict were that the managers were to be called to account for their wartime activities, and the internal structures of the company were to be democratised.

Immediately after Japan's surrender in 1945, a group of white-collar vice-heads of divisions organised a number of meetings which discussed conclusions to be drawn from the management's cooperation with the government during the war. As a result of these discussions, a meeting of all employees was convened on 23 October 1945. The meeting's participants adopted a list of demands and called for the resignation of all managers and division heads, but especially of the managing director, Matsutarō Shōriki. They requested a democratisation of the company's internal structures, better treatment of employees, and so forth. Matsutarō Shōriki immediately rejected these demands. He did not stop there, however, but sacked five leading members of the rebellious group, among them Tōmin Suzuki. Now the employees founded a struggle committee headed by Tōmin Suzuki and published a declaration underlining their willingness to enter into an all-out conflict. The struggle committee further declared its intention to control the editing of the paper, refusing to grant the managing director and his fellow managers any influence over the work of the editorial staff, and began independent production of the newspaper.

The Yomiuri conflict had a great impact on society, as it not only gave a signal for the founding of labour unions in other publishing companies, but marked the beginning of struggles for production control throughout the country. The government attempted to intervene, establishing a mediation committee for the Tokyo area. Managing director Shōriki showed no interest whatsoever in mediation, thereby prolonging the conflict. Finally, however, the management accepted the struggle committee's proposals after Shōriki had been notified by GHQ that he would be indicted as a war criminal (12 December 1945). Thus the struggle ended after fifty days with a complete victory for the employees. Shōriki and four managers withdrew from their positions, Tōmin Suzuki was promoted to the post of chief editor and a management consultative group was set up jointly by the employees and the management, giving the employees a say in company matters which extended to the control of the newspaper's production.

Struggles for production control now erupted throughout the country, and as a result of the Yomiuri conflict a management consultative group was founded in every company.

## The Second Yomiuri Dispute (1946)

In the Second Yomiuri Dispute, the struggle between management and employees began over the question of who had authority over editorial policy (a special aspect of the entrepreneurial prerogative peculiar to the news media sector), and resulted in the unjustified sacking of union leaders which constituted the first post-war purge of left-wing elements (the red purge). The employees, having won a decisive victory during the first conflict, were able to promote democratisation of the company's internal structures through negotiations within the management consultative group. In a leading article they declared that the newspaper would henceforth be 'a voice of the people', whose production would be guided by the spirit of self-management (which is why they called the paper '*Democratic Yomiuri*'). In contrast to the democratisation policies promulgated by GHQ, the *Democratic Yomiuri* aimed at taking the leadership of a democratic revolution based on a broad people's movement.

GHQ therefore refused to accept the *Democratic Yomiuri*, and the company's management attacked the union for taking over control of editorial policy. Both GHQ and the company's management were trying to regain their influence on the paper and arranged to dismiss the union leadership. At this point GHQ used a rather insignificant article on the title page of the paper as a pretext for intervening against a 'breach of the press code'. The management called the responsible editors to account and enforced the dismissal of the six chief editors headed by Tōmin Suzuki (on 12 June 1946). This led to a second strike which lasted 128 days and concentrated on the control of editorial policy and the unjustified dismissals.

In the meantime, support for the Yomiuri Dispute grew among the organised employees of newspapers, news agencies and the broadcasting service, who were trying to build up an industrial federation with subdivisions based on the closed-shop system (Shinbun Tan'itsu, the Industrial Union of Newspaper, News Agency and Broadcasting Employees, IUNNBE, was founded on 12 July 1946). In autumn, this struggle became part of the so-called October Struggle of Sanbetsu Kaigi, and a strike of all newspaper, news agency and broadcasting employees was launched on 5 October 1946 (however, it was joined only by workers of local newspapers and the broadcasting sector). This development intensified the effect of the Yomiuri conflict on the social confrontations of this time.

Then one day 500 armed police officers stormed the offices of the publishing company and arrested 56 union members, most of them journalists. A lock-out was ordered by the management. The confrontation proceeded with the workers forming a struggle committee and establishing their headquarters in a burnt-out building which came under siege. Meanwhile a second union, which was prepared to concede control of editorial policy to the management, gathered support. With acceptance of the condition that the group of six editors headed by Tōmin Suzuki would retire 'voluntarily' from the company and that thirty-one employees, among them Tasuke Masuyama, would hand in their immediate resignation, the strike ended in a defeat for the workers (on 16 October 1946).

### Results

Following this conflict, both unions reunited and formed the Yomiuri union which still exists today. Further Yomiuri labour disputes were mainly initiated by the management and aimed at restoring its entrepreneurial authority by enforcing the dismissal of leading union officials. In the course of these conflicts of the management counter-offensive type, a second union split off, with the result that the employees were always on the losing side. The Yomiuri conflict can therefore be regarded as an early paradigm of this development. With regard to control of editorial policy, the principle was established that 'the editorial guidelines and the contents of newspaper articles are determined by the management'. This principle is the basis of today's 'ethical principles in the newspaper sector'.

## II Lecture by Tasuke Masuyama

Nearly thirty-eight years ago now, on 14 August 1945, a cabinet meeting took place 'in the presence of His Majesty the Emperor' (as it was officially announced), during which the Potsdam Declaration was accepted. Japan had lost the war. On the following day, 15 August 1945, a speech of the emperor was broadcast on the radio. At this time I was working as an accountant at the 3rd Tokyo Provisional Army Hospital at Sagamihara in Kanagawa prefecture. My work as an accountant consisted of organising food and clothing for the patients and managing the book-keeping department of the hospital. In the official terminology, I was an 'army accountant with the rank of a commissioned officer'.

In 1939 I had graduated from the Kyoto University and joined the Yomiuri publishing company. Reputedly this was the first time the *Yomiuri* newspaper had hired fresh graduates. Today, the *Yomiuri* is one of the three leading Japanese newspapers, but then it was still strongly influenced by its former status as a literary paper. It was said that 'what Kodansha is among the publishing houses, the *Yomiuri* is among the papers' which meant that this newspaper concentrated on literature. In those days students were exempt from military service until they graduated but were drafted after they had completed their studies. Being an enthusiastic basketball player because of my height, there was no chance of evading the draft. Therefore I racked my brains over whether I should become a war correspondent or a soldier. My superior advised me to become a war correspondent in order to avoid being enlisted as a serviceman, but in the end I decided on the army. I spent my time as accountant of the 3rd Tokyo Provisional Army Hospital and was not sent to the front. During the five years until Japan's defeat I organised food, clothing and shelter for the patients and was completely absorbed in managing the hospital.

## The period immediately following Japan's surrender

When the speech of the emperor was broadcast on 15 August, most patients, with the exception of the most seriously injured, gathered in the courtyard of the hospital to listen to the radio. As is generally known, the emperor's way of expressing himself is not exactly colloquial. He spoke in the so-called 'Divine Language' which is why nobody understood much of what he said. When, after his speech, an announcer gave some explanations, we realised for the first time that Japan had lost the war. The military surgeons were mostly university lecturers from the medical faculties who had been drafted. The army hospital was a somewhat special facility, as it concentrated on after-treatment – today we would call it rehabilitation – fitting artificial limbs for patients who had had their arms or legs amputated and giving them some vocational training in order to facilitate their reintegration into society. When surrender came, the hospital was grossly overcrowded, as disabled patients were sent home from the south of the country, arriving in a condition more dead than alive and suffering badly from malnutrition. More than 3,000 of them were admitted. This hospital was the only one of its kind in Japan and therefore an exceptional place. Apart from those who could not move, all had gathered in the courtyard. When they finally realised that the war was lost and over, patients, military doctors and nurses became very quiet; everyone was utterly shaken. During the following two days, the hospital was an utterly silent place.

I was not required to live in the barracks but commuted from my apartment to the hospital every day. Since the Edo era[1] my family has lived in Tokyo. Being born in Nihonbashi, I lived in Tokyo and had no other hometown in the country. When in April 1945 our house was destroyed in an air-raid we were ordered to move to Haramachida. My work as an accountant gave me ample opportunity to maintain contacts with the outside world, and often I visited the Yomiuri publishing company. During the war, newspapers offered the only means of access to news from abroad which went beyond the official news bulletins, except for short-wave radio. So we were already aware of the fact that Japan was losing the war well before the atomic bomb was dropped on Hiroshima. We also knew in advance of the radio broadcast that Japan had accepted the Potsdam Declaration and thereby surrendered. Thus I continued my work in Sagamihara in anticipation of Japan's defeat.

The Atsugi airfield is very close to Sagamihara. At that time there were the Sōbudai Officer Candidate School, our hospital and also a couple of regiments. Right until the end of the war, the government and the army planned to transform Sagamihara into the biggest garrison town in this part of the country. As General MacArthur intended to land on Atsugi airfield and an advance detachment was scheduled to arrive soon, the whole area around Sagamihara was in a state of confusion. When news of the impending surrender had finally got around, an incident occurred: the young cadets of the OCS entrenched themselves with weapons and ammunition in the Tanzawa mountains and vowed to fight against the Americans. The fighter squadron stationed at Atsugi airfield dropped leaflets in low-level flight; these read 'Japan's surrender is a communist conspiracy. We must be determined to fight to the end.'

When MacArthur's advance detachment finally arrived at Atsugi, all women in the area changed into men's clothes, cut their hair and fled to the nearby mountains. Panic spread among the people. Now that the occupation army was due to arrive, all were worked up to a frenzy. They had been brought up with the slogan 'Destroy the American Satans!' and the propaganda had convinced them that all Americans were devils.

One could see people moving about, racking their brains over how they should feed themselves and what would become of them. Mothers with young children, physically too weak to nurse their babies, were in an especially desperate situation. I too lost one of my children during the war. If a child fell ill during these times, there was hardly any hope of survival. On 30 August, MacArthur arrived at Yokohama. Two weeks after Japan had accepted the Potsdam Declaration and surrendered, MacArthur moved into the New Grand Hotel in Yokohama. Some days later, he was on his way to Tokyo.

## Preparing the Yomiuri Dispute – the 'Democracy Study Group'

Being aware that Japan would lose the war, I had already met with some friends from the *Yomiuri* and others during the final phase of the war to discuss what to do after the surrender. During my studies at the Kyoto University I had been the leader of a student council, and the secret police had arrested me because of my resistance against the war and anti-fascist activities. This experience had caused me to keep in touch with friends from the anti-war movement, and I had offered resistance on a moderate level.

Well before the broadcast speech of the emperor I had visited friends from the *Yomiuri* and we had repeatedly discussed a course of action to be followed after the defeat. These meetings led to the establishment of an organisation within the *Yomiuri* newspaper which we called the 'Democracy Study Group'.

I was among the first to be demobilised, and returned home in September. When I speak of demobilisation and coming home, many will not comprehend what I am talking about. When times are changing, everything is at sixes and sevens. In the case of Japan this meant that once the army had finally been disbanded, the whole chain of command broke down. The army seems to have a very solid organisational structure, but once the chain of command from the top to the bottom is gone, everything goes to pieces. The people who had heard the speech of the emperor all thought, 'Let's get the hell out of here', and everybody asked to be released immediately or simply went home. At the hospital, the inmates wanted to return to their families and demanded to be allowed to leave. As MacArthur was due to arrive, all patients and personnel who had been temporarily speechless after the shock of Japan's defeat now suddenly felt as if they had been freed from their chains.

As I said, I returned home as one of the first to be demobilised. Immediately I met with friends from the *Yomiuri* to discuss what to do in this situation and how we could help in building a new Japan. It would probably be correct to regard these meetings as the beginning of the Yomiuri Disputes. The *Yomiuri* offices had been on the Ginza,[2] but after an air-raid the building had suffered fire damage and provisional offices were set up in the Honganji temple in Tsukiji. When I went to the Ginza, I saw that in this burnt-out wilderness the company's building had been among those consumed by the flames and was completely destroyed. The *Yomiuri* newspaper then bought another paper, the *Hōchi* sports magazine, and changed its name to *Yomiuri-Hōchi*. The former offices of the *Hōchi* paper were near the Yūrakuchō station where today the Sōgō department store is located. As the Hōchi building had not been burnt down, we left the Honganji temple and moved to these offices. This was the start of the post-war *Yomiuri* newspaper.

At that time, the only other facility around Yūrakuchō was the black market. When dusk fell the area around Sukiyabashi filled with repatriated soldiers, and a little later with whores. These were the circumstances under which the First Yomiuri Dispute developed.

## The GHQ media policy

During the autumn and winter of 1945, the number of people in Yūrakuchō who were dying from starvation rose so sharply that we could see it with our own eyes. The Ministry of Health and Welfare published some figures, but as the weather during the year following the surrender was very bad, Japan experienced the worst crop failure since the Meiji era, and I think that the death toll was much higher than officially announced. During the two weeks between the declaration of surrender and MacArthur's arrival and in the few weeks following there was no sign that the Japanese workers would rise up. Matsutarō Shōriki, the owner of the Yomiuri Publishing Company, had been a high-ranking officer with the security police and was a police expert. In our presence he stated: 'Things can't remain as they are. There certainly will be a communist uprising. Then I will be the only one who can put it down.'

But contrary to Matsutarō Shōriki's expectation, the Japanese workers remained calm. Immediately after the surrender workers at the Hokkaidō coal mines staged a rebellion, but they were in fact Chinese prisoners of war belonging to the communist 'Eighth Route Army' and workers from Korea who after the end of the war stood up and demanded their freedom. The Japanese workers didn't rise until much later. The ruling classes were certainly aware of the fact that they could not prolong the war. Nevertheless they issued rallying cries such as: 'Decisive battle for the main islands! Hundred million jointly face an honourable death!' But they knew that a revolution would break out once fighting began on the main islands. While publicly accepting the terms of the Potsdam Declaration, they desperately attempted to establish a system which would save Japan from the threat of revolution. Following MacArthur's arrival, democratisation policies in Japan were implemented against this background.

When foreign troops occupy an enemy country, they first attempt to secure their control over the population in the occupied territory by means of propaganda. Newspapers and the broadcasting services are very useful means to this end. Therefore the occupation army tried to bring them under their supervision. During the war the Japanese military had maintained tight control of newspapers and the broadcasting service; now GHQ under MacArthur did the same. On Okinawa all newspapers were suspended, leaving only a propaganda paper issued by the occupation army. In Germany, which had also been defeated, all existing newspapers were superseded by new ones. It was expected that the same strategy would be applied in Japan as well.

The Japanese monarchy – the so-called emperor system – faced problems of a similar nature. Voices calling for the emperor's resignation were numerous among the Allies, but the same demand was heard also among the Japanese people. Until the middle of December, the overwhelming majority of newspaper editors were convinced that the emperor should be forced to resign. But then the occupation authorities changed their stance on the issue and decided to use the emperor to exert indirect control over Japan.

The same method was applied with regard to the news media: the old newspapers were not closed in favour of new ones, but the already well-established newspapers were used to support the implementation of occupation policies. However, in comparison with other newspapers, the attitude of the occupation army towards the *Yomiuri* was exceptionally negative. The *Yomiuri* had carried a lot of heroic and sentimental pro-army propaganda stories. During the fifteen years of war, a wide variety of sentimental serialised novels, such as *Three Heroic Bombardiers*, had been published. Right until the end of the war the paper carried a mawkish series about some young cadets of a suicide command 'Kamikaze' base in Kyūshū going to the front. Whereas other newspapers published appeals for patriotism, the *Yomiuri* used such stories to incite its readers to militarism and loyalty to the emperor. In this respect the influence of the *Yomiuri* on the average citizen was much greater than that of the *Asahi* or the *Mainichi* newspapers. Consequently the pressure exerted by the occupation authority on the *Yomiuri* was stronger. Matsutarō Shōriki on the other hand boasted that his paper had no reason to indulge in self-criticism. If the occupation forces should close down his paper, he as the owner would simply abandon it, build an apartment block on the site of the burnt-down company building and provide housing for homeless people of whom there were enough after all.

## The outbreak of the Yomiuri Dispute

Under these circumstances we gradually reached a consensus concerning the need to democratise the *Yomiuri* in order to transform it into a newspaper which supported democracy in Japan. We called it a 'democratic revolution'. However, many people in Japan simply did not understand the meaning of the word 'democracy', and there were conflicting views about its concrete substance. I was born at the beginning of the Taishō era,[3] a period which is often referred to as the Taishō democracy. But as the war approached, the doctrine promulgated by the education system changed rapidly. When the student militias became active, the imperialistic interpretation of history caused young men to enthusiastically sacrifice their lives for their country. In view of this development, the fifteen-year-long Taishō era can hardly be regarded as a successful step towards democracy.

In 1933, not long before I started my studies, the so-called Takigawa incident occurred at Kyoto University. A short while ago we convened a commemorative meeting on the fiftieth anniversary of this incident. At the time it occurred academic freedom had been abolished by the government and the military. This caused 15 professors of the law faculty to resign, and all of the students to leave the university prematurely. This incident was reputedly the last protest action by students before the war broke out. Afterwards, with Japan's growing involvement in the fifteen-year-long war, militaristic education was intensified. It was therefore hardly surprising that among people who had been educated in the spirit of militarism before the war and who now produced the *Yomiuri* newspaper – among them also my friends – ideas about the substance of democracy diverged. If one spoke of democracy, some people immediately thought of communism, while others more or less had the American system in mind; still others had a notion of democracy more in line with the English concept. Within the labour movement there were a number of even more sharply contrasting positions.

This situation led to the establishment of the Democracy Study Group for the comprehensive study of these problems. The group agreed on a list of five demands which on 13 September was orally brought to the attention of Mr Shōriki. The demands included the transformation of the *Yomiuri* into a democratic newspaper which would support the democratisation of Japan; in the end they caused the outbreak of the Yomiuri Dispute. Mr Shōriki was not prepared to accept them, of course. Quite to the contrary, he told us to shut up, and that it was for him to decide what the company would do.

Meanwhile, on 10 October all political prisoners were released, among them communists and others who had opposed the war effort. The Japanese government had intended to kill them in the prisons one way or another. One plan had been to weaken their physical condition by gradually reducing their food rations until they would die. In the Fuchū prison, sixteen were still held in preventive custody, among them Kyūichi Tokuda, Yoshio Shiga and other leading members of the Communist Party. Another group of four was made up of followers of the Tenrikyō sect[4] and a Christian sect, and participants in the Korean independence movement. Twelve prisoners were communists who had stubbornly refused to convert; they had already completed their prison term but had not been released. These political prisoners were freed by the Allied occupation forces.

Some days later MacArthur announced his reform plan consisting of five major reforms which were to become the basis of democratisation. It called for legal equality of men and women, asserted the right of workers to form associations, and demanded the liberalisation of education, the abolition of repressive legislation and the democratisation of the economy.

This occupation policy declaration strengthened the resolve of the *Yomiuri* employees to start a conflict. On 18 October, in the name of the founding members of the Democracy Study Group which included all middle-ranking employees, we again presented our demands to Mr Shōriki, this time in written form. Now the struggle began to unfold.

In the Yomiuri publishing company, two labour conflicts were launched, the First and the Second Yomiuri Dispute. Between these conflicts was a period of six months during which the employees took the initiative and published a newspaper under the title *Democratic Yomiuri*. Normally, the first conflict, the period of independent publication of the newspaper, and the second conflict are jointly referred to as the Yomiuri Dispute.

## The five-point list of demands

During wartime, all-Japanese journalists had written articles based on official army bulletins which often described the sinking of enemy warships or transformed defeats suffered by Japanese troops into great victories. It is a fact that only militaristic press releases were allowed to be printed in the papers, but nevertheless within this limited framework journalists had offered resistance in a number of ways. Luckily, I had not written a single article on the war. In my capacity as a journalist specialising on economic matters I certainly would have had the opportunity to do so, but I declined. Among those who chose to become war correspondents were people such as Ashihei Hino[5] who in his book *Wheat and Soldiers* described landscapes but did not include a single eye-witness account of a battle scene. But there were in fact journalists who opposed the war and who used every means to avoid publishing lies.

In any case, our first duty was to uncover the war responsibility of our superiors who had forced journalists to write such articles by threatening them. A further important demand was the democratisation of the internal structures of the company. This was especially relevant in the case of the *Yomiuri* which was controlled by Mr Shōriki, a veteran police officer who was surrounded by ex-bureaucrats from the Ministry of Internal Affairs and the police forces. The paper was controlled by a system he had established. Within the company a network of spies existed, and if anyone was careless enough to make a disparaging remark about Shōriki, the latter would know it within half an hour. As this mechanism of control had forced journalists to glorify the war effort, it was essential to call the war criminals within the management to account and to democratise the decision-making process. In comparison with the *Asahi* and the *Mainichi* newspapers, this matter was of special relevance for the *Yomiuri*.

Moreover, we demanded improvements in working conditions. Workers were treated badly and their wages were so low that they were constantly on the brink of starvation. When I was with the company, Shōriki used to call each employee into his office and tell him, as if he kept all employees under close surveillance, 'This month you have done well, therefore you'll get more than your colleagues, but don't tell any of them!', and then he would hand over the money. But when the employee returned to his office in a happy mood and talked with his colleagues, he learned that Shōriki had said the same to each and every one of them. So when people compared their wages in order to see who had got most, they realised that the amount was almost the same. The *Yomiuri* was a major paper, but the way payment of wages was handled shows that feudalistic structures were dominant. This was a situation we intended to change. Another demand concerned the separation of capital holders and management on the one hand and editorial policy on the other.

## Attempting to achieve production control

Our demands were summarily rejected by Shōriki, and four of those who had signed the list and thereby exposed themselves to his wrath were told that they had been fired. When this happened, we decided to launch a struggle for self-management. We decided to publish our own newspaper, take over control of the company and keep on fighting until the other side gave in to our demands. This marked the beginning of the struggle for self-management which later was referred to as the fight for production control. At first, production control was just one important strategic instrument of our union in the struggle, but soon it became an issue through which we acquired an astonishing influence on the whole Japanese labour movement.

In the beginning nobody was really convinced that the newspaper could be published if it relied solely on the strength of the workers. But because we were determined to give it a try, the editorial staff and the departments of production and distribution got together and began their struggle for self-management. People from the book-keeping and sales departments at first were reluctant to join us. But when the paper actually went into print (at that time with 1,500,000 copies daily) they could not pay any wages because they were not involved in selling it and consequently had no proceeds. Therefore book-keeping and sales people reluctantly decided to join us. Now the struggle for self-management gathered momentum.

During this conflict, we produced the paper according to the principle of trial and error in order to find out how the newspaper we wanted should actually look. While we continued our battle with the management, the workers went on producing the paper. The First Yomiuri Dispute lasted until 12 December, and until that date we had a meeting each day to identify mistakes and decide how we should produce an even better newspaper. On the whole, it was a never-ending endeavour. Until that time articles had been written only on order from above, and when no orders came the journalists went home without having written anything at all. But now all employees got together and made their own paper. Workers in the production department read the articles and communicated their objections to the editorial staff. This intensive exchange with the workers enabled us to publish the sort of newspaper we had envisaged.

## Joint struggle with workers from other companies

The more we proceeded with our struggle for self-management, the more contacts we established with workers from other companies. For instance, the rotary printing machine of the Yomiuri company had been severely damaged in the air-raid and was unusable, but the company had not had it repaired. We took it to the Tokyo Machine Company and the workers there fixed it right away, saying that they too would like to share some responsibility.

Distribution of the *Asahi* newspaper was always thirty minutes ahead of the *Yomiuri*, even though the articles were completed at the same time. The Asahi publishing company had high-quality machines. Therefore its newspapers arrived at the railway freight terminal thirty minutes earlier, and by the time they finally reached their readers in the country, the time difference had become considerable. We decided to get together with the workers of the National Railways. When the papers were loaded into the freight carriages at Yūrakuchō station, a couple of their workers clung to the outside of the carriages and prevented the train from departing. Then they waited until the *Yomiuri* arrived and loaded our paper into the carriages together with the others. From then on the *Asahi* and the *Yomiuri* were always shipped on the same train. After a union had been established within the transport company which brought our paper to the station, the drivers raced their trucks to Ueno without stopping and made sure that the *Yomiuri* was dispatched together with the *Mainichi* and the *Asahi* newspapers.

The struggle became a bigger success than we had expected. The fact that the employees of the *Yomiuri* advocated the prosecution of war criminals and made a contribution towards the democratisation of Japan was a hard blow to Shōriki in particular and the management of our company in general. Shōriki was utterly dismayed and vowed that he would not give another penny for this newspaper.

## Victory

As the events of the Yomiuri Dispute unfolded, a number of matters became clear to us. The Yomiuri publishing company was a stock corporation whose shareholders remained anonymous. When Matsutarō Shōriki was appointed managing director, the shareholders had invested their capital but their names remained secret. We found out that these people came from the top ranks of Japanese financial circles, and that they had placed Shōriki in his position so that he could make a newspaper which supported the interests of big business. For this purpose they had chosen the *Yomiuri* paper. Without even being aware of it we had entered into a confrontation with the *zaibatsu* – the big family corporations.

This newspaper, financed with the money of the ruling classes of Japan and the top-ranking financial circles, carried articles every day which called for thorough democratisation and the liberation of workers. To those who had invested their money in the company, this was an unbearable situation. Shōriki therefore declared he would not support such a newspaper any more. We, on the other hand, were determined to continue publication of the newspaper and our fight for the prosecution of war criminals. Acceptance of our position by the company's board of management marked the end of the First Yomiuri Dispute, in which the union achieved a decisive victory. Matsutarō Shōriki was indicted as a Class A war criminal by the occupation authorities and taken to the Sugamo prison. He gave up, and this removed the last obstacle to a successful mediation. The First Yomiuri Dispute ended on 12 December.

At this stage the process of establishing labour unions was still in its infancy. Labour conflicts such as that in the coal mines on Hokkaidō or the Ishii Metals Factory in Tokyo were only isolated incidents. These were the circumstances under which the First Yomiuri Dispute took place.

## The cooperation of intellectuals

In the course of our struggle we also encouraged intellectuals who either had cooperated with the military during the war or had not been able to show resistance against fascism to cooperate with our paper. However, almost all of them thought it presumptuous to take a leading role in the post-war democratisation process as they had not opposed the war in the first place. They therefore declined to write for us.

As you may know, Shimizu Ikutaro, who later became professor of sociology, wrote leading articles for the *Yomiuri* newspaper. During the war he had been in charge of the youth movement and had actively promoted militarism. He feared being sentenced to death when the occupation forces entered Japan. Now he declared his determination to take part in our struggle as a sort of self-criticism. From this time onwards, he wrote articles strongly encouraging youth to support the revolution. Although he promoted the struggle against the Japanese–American security treaty during the 1960s by writing articles such as 'March on the Parliament!', he has recently become active again as a right-wing ideologue. There were many like him who constantly changed their position.

But the majority of intellectuals was more or less absorbed in introspection and self-examination. As a consequence, only a few of them were prepared to take a role in making a new sort of newspaper and write articles for us. We tried to encourage them and asked them to support us in our struggle for a new and democratic paper, and in this way to express their doubts about their own behaviour during the war. Gradually cooperation with the intellectuals did develop. As Masao Maruyama[6] put it, they formed a sort of 'remorse community'. Those who wanted to avoid making the same mistakes again really helped us considerably in producing our paper. (However, during the First Yomiuri Dispute very few of them gave any active support.)

The head of the mediation committee which had been set up during this conflict, Professor Izutarō Suehiro,[7] offered a theoretical underpinning for the separation of capital and management on the one hand and editorial policy on the other. He declared: 'It would be desirable to have a system where the newspaper can be edited without interference from the capital owners and the management, and to create a management consultative group jointly formed by the workers and the management through which the workers can have an influence on management affairs.' Professor Suehiro's statement gave our strategy of production control added legitimacy.

## The era of the *Democratic Yomiuri*

Now we conducted an in-depth study into what is called 'democracy'. Not wanting to have the same bad experiences as those who had written articles in praise of the *yokusan* organisations, but intending to produce a real newspaper, we included in the edition of 1 January 1946 a declaration beginning with the words: 'From now on the *Yomiuri* newspaper will be an organ of the people.' The new year's issue normally carried a picture of some delightful scene, such as Mount Fuji or the rising sun. We decided to put on the title page a photograph showing a workers' demonstration. On the second page was a picture of workers producing salt on Shikoku. By including these two pictures we totally destroyed the normal image of a new year's edition. According to the government and the high financial circles we had gone a step too far. We ourselves simply wanted to demonstrate with these pictures how the process of democratisation in Japan could be promoted. This edition marked the beginning of the *Democratic Yomiuri*.

What were the intentions of the *Democratic Yomiuri*? In the first edition we reported on the people around Yamakawa Hitoshi who intended to set up a democratic people's alliance which would promote democracy by uniting the people into one body. We supported this movement because the need to destroy the still existing militaristic and despotic power structures and to create a new political system in Japan had been our initial motivation for producing the *Democratic Yomiuri.*

We did not, however, become the voice of the democratic people's alliance, but in general we shared the goals of this movement. Writing articles at that time – and this is still the case today – meant joining the press clubs of the employers' associations, investigating only matters the ruling classes wanted to be published and writing the corresponding articles. This is the way newspapers are made. When a journalist intends to collect material reflecting the views of the people, he has to deduce from the publications of the ruling classes not only their intentions but also the way they want reality to be portrayed. If he has access only to this kind of information and relies on it in composing his own articles, he is in the same situation as that during the war: merely copying the official announcements issued by the imperial army headquarters, reporting that there have been some battles and that enemy warships have been sunk in great numbers. The readers will accept this as the truth. But it is the task of newspapers to check whether such announcements by the ruling classes are in fact true or not. Therefore a journalist must not simply hang around the press clubs run by the public relations departments of the ruling classes and use only their material in his articles. We have always tried to create a paper which informed its readers about the real intentions of such articles.

## The Second Yomiuri Dispute

There was one particular article which provoked the outbreak of the Second Yomiuri Dispute. This article was interpreted as an offence against the occupation policy, whereupon we received a severe reprimand from GHQ. Immediately afterwards, the occupation authorities declared their intention to destroy the *Yomiuri* newspaper. At that time, the government took measures to bring down prices by buying potatoes from the tenant farmers, while at the same time the price of rice remained high, even though there was a surplus of it stored in the warehouses of the landowners, and despite the fact that there was a famine. This policy was clearly designed to favour the landowners' interests over those of the tenant farmers, which is what we wrote in our article. We were then told that we had criticised the occupation policy. Today news and commentaries are separated, but then, because of lack of space among other reasons, we placed our critical comments at the end of an article. As this was deemed to contradict the rules of objective reporting and, to make things worse, to reflect the subjective opinion of the journalist, we came under pressure. Concerning the declarations from the government side, we stated that it was our task to mention how things looked from the people's point of view. The people's voices and their criticism of the government's measures must be included in a newspaper. This was the kind of paper we wanted to make, but the occupation authorities expected us to produce a democratic paper which stayed within the framework of GHQ's democratisation policies and supported them. This issue brought to light a sharp contrast between ourselves and occupation authorities.

GHQ and the government attacked us, arguing that the *Yomiuri* always spoke of a democratic revolution but in reality was a red paper advocating a socialist revolution. If you actually read the *Democratic Yomiuri* of those six months, you will find no word about any such thing. At that time, the word 'revolution' was in everybody's mouth. It was a time in which speaking of a revolution didn't carry any sinister meaning, because everything was termed a 'revolution' or a 'democratic revolution'. Today you immediately face a big problem when you use this word, but in those tumultuous times directly after the war we all used the word in the sense of 'democratic revolution' with the aim of building a democratic Japan. Therefore in each and every number of the *Democratic Yomiuri* the term 'democratic revolution' was widely used, while the words 'socialism' or 'communism' did not appear at all. So much regarding the contents of the *Democratic Yomiuri*.

Reprints of the *Yomiuri* newspapers do not include copies for the six months during which we produced the paper. It was said that these editions were a disgrace for the *Yomiuri* and therefore could not be reprinted. You can find them, however, on microfilm in the parliament library. If any of you is interested, you can have a look at them. From today's point of view it is not a very attractive newspaper; its slanting characters made it difficult to read. But by taking a look at it, you may be able to understand the general situation of those times.

## All-out confrontation with GHQ

There was a wide gap between the goals of the basic policies promulgated by the GHQ and democratic newspaper as we envisaged it. The American line which was represented by MacArthur was incompatible with our demand that the Potsdam Declaration must be followed to the letter. MacArthur and his occupation forces stood for American interests which caused them to deviate from the Potsdam Declaration. This inconsistency was reflected in the course of action taken with regard to newspapers.

To give an example, there were certain types of incidents which happened quite frequently. Because railway crossings had been destroyed, children were killed by passing trains. Japanese girls and women were raped by members of the occupation forces and were found in the Hibiya Park, covered with blood. Such incidents often occurred, but censorship strictly forbade us to report on them. Utilising the newspapers, the occupation forces controlling Japan intended to communicate to the world an image of Japan under their rule as being a sort of paradise. These intentions determined the way censorship treated the papers. Accordingly, no articles could be published which did not concur with this position. But it is also true that a number of copiously bleeding young women fled into the offices of the *Yomiuri*, seeking protection after they had been molested by American soldiers. Determined to protect these women, young members of our union clashed with the American military police. These young colleagues who had just returned from the war could not bear to watch how Japanese girls of their own age were raped by American soldiers. For this reason employees of the *Yomiuri* newspaper fell out with the military police or soldiers of the occupation army. Although such incidents frequently occurred, they hardly ever made the news. The measures taken by the occupation forces with regard to the newspapers always required us to declare what a great success occupation policies were. A democratic paper was acceptable only if it operated within this framework. Our position, however, deviated. Our newspaper was to be a tool used in the construction of a democratic system by the people, and its declared aim was to uproot militaristic and fascist tendencies.

At this stage American occupation policies took a new direction. On 5 February 1946 Churchill delivered his famous speech about the 'Iron Curtain'. Among the Allies of the anti-fascist camp who had crushed the fascism of the tripartite pact of Japan, Germany and Italy, serious divisions developed. Against the background of the revolution gathering momentum in China, the United States started a policy of integration, with the goal of transforming Japan into a bulwark against the influence of socialist states. This is what Churchill had meant when he used the term 'Iron Curtain' in his February speech in Fulton.

On 1 May of that year, May Day was celebrated for the first time since the war. People turned out in large numbers. Nearly every member of the *Yomiuri* union attended the celebration. As in our opinion a newspaper had the duty of reporting on this festival of the workers, and because we opposed the view that papers had to refrain from actively engaging in any sort of struggle, almost all of us turned up, and we decided to write articles about this event.

Subsequently a number of incidents led to a sudden intensification of popular struggles, such as the so-called 'Food May Day'. At the same time the policies of the occupation authorities became more and more conservative. Under these circumstances the Second Yomiuri Dispute broke out. It was bound to become an all-out confrontation between us and the occupation authorities.

## The lines of confrontation in this labour conflict

At this time the company decided to announce redundancies. Then one day, in broad daylight, police stormed our offices and we were arrested. Pre-war and post-war, this was the first and only incident of police storming the offices of a large newspaper and arresting journalists. On the same day union members of the *Mainichi* and the *Asahi* newspapers together with people from other unions marched to the police station of Marunouchi which was located in the vicinity of GHQ's main offices, and formed a circle around it. They demanded the immediate release from custody of all their *Yomiuri* colleagues. Except for five persons their demand was fulfilled in the end. After this incident threats were uttered that the Yomiuri publishing company would be closed down if we refused to accept the demands of the management. These demands included a change in the editorial policy of the *Democratic Yomiuri*, the discharge of union officials and submission to the course stipulated by the occupation authorities. We reacted by calling a five-day strike. When we were locked out of the company offices, we formed an action group and continued our struggle outside the company. That was on 16 July 1946.

Freedom of opinion was the main point of controversy during the Second Yomiuri Dispute. On no account could we accept that a journalist who had written a certain article be submitted to an ideological screening and then discharged. To us, freedom of thought and a journalist's freedom to follow his own principles were matters to be defended at any cost. Unquestionably, the right to decide whether a certain article is printed or not lies with chief editor, but marking a journalist as a communist and then firing him because of an article he has written is simply unacceptable. If we gave in to such a practice, the journalist's freedom of opinion would be lost forever. We were not robots conditioned to write only what the rulers allowed us to write. Given the terrible experiences all of us had had during the war, we were in no position to surrender. This was one of the controversial issues which motivated our struggle.

Another concerned the nature of a democratic newspaper as we envisaged it, now the war was over. In our opinion a newspaper could only be called democratic if its staff was granted unrestricted access to information sources and the right to investigate the truth. The right of access to information sources and to collect information about relevant matters was not legally conceded to newspapers and their staff during the period immediately after the war. To give just one example, a change in the government or a cabinet reshuffle is a very important matter. But normally those who had a hand in the matter remained utterly silent. At that time it was deemed advisable not to issue any public statement. An appointment to a cabinet position was inevitably accompanied by a lot of wheeling and dealing behind closed doors. The same is still true today, no doubt. We had to pussyfoot around those in power in order to extract some information. If you do not do this sort of information-gathering and rely only on the official announcements of the rulers, you will end up writing lies. Moreover, the unrelenting competition which already existed between the newspapers in those days forced us to use such methods in order to write the best stories.

Today there exists a very fine-tuned mechanism for controlling the mass media. Readers are given the impression that statements by the government or the police always reflect the truth. In fact, that is not the case. Because of certain intentions, only information filtered in advance is released. Information is actually tightly controlled; this is a reality.

Presently, there are hardly any scandals. Once a cabinet has been assembled, only the names of those appointed to a ministerial post are announced. A journalist, however, must be allowed to put together an exact picture of the decision-making process involved. A democratic newspaper has the right to contact those who are in possession of relevant information in order to conduct an investigation. The acceptance of this right as one of the cornerstones of a democratic newspaper was what we demanded.

A third controversial point concerned the opinion of the occupation authorities that the right to determine editorial policy was part of the entrepreneurial prerogative. Accordingly, the appropriation of this right by the workers was an unacceptable infringement. This position directly contradicted our strategy of self-management and therefore became one of the main issues of controversy.

A fourth matter was the dismissal of the complete board of union officials and the leading editorial staff on the grounds that they had committed legal offences against the occupation policy. This was a manifest and unwarranted infringement of our rights. Except for one or two persons, all members of the union's executive organ had been fired. But firing people simply because you don't like their opinion violates the rights of the union and therefore cannot be tolerated. For this reason, the retraction of the discharges was another controversial matter.

## General strike of Newspaper, News Agency and the Broadcasting Service Employees

While the occupation policy drifted further to the right, the worker's movement rapidly and spontaneously gathered strength. We had been locked out and entrenched ourselves in a transformer station near the Yūrakuchō station, right next to where the food centre is located today, in order to continue our struggle. At the same time a large number of National Railway workers and seamen were dismissed, so we joined forces with them.

More and more soldiers returned from the front-lines, a fact that produced a surplus of workers and led to more dismissals. The National Railways, however, did not fire employees with family dependants, so the majority of those who were fired were young men eager to join the fight. Their struggle took on such proportions that it developed into the so-called October Struggle of Sanbetsu Kaigi.

While actively supporting their cause, we also participated in the October Struggle. The decisive battle during the Second Yomiuri Dispute was a general strike of all employees of newspapers, news agencies and the broadcasting sector which we continued until our demand that the dismissals be retracted was fulfilled. Today a situation like that would be inconceivable – a strike of the entire workforce of news agencies and broadcasting stations whose object was to have the dismissal or forced transfer of only thirty people revoked. Only then was such a thing possible.

One of the foremost duties of any union is to protect the livelihood of workers, and to fight against unjustified dismissals and transfers which those who are concerned do not want. Today the unions hardly ever oppose such dismissals and similar measures, which are termed 'voluntary retirement from the company'. We on the other hand were determined to fight together with all workers of the same branch if only one of us was fired or transferred; that is just what we did in the October Struggle. The other side, however, fought back, and the *Asahi* paper which had been the mainstay of the joint struggle left the strike front. In the end, only small and middle-sized newspapers and the broadcasting service continued the struggle. The employees of the broadcasting sector prevented all broadcasts and kept on fighting together with us for twenty days.

During a lecture I recently gave on this struggle, I was asked whether stopping the NHK broadcasts could be used as an instrument in a labour conflict as it contravenes the broadcasting law. I was a bit surprised at this unexpected question. Undoubtedly this was a breach of the law. If the power stations cut the power supply, this too is against the law. It seems as if the workers of today think that going on strike is a law-abiding matter, such as staying in bed at home. In essence their question seems to be whether you can call it a strike when the machines are stopped, the power supply is cut or broadcasts are prevented. In our opinion a strike meant stopping production, so that the workers, at least if they wanted to maintain their strength, could for the first time achieve a level of power equal to that of their opponents. Therefore the NHK with its excellent technicians also joined the struggle by preventing all broadcasts. Once a demand had been fulfilled, the technicians used their knowledge and repaired the equipment within minutes on behalf of the workers who did not have the capacity to do this. By doing this, they showed their determination to play a part in the conflict. This is what we used to call a strike.

## The lessons from this labour conflict

Unfortunately, the Second Yomiuri Dispute and the general strike of media workers broke down and ended in defeat. The unfair dismissals were retracted and we were permitted to rejoin our company. However, as the members of the second union which had split off feared being subjected to a sort of lynch law once the strikers returned, we were told that the return of myself and a number of other persons would on no account be accepted, and that our resignation was a condition for the reunification of the first and the second union. Thus we resigned. This marked the end of the Second Yomiuri Dispute.

I have given you a broad outline of the events which constituted the whole Yomiuri Dispute. So far I have explained what the Yomiuri Dispute was all about, what kind of newspaper we intended to publish, and how we established self-management in order to reach our goals.

Finally, I want to make some remarks on the problems facing today's newspapers. In the age of mass media, newspapers have undergone considerable change due to increased circulation and new printing technology. It has become very difficult for a newspaper to report on the real living conditions of ordinary people and on their necessities. When we produced our paper, we concentrated on the unions and the activities of working people and reported on their affairs extensively; consequently we came under criticism as this was considered to be disgraceful behaviour for a normal newspaper. Today not enough is written about the demands of the workers. Reports on workplace matters appear only if there has been some kind of incident. Workers have to live under special conditions. In my opinion, explaining to other workers the rights which have been gained by fighting under these conditions, and standing together in order to secure these rights, is the essence of the labour movement; this is the true meaning of words such as 'solidarity'.

By the way, the standpoint 'Everything's okay if I'm okay' is unacceptable. During the Yomiuri Dispute for instance, there was only one bathroom, and the time it could be used had to be divided up between men and women. We fought for a separate bathroom for the women and we got it. It is important to create a humane working environment. This is why we need a labour movement which ensures that the workers' demands are actually fulfilled. Let's take a look at the problem of equality: women who got a job at the time when students were drafted to the army, and who were dismissed once the war was over, had nothing to eat. Even though they wanted to stay in their jobs, the companies dismissed them for the simple reason that the men gradually returned from the war. Thus the fight for securing women's jobs became one of the main goals of the labour movement of those days. As women at work were exploited for all sorts of chores, we fought against such practices, and we asked 'Why can't women be given the same jobs as men?' I believe that such ordinary, small-scale struggles are very important.

## The newspapers' way of reporting

Because the *Yomiuri* was considered a normal newspaper, we were criticised for carrying articles on such 'trivial' matters. However, we believed that the readers had a right to know about such demands. When there is a strike and the national railways suspend their services, there are all sorts of complaints: people have to walk, the unions do not show any consideration for the normal people who cannot go about their business and so on. Certainly, when train services are suspended, people are bound to experience some discomfort; but *why* did the railway workers call for such an action, and *why* are their demands in effect also our demands – these are matters readers cannot comprehend if they are not properly explained by the newspapers. I believe that if we had only had the chance to go on for another six months, we could have shown how such issues can be dealt with in a newspaper.

During the war, journalists employed the strategy of addressing problems by hiding seemingly insignificant remarks within certain articles. Even today it often happens that a quite important matter is hidden within a leading article. The trick is reading between the lines. Today, the major articles of all leading newspapers are nearly identical. But today, as during the war, we find within some of the smaller articles often one or two lines in which the journalist managed to express what he intended to say.

Today everybody seems to believe that the workers have no more demands, but this is not true. I think they actually have many demands. In my opinion it is a mistake to think that the workers generally regard themselves as part of the middle class and therefore feel that they do not need a labour movement. The task of a newspaper is to inform its readers about the workers' demands, well before the problems they face lead to a labour conflict. The overall goal of the *Democratic Yomiuri* was exactly to fulfil these expectations.

## The spread of the struggle for production control

The push for self-management which formed part of the Yomiuri Dispute spread to a number of other industries where it was referred to as a struggle for production control. On the day before the First Yomiuri Dispute ended (11 December 1945), employees of the Keisei railway line started a struggle for self-management concerning wages which lasted until 29 December. Those who had initiated the union meeting immediately took a train and went to the main offices of their company, issued their demands and from that day took over control of fares. This led to their victory, because although the management had maintained that the demands for higher wages were impossible to meet, the workers, by taking control of the collection of fares, realised that the total amount paid in wages to the workers constituted only a small part of the earnings of the company. Moreover, the workers immediately began to repair the many buses on the Keisei line which had been damaged during the war; they even organised night shifts. For people who went to the country to buy food, a special train service was established, which led to even higher proceeds.

Then there was the famous labour conflict in the Kinuta film studios of the Tōhō company. Their union had organised people from many different professions, because they were aware of the fact that for making a good film one does not only need the directors, but also the actors, stage workers, lighting technicians and so forth. In order to produce democratic films, the union established production control. The reaction of GHQ and the management was the same as in the case of the *Yomiuri* newspaper. Arguing that the right to make films rested with the management alone, they suppressed the union. This marked the beginning of the Tōhō Dispute.

Many different struggles for production control occurred, but most centred around wage issues. In those days there was a food shortage, and workers urgently demanded leave in order to go to the countryside and obtain some foodstuffs. Rations alone were not sufficient to survive, so everybody had to procure more food one way or another. But in the villages they would not get any groceries or rice if they did not bring something for bartering. In the factories, raw materials originally intended for military purposes lay around unused. Factory owners refused to re-start production. Because they had cooperated in the war effort, they demanded indemnity payments from the government, and declined to start production before their demand was met. Moreover, the raw materials could be sold at a high price on the black market. As a consequence, the workers took over control of production and used the raw materials to make pots which they took to the villages. There they bartered them for the food they needed to feed their children.

In February 1946, GHQ and the government issued a declaration condemning production control in the hope that this would stop the movement in its tracks. However, in Tokyo just the opposite happened and the production-control movement gained momentum. In its heyday in May and June, wherever you went, the workers were exercising control over production. Because these tactics had emanated from the *Yomiuri* newspaper, we often had visitors who wanted to learn how to apply them successfully, and we even went out and offered our help as organisers. To my mind this is a clear indication of how strong an influence the Yomiuri Dispute had.

As a matter of fact, if one compares the struggle for production control in Japan immediately after the war with the takeover of factories by striking workers in Italy in August 1920, which occurred in Milan and Turin, our struggle was far more extensive. Even the official statistics for the year 1946 document 400 cases with 230,634 participants for the whole of Japan. With regard to the number of cases, Tokyo heads the list, followed by Hokkaido, Kanagawa, Akita and Saitama. Ranking the number of participants, Hyogo comes first, then Hokkaido, Tokyo, Kanagawa, Niigata and so on. These data show the distribution of the struggles throughout the country. Another characteristic feature was the length of the conflicts.

## The development of union democracy

The Yomiuri Dispute had a special influence on the attitude of employees towards their unions. During the First Yomiuri Dispute, there was actually no union at all. In each and every workplace we organised workers' meetings and established a so-called struggle committee, the members of which were directly elected. These shop-floor struggle committees later formed the company-wide struggle committee which led the First Yomiuri Dispute. This was the way the union was founded. We believed that workers first had to secure their three basic labour rights and only then should form the joint organisation which we refer to as a union. We wanted to establish a union which was based on the recognition of every worker's freedom to strike. Consequently, the decision to join the union should be a matter of personal conviction. Even by the end of the First Yomiuri Dispute, no more than about 70 per cent of the company staff were union members. In our opinion it was good also if non-union members came together, formulated their demands, and then participated in the struggle committee which organised the active measures. In the end, the union was established according to these principles. To our mind, this was the true meaning of democracy.

With the *Asahi* newspaper there was a man named Kyozo Mori. He was one of the leaders of the group which had sabotaged the general strike of our united union, 'Shinbun Tan'itsu'. This man has assumed the posture of a post-war democracy hero, but among other things he wrote in his books that it was impossible to get things done if one acted like the *Yomiuri* workers, and therefore democracy meant the election of an executive organ to which all responsibility is delegated. He advocated the introduction of the formal democratic system to the unions. Then elections should be held and everything which went beyond the mere casting of votes should be left to the elected executive organ.

Convening union meetings and such matters during work hours was detrimental to production. These opinions were promoted also by the Mindō movement which later joined Sōhyō.

The type of democratic trade unionism propagated by the occupation authority stipulated that a conflict between labour and management should be resolved by collective bargaining and, if these attempts failed, that a body of impartial mediators should try to achieve an agreement. This approach reflected their fear of labour conflicts turning into political struggles which could strengthen the influence of the left on the labour movement; in fact, the freedom to strike should not be exercised. However, in our view a strike was a means by which the inherently weak workers could achieve equality with the capitalists. The workers of the *Yomiuri* therefore thought that by using their freedom to strike on a broad scale the workers of an industrial branch could be united, which then would lead to the establishment of industrial unions.

## The goals of the Yomiuri Dispute

Right up to the present day, no industry-wide unions have been established in Japan; existing unions are all of the company or enterprise union type. 'Shinbun Tan'itsu' intended to gain the right of collective bargaining as an industrial union and to conclude wage agreements with the goal of improving working conditions. If, for instance, I were to leave the *Yomiuri* and join another newspaper, my achievements with the *Yomiuri* should have a bearing on how my wage is calculated. The union was also meant to serve the interests of journalists and agency workers who were not employed on a permanent basis. We wanted to have a branch union which would demand collective agreements and the determination of wages and salaries according to performance; whether someone was working for the *Yomiuri* or the *Asahi* or as a freelance journalist would be irrelevant. Only experience and professional performance as a journalist would count, regardless of the newspaper where he was employed.

As a matter of fact, however, after the Yomiuri Dispute enterprise unions were established in all companies. If such a company does not make any profit, wages are not increased – wherever this type of union exists, the workers tend to develop an accommodating attitude to this practice. Consequently, their workload has been increased and people now think only of their own careers. If they want to rise within the company and get a higher salary, they can win their promotion only at the expense of their colleagues. Workers have become prisoners of the enterprise union system. This is the main feature, and at the same time the weakness, of the Japanese unions.

There are a number of reasons why unions in Japan were established only as enterprise or company unions. To my mind, however, the influence of the wartime Dai Nippon Sangyō-Hōkoku-Kai (Sanpō, the Association for Service to the State through Industry) was paramount. The occupation army did order the dissolution of the central Sanpō, but used the so-called 'Shop-floor Sanpō' which still existed in every workplace to speed up the founding of unions. In my opinion, the results of this policy were a most important factor.

On the other hand, the workers of the *Yomiuri* newspaper organised an industrial federation called Shinbun Tan'itsu which became an integral part of the national centre Sanbetsu Kaigi. As this centre became the mainstream of the labour movement in post-war Japan, it is no exaggeration to maintain that the workers' movement of the *Yomiuri* had considerable general influence on the labour movement of those days.

Now every one of you will assume that unions are primarily concerned with the struggle for higher wages. However, this was by no means our ultimate goal during the Yomiuri Dispute. Of course, we did fight for higher wages, as well. Moreover we sought to abolish the differences between temporary and regular employees and give everyone the rank of a regular employee. But our main objective was to determine the newspaper's share of responsibility for the war and, based on this self-critical attitude, to build real democracy in Japan. Therefore we wanted the *Yomiuri* to be a newspaper of the people and tried to achieve our goals by taking the management of the company into our own hands.

But conflicts arose among ourselves on the one hand and with capital owners and the occupation forces on the other. Their resistance led to the First and the Second Yomiuri Disputes which ended before we had fully achieved our goals. Following these conflicts, the *Yomiuri* was rapidly and completely turned around by the other side; every day articles were published which denounced the labour movement. It is amazing that such a change could occur. We had written that 'the Yomiuri newspaper will forever be a paper of the people', but in the end it became a very different paper.

Perhaps my lecture was somewhat difficult for you to understand, as you have grown up in a period when the post-war democracy was already well established. But if you take a historical perspective on this post-war democracy and use my lecture as a source of information on which movements played a part immediately following the surrender, how they tried to build this democracy, what became of it afterwards and how today's situation came about, I would be very happy indeed.

The Yomiuri Dispute did not only concern wages or other economic matters. In order to give you a comprehensive picture of the Yomiuri Dispute, I have in this lecture tried to give you an outline of what our intentions were at that time.

## Notes

1. Edo era: period of rule of the Shōguns from the Tokugawa family, thereby also known as the Tokugawa era.
2. The Ginza: a big shopping street and business centre in Tokyo.
3. Taishō era: the period of the Taishō Emperor (1912–26).
4. Tenrikyō: a sect in the tradition of the Japanese native religion, founded by a peasant woman in 1838. Its present number of followers is estimated at over 1 million.
5. Ashihei Hino: author and journalist who glorified the war effort in his books and articles.
6. Masao Maruyama (1914–96): one of the most influential Japanese political scientists.
7. Izutarō Suehiro (1888–1951): jurist (civil law); co-author of the Japanese labour law.

# 3 The Labour Conflicts of Tōhō Motion Pictures, 1946–50

*Takeo Itō*

**Takeo Itō**

| | |
|---|---|
| 1910 | Born on 17 July in Fukui prefecture |
| 1934 | Graduated from the Faculty of Letters of Waseda University and joined the Film Department of the Ōsawa Company (later to become Tōhō) |
| 1941 | Promoted to producer |
| 1948 | Voluntary resignation |
| 1950– | Managing director of Shinsei-Film, production of *And Yet We Live* (Dokkoi ikiteiru, 1952) and *Storm Clouds over Hakone* (Hakone fuunroku, 1953)<br>Subsequent production of the following films as an independent producer: *City of Violence* (Bōryoku no machi, 1951), *The Tower of Lilies* (Himeyuri no tō, 1953), *Hiroshima* (1955), *As Far as the Clouds Sail* (Kumo nagaruru hate ni, 1956), *Muddy Pictures* (Nigorie, 1956), *The Human Wall* (Ningen no kabe, 1960), *Fight Without Weapons* (Buki naki tatakai, 1961), *The Factory of Slaves* (Dorei kōjō, 1966), *Takiji Kobayashi* (1974), *Nomugi Pass* (Nomugi tōge, 1979), *The Southern Cross* (Minami Jūjisei, 1982).<br>For the Daiei company he produced the series *The Scout* (Shinobi no mono), *The Giant White Tower* (Shiroi kyotō) and *Annular Solar Eclipse* (Kinkanshoku)<br>At present, Takeo Itō is in charge of administrative affairs of the Society for the Preservation of Independent Film Production Companies |

### Trade union functions

1946 Chairman of the Tōhō Employees Union
1947 Chairman of the Union of Japanese Film and Theatre Workers (Nichieien)
1952 Resigned as chairman of Nichieien

### Publications

The chapter 'The Tōhō conflict – the only thing which was lacking were the warships' (Gunkan dake konakatta Tōhō sōgi) in: Ichiro Mikuni, *Reports on Shōwa History,* Banchō Shobō, 1975

## I Editor's Overview

The Tōhō Labour Conflict (in particular, the Third Conflict in 1948) followed the pattern of post-war labour conflicts which had been established with the Yomiuri struggle. It belongs to the 'management counter-offensive' type. This type of conflict is characterised by attempts on the part of management to regain its entrepreneurial authority by forcing the resignation of union officials and to provoke conflicts by splitting a union. In the case considered here, management also tried to restructure the company. The Tōhō labour conflict can be divided into four phases, and, as this conflict concerned the film industry which by its very nature draws the attention of ordinary people, it was extensively discussed by the public. The third strike in particular, in which 2,000 policemen were mobilised to disperse the strikers entrenched in the studios, a company of US soldiers with three tanks and six armoured vehicles appeared on the scene, and three fighter planes circled above, was such a remarkable event that later on it was described with the words: 'The only thing which was lacking were the warships.'

During this conflict, the management, adopting the motto 'elimination of the two red evils' (which meant the company's deficit and the union) staged an offensive against the union which had the full support of the Nikkeiren.[1] The union on the other hand regarded this development as a preliminary skirmish against an impending nation-wide wave of mass dismissals and, supported by Sanbetsu Kaigi, formed a 'united resistance front'. Thus the conflict became the focus of a nation-wide confrontation between capital and labour.

The management's success in this conflict gave rise to the management counter-offensive in the Tōshiba Labour Conflict during the following year and led to incidents which resulted in a fundamental shift of power between management and labour in post-war Japan.

## The First Tōhō Labour Conflict, 1946

The Tōhō Stock Company was founded in 1943 by a merger of the Tokyo Takarazuka Theatre and the Tōhō Motion Pictures Stock Corporation. The former company had been founded by Ichizo Kobayashi of the Hankyū Railway Company in 1932, the latter by Yoshio Ōsawa of the Institute of Photochemistry in 1937.

After the merger, the Tōhō-Kinuta studios formed the main element of the Tōhō Motion Pictures Stock Corporation headed by Yoshio Ōsawa, which itself was part of the Tōhō Stock Company under the leadership of Ichizō Kobayashi. The fact that both men had incompatible characters became apparent in the subsequent period and had a strong influence on the Tōhō labour conflicts.

The first union to be formed in the post-war film industry was the union of employees of the Tōhō-Kinuta studios (founded on 5 December 1945). This later was transformed into the Tōhō employees' union (17 February 1946) which after a short while comprised the entire Tōhō staff. Immediately following its establishment, the union initiated the First Labour Conflict (21 March 1946), using production control as its main strategy. It ended on 6 April after the union had succeeded in pushing through its demands: a collective agreement was reached which resulted in an improvement of the salary system. This meant an almost complete victory for the union.

## The Second Tōhō Labour Conflict, 1946

After the strike, the Tōhō union began organising an industrial federation of film and theatre unions with subdivisions formed by the various company unions. At the same time, Nichieien (the Industrial Union of Japanese Film and Theatre Workers, which was founded on 28 April 1946 and had 12,000 members) was established in cooperation with the employees of the companies Shōchiku and Daiei.

In October 1946, Nichieien joined a strike for higher wages and salaries which was coordinated with the October Struggle of Sanbetsu Kaigi. Because the companies refused to recognise the right of Nichieien to engage in collective bargaining as an industrial federation with subdivisions, negotiations stalled. However, when union groups in the various companies started strike action one after another, most of the strike's goals were achieved within a few days.

Only the Tōhō subdivision needed considerably longer, taking about fifty days to reach a conclusion, as the management insisted on an absolutely unambiguous collective agreement. Finally, the company's management agreed with the demands of Nichieien, and the conflict ended with the conclusion of a labour agreement according to American standards, which reflected the point of view of the managing director, Mr Yoshio Ōsawa. It called for the establishment of a consultative system jointly formed by employees and employers at the workplace, the appointment of shop stewards and a democratisation of the internal structures of the company by means of management consultative groups. As a result, the union acquired a say in the planning and production of films and the entrepreneurial prerogatives of the management were curtailed. However, during this conflict a group emerged around the film stars Denjirō Ōkōchi, Kazuo Hasegawa, Setsuko Hara and others, which called itself 'Group of the Flag of the Ten' and opposed the joint struggle of Nichieien. This soon led to a split in the union leadership and the establishment of a third union (a second union had already been founded by the management during the First Tōhō Conflict). The management, together with members of the second and the third union, then founded the Shin Tōhō Stock Company.

## The Third Tōhō Labour Conflict, 1948

According to the management's point of view, the company's deficit was caused primarily by the influence of the union on management affairs as a result of the agreement mentioned above; the management therefore tried to regain the prerogative lost to the union. The group around Ichizō Kobayashi took the initiative by calling for the resignation of Mr Yoshio Ōsawa. After having consolidated their position within both camps of the managing board, they enforced the dismissal of 1,200 persons, among them 270 employees of the Tōhō-Kinuta studios who comprised the main forces within Nichieien. Resisting this move, the union leadership issued a 'Manifesto of Disobedience' and instituted measures to mobilise support throughout the country following a call to support strike action. For instance, Toshiro Mifune, Yoshiko Kuga and others of the so-called 'new faces' used street propaganda as a means of advocating the common cause and tried to win broader support among the general public. As a result, a group of sympathisers formed a 'joint defence group' of about 3,000 persons which proceeded to occupy the Tōhō studios; thus the Tōhō struggle developed into a major social conflict.

While the strike dragged on, the Mindō faction organised itself within the union and soon caused a split. The company and this new union reached an agreement on re-opening the studios which formed the basis for a decision of the Tokyo municipal court on 19 August ordering the expulsion by force of the occupants of the studios. Then the authorities resorted on a broad scale to repressive measures. A confrontation was avoided, however, when the occupants left the studios. Thereupon twenty union officials handed in their resignations (among them the chairman of Nichieien, Takeo Itō, the directors Satsuo Yamamoto and Fumio Kamei and the cameraman Yoshio Miyajima), and the strike ended in a defeat for the union.

## Results

At the end of the strike, 386 left the union, but the majority (698 members) remained. Those who left joined the Zen'eien (Federation of Cinema and Theatre Workers' Union). In 1950, another 1,315 employees were dismissed, about 35 per cent of the staff. As the majority of those dismissed were members of Nichieien, its influence was considerably diminished. In a parallel development, on 25 August GHQ ordered the dissolution of the Communist Party cells within the Tōhō-Kinuta studios. Even in the context of the chain of events referred to as the 'red purge', this measure was of unprecedented rigour. When in 1951 the Shōchiku subdivision also left it, Nichieien, which in effect had been transformed into a neutral, independent union, abandoned its former structure as an industrial federation and was reorganised as a loose association. The Tōhō subdivision changed its name to Tōhō Enterprise Union, under which it still exists today.

Those who had been dismissed during the Tōhō conflict founded independent production companies and continued to produce films dedicated to the spirit of the Tōhō struggles. It is no exaggeration to claim that the structure of today's Japanese film industry is a result of the Tōhō labour conflicts. Production is mainly done by independent production companies, while the marketing business lies in the hands of the big corporations.

## II Lecture by Takeo Itō

The Tōhō Labour Conflict extended over a period of five years, beginning in March 1946 – a year after the Allies had landed in Japan – and ending in December 1950. The first conflict began on 21 March 1946 with the object of achieving production control; the second was the so-called 'October Struggle' during the same year; the third struggle, which lasted for 200 days, opposed the unjustified dismissals (the 'red purge') in 1948, and was later described with the words, 'The only thing which was lacking were the warships'; and the fourth conflict focused on a second wave of dismissals (a second red purge) in 1950, which was the final blow directed by the management against the union. The term 'Tōhō Labour Conflict' thus covers these four labour disputes which occurred within a period of five years. Immediately after the war, nobody had thought it possible that the Tōhō film workers would stage such a spectacular fight.

In two respects, the Tōhō Labour Conflict was a war by proxy. For the entire Japanese film industry, the first and the second conflicts had a decisive impact on the future development of the post-war Japanese film. The third and fourth conflicts were widely regarded not merely as between management and labour within the film industry, but as representing in general the type of struggle which occurred everywhere in Japan during that period. This view was taken by the mass media, which covered the subject extensively. I hope that my lecture, which will focus on these two points, will give you a broader understanding of the position of the Tōhō Labour Conflicts within the history of the Japanese film and the history of the relations between capital and labour in Japan.

## The film and theatre policy of GHQ

It was in September 1945 that the commander of the Allied occupation forces in Japan, General MacArthur, who at first sight had the relaxed manner of a pipe smoker, made his headquarters in the building of the Daiichi life insurance company in Hibiya. The task he saw himself confronted with was to build on the Japanese island chain a democratic state which had the support of the people. Although MacArthur was generally known as the 'Caesar of the Pacific', he did not seem to possess much confidence where matters of civil administration were concerned, as he brought in a whole team of proponents of the New Deal as consultants. These New Dealers, who had proved their abilities after the 1929 world economic crisis, were the favourites of former US President Roosevelt.

On 10 October 1945, MacArthur ordered the release of sixteen political prisoners held in the prisons of Fuchō and Toyotama, among them twelve leading members of the Communist Party including Kyūichi Tokuda and Yoshio Shiga, and four religious conscientious objectors. Following these first releases, about 3,000 other political prisoners were freed according to the human rights directive, while the leading ranks of the armed forces and the navy, members of the financial and the political elite, and the leaders of right-wing organisations, took their places behind bars. Concerning the drafting of a new constitution, MacArthur stressed the importance of the people's sovereignty and the renunciation of war; trade unions were formed and MacArthur issued orders calling for the organisation of workers into unions throughout the country. Further measures such as land reform, the introduction of women's suffrage and so forth, laid the foundation for a far-reaching democratisation of Japan. The Allies promulgated guidelines for the occupation of Japan according to the Potsdam Declaration, and the Far Eastern Commission based in Washington, which comprised delegates of eleven nations, supervised MacArthur's administrative measures through its Tokyo subsidiary, the Allied Council for Japan.

On 22 September, Iwao Mori, the executive director of the Tōhō-Kinuta studios, attended a meeting at the Civil Information and Education Section (CIE) of GHQ. Shōchiku likewise had sent its vice president, Shirō Kido, and Daiei was represented by its president, Kan Kikuchi, and vice president, Eiichi Nagata. Among the companies producing short films, Asahi News Pictures had sent its executive director, Einosuke Ōmura, and some other top figures. The reason for their appearance was that they had been summoned by the man in charge of matters concerning film and theatre, Mr David Conde, who wanted to hear what these dignitaries had to tell him. Conde was a leading light among the New Dealers. The idea of educating the film-loving Japanese people through this medium made his heart beat faster. He had graduated in Japanese Studies in the United States, was familiar with the contemporary history of the country, had, after the landing in Manila, visited POW camps to interview Japanese prisoners about the current situation of the Japanese film industry in detail and was generally well prepared. He arrived in Japan burning for action. Conde had printed some guidelines concerning Japanese films; these he now handed over to the leading representatives of the Japanese film industry. In his eloquent manner, he explained some of the rules. For instance, historical dramas, especially bloody vendetta stories such as *Chūshingura*,[2] were prohibited; on the other hand, films exposing Japanese war crimes and about the friendly reception at home of Japanese POWs were welcome. Films were to be made which proved the wrongness of feudalistic attitudes, e.g. that captivity in war was the worst disgrace. Accordingly I immediately started the production of *Green Homeland* (Midori no kokyō, January 1946), in which Setsuko Hara plays a woman who has hidden herself at home throughout the war out of shame for her elder brother, who had been captured in battle. But now she comes out to tell the world: 'Is being a prisoner of war really such a disgraceful thing?' This was in December of the year the war ended.

During the subsequent period, Conde often came to our studios, encouraging us when we were busy producing films such as, for instance, Keisuke Kinoshita's *Morning for the Osone Family* (Ōsoneke no Asa), Tadashi Imai's *An Enemy of the People* (Minshu no teki), Fumio Kamei's *Japanese Tragedy* (Nihon no higeki) or Kiyoshi Kusuda's *As Long as I Live* (Inochi aru kagiri, based on the memoirs of Hotsumi Ōzaki). Even though it did not come under his jurisdiction, he strongly supported the establishment of unions of film workers. Because the division of GHQ in charge of such matters (the Labour Division) had its offices next to his room, he presumably coordinated his actions with the people there.

Supported by these efforts to help along the democratisation process, the Japanese, who had been completely demoralised by their defeat, began to regain some courage. But when in June 1946 the United States, in view of the growing antagonism between the superpowers which was to become the Cold War, adopted an openly anti-communist stance, Conde and the other New Dealers were fired and replaced by Washington right-wingers. The Japanese capitalists, who had gone through a difficult time because of their uncertainty over where the democratisation policies might lead, must have heaved sighs of relief.

## The founding of the Tōhō Employees' Union

About half a year after Japan's unconditional surrender, on 17 February 1946, the Tōhō Employees' Union was founded in the Mitsukoshi hall; I was elected chairman. I accepted this position because in my opinion the union had to fulfil the important task of promoting the production of films, but especially of furthering unity among workers. Other companies followed suit and founded their own unions: Kajiro Yamamoto became chairman at the Tōhō-Kinuta studios; at Shōchiku Ōfuna it was Kenji Mizoguchi who held this post, and at Shōchiku-Shimogamo it was Masahiro Makino. The fact that these famous directors were elected chairmen of unions immediately drew the attention of the general public.

The first conflict, starting in March 1946, was a struggle for production control. Owing to the shock of Japan's defeat, the capitalists were not very eager to do business. Therefore the employees started to produce films on their own. Having taken this first step, they then decided to do the work of the managers as well. Moreover, people were driven to starvation by the lack of goods and a high rate of inflation which required a steep increase in wages.

On 21 March, the union of the Tōhō-Kinuta studios began negotiations with the management, but these soon failed. Three days later, the Tōhō supreme struggle committee was established by delegates from all over the country who had gathered on a stage on the studio site. We decided on production control by the employees as a strategy for our fight – the management at that time consisted only of the managing director, while the department heads and their deputies as well as the secretarial staff, had joined the workers' side. On top of that, the union was supported by GHQ in accordance with the spirit of the Potsdam Declaration; it is by no means surprising that its position was quite strong.

Nevertheless, managing director Yoshio Ōsawa, who had graduated from Princeton University and adopted the American view on labour relations, had his own ideas concerning trade unions. During discussion, for instance, of the use of staff during a strike or of the selection of negotiators for collective bargaining, he always wanted to begin by debating the basics of trade unionism. The union on the other hand gave in to this, and it took five days for a settlement to be reached. During this strike we often felt as if we were attending a lecture on the question 'What are trade unions?' While exercising production control, the union produced the film *The People Creating Tomorrow* (Ashita o tsukuru hitobito), which was shown free of charge in some cinemas.

Soon afterwards, on 28 April, the employees of the Japanese film and theatre companies united and founded an industrial union with subdivisions – Nichieien. Yoshio Miyajima from Tōhō, who had led the strike for one day, was elected chairman. The union comprised 10,800 members, of which the majority, 5,600 persons, came from Tōhō. The grand master of the Japanese scriptwriters, Yasutarō Yagi, became chairman of the executive committee. Yasutarō Yagi was one of the scriptwriters who in 1935 had contributed to the rise of the Japanese film. He had written the script for *Never Ending Progress* (Kagirinaki zenshin, directed by Tomotaka Tasaka, with Isamu Kosugi in the leading role), a wonderful film showing the tragedy of an employee. Now he became the first chairman, and I was elected chairman of the Tōhō division. One year later (1947) I succeeded him and became chairman of Nichieien.

## Japanese film before and after the war

At this stage I have to explain how it was possible that the Japanese film workers were able successfully to exercise production control not even a year after the war, and why they could establish such an industrial federation with subdivisions as

Nichieien. Their achievements must be seen against the background of a situation in which, before the war, the Japanese film had already reached a cinematic standard which, internationally, was rightfully a source of pride.

During the war there had been rumours that Tōhō offered better working conditions, and a number of famous stars and directors joined us. Because Tōhō was a younger company than Shōchiku and Daiei, superstars such as Denjirō Ōkōchi and Kazuo Hasegawa were enticed away from other firms, moves which even led to an attack on Hasegawa during which he suffered facial injuries from knife cuts. In spite of this incident, Tōhō managed to attract many such superstars.

Some famous directors also went over to Tōhō. One of them, Mikio Naruse, had been a director with Shōchiku where he had roused high hopes. Already during our studies at Waseda University he had produced some wonderful films and was generally regarded as a young hotshot director. His older colleague Yasujirō Ozu, was also at Shōchiku and fascinated cinema fans all over Japan with his films about the *petit bourgeois*. Mikio Naruse joined Tōhō at the same time that I started working for the company.

Satsuo Yamamoto, who had studied at Waseda University at the same time as me, began making films at an early age, as he had been expelled from university because of his activities in the students' movement. He worked as assistant director for Shōchiku Ōfuna under the supervision of Mikio Naruse. When Naruse left for Tōhō, he asked Yamamoto to join him. He accepted, and working there as Naruse's assistant director he produced *Wife, Be Like a Rose!* (Tsuma yo bara no yō ni, 1935). When this film was named the best of that year, everyone said that it was easy to make films at Tōhō, and very good ones, too. There were even rumours that Mikio Naruse had proposed marriage to Sachiko Chiba who had played the leading role.

Satsuo Yamamoto had learned a lot during his time under Mikio Naruse, and being a bright young guy he soon became a director himself, making his debut in 1937 with Nobuko Yoshiya's *Miss* (Ojōsan). During the same year, both parts of *Mother's Song* (Haha no kyoku) were shot also. The story was again written by Nobuko Yoshiya. When this film had its premiere, people turned up in such large numbers that the queue went three times around the building. It will be shown time and again in the future. It is great, isn't it, to have achieved such things at an age of twenty-five or twenty-six?

Having just finished this film, Satsuo Yamamoto announced that he was fed up with doing that sort of thing. He was allowed to produce films on subjects he himself liked, such as Andre Gide's *Pastorale* (Den'en kōkyōgaku, 1938) and Tomoji Abe's *The City* (Machi, 1939). Then he did one that even the company liked – *Tange Sazen* (1939), in which Denjirō Ōkōchi plays a man who goes around with a sword and a contemptuous look on his face, killing people – and it was widely acclaimed. Afterwards he could just do as he pleased, and when the war was finally over he had already made three masterpieces.

Teinosuke Kinugasa once said: 'The Japanese film and I are of the same age.' He died two years ago (1981) at the age of eighty-seven, which means that the Japanese film is about ninety years old. Teinosuke Kinugasa was an even brighter lad than most of the other directors. Unsatisfied with Japanese films, he went to Russia at the age of twenty-two or twenty-three to visit the locations where Eisenstein's *The Battleship Potemkin*, a film enjoying global acclaim at that time, had been shot. Even if some may disagree, this film is still among the best ever made.

Thus among the great directors of that time, the following worked for Tōhō: Kajiro Yamamoto (*Horses* [Uma], 1941); Heinosuke Gosho, who had come from Shōchiku-Ōfuna; Shiro Toyoda (*Spring on a Small Island* [Kojima no haru], 1940); Tadashi Imai (*The Tajinko Village* [Tanjiko mura], 1940; *Furious Seas* [Ikari no umi], 1944); and Akira Kurosawa, whose debut film *Sugata Sanshiro* (Sugata Sanshiro, 1943) had fascinated cinema-goers. At Shōchiku-Ōfuna, Keisuke Kinoshita sat in wait for the right moment to follow Akira Kurosawa to Tōhō.

But with the other companies there were also great masters such as Kenji Mizoguchi, Daisuke Itō and Hiroshi Inagaki, all of them a little older than Naruse or Toyoda. From 1935 onwards, the Japanese film had reached a high artistic level, and these powerful cinematic forces pressed ahead now that the war was over.

## The background to the second strike (the October Struggle)

Now let us talk about the second strike. On 15 May 1946, the head of the Allied Council for Japan, Acheson, delivered a strongly anti-communist speech in which he said: 'Our occupation forces do not encourage communism.' In the presence of the Soviet delegate, he announced a sharp change in the occupation policies. Acheson had been MacArthur's staff officer since their arrival in Japan and enjoyed his complete confidence. Therefore one can be sure that MacArthur approved of Acheson's words, because the latter undoubtedly had checked every move with him beforehand.

Three months earlier, on 5 March, British Prime Minister Winston Churchill had delivered his famous 'Iron Curtain' speech in Fulton, Missouri. In a sharply worded note he expressed his conviction that an unfortunate development was taking place in which the Eastern European countries, which the Soviets regarded as their sphere of influence, were being turned into an 'iron curtain' protecting the Soviet Union. This anti-Soviet speech by Churchill received world-wide attention as a harbinger of the Cold War. Only seven months after his arrival in Japan, it seemed as if MacArthur regarded the Potsdam Declaration as mere rubbish. The shipload of New Dealers which had been brought in from the United States had already been sent home. David Conde, who could not tear himself away from Japan, showed great tenacity by engaging in research for his book *War in Korea* (published by the Iwanami publishing company) which enabled him to shuttle between the Korean peninsula and Japan, playing for time. But in March of the following year, he was ordered by GHQ to leave Japan within a week, and sore at heart he finally returned to the United States.

The Japanese capitalists had been encouraged by the speeches of Acheson and Churchill, and during the summer they started suppressing the Second Yomiuri Conflict. In this period, during which the workers found it extremely difficult to find enough food to survive, the capitalists enforced rationalisations combined with dismissals: 75,000 employees of the National Railways and 43,000 seamen were told to leave. To prepare for battle, Shinbun Tan'itsu proposed the foundation of Sanbetsu Kaigi, which came into existence at a plenary meeting held from 19 to 21 August at the Kanda city hall. This new organisation had 1.64 million members. At the plenary meeting, Nichieien formally joined Sanbetsu Kaigi.

When, in October of that year, workers throughout the country went on the offensive, Nichieien joined the attack. This was the Second Tōhō Conflict.

## The collective bargaining agreement

Unexpectedly, the Second Tōhō Conflict turned into a massive fifty-day strike. It became a war by proxy in the sense that it also aimed at the recognition of Nichieien by both Shōchiku and Daiei as an organisation affiliated to Sanbetsu Kaigi.

At a national plenary meeting held on 5 October, Nichieien called for strike action in the entire film industry; on 15 October, unified demands were presented and the individual companies were informed that a general strike had been called. One after the other their unions joined in. The management of Shōchiku and Daiei refused to recognise Nichieien's role as an industrial federation and entered into negotiations with their company unions, which after several days led to agreements. Only Tōhō acted differently because, just as during the first conflict, managing director Yoshio Ōsawa again had his own ideas. In his opinion, firmly institutionalised labour relations were of great importance for the future development of Japan. Therefore he wanted to accept only a 'perfect' collective agreement. 'Perfect' meant to him that the collective agreement should include a mechanism for routine mediation in case of controversies arising between labour and management, so that strikes could be avoided. Concerning workers' participation and personnel matters, the union should be granted considerable influence. Company employees should almost automatically become union members, and he also wanted to implement the principle of 'one company, one union'. He intended to use Tōhō as a test case for these ideas.

As Yoshio Ōsawa liked the word 'shop', all departments were renamed as shops; there was a general affairs shop, a planning shop, a production shop and a shooting shop. Each shop had a representative called a shop steward who formerly had been the head of department or a group leader. Union officials negotiating with them were called foremen. For all functions, English terms were used. 'Moreover,' he said, 'we should organise a management consultative body as follows: in every workplace there will be a *grievance machinery*, i.e. an appeal committee through which the opinions of the workers can be brought to the management's attention. In the first step there will be consultations between the department and sub-department heads. The next level is the studio director, and on the highest level there are consultations with the main office.'

Because I was the chairman of the Tōhō subdivision, during the era of Mr Conde, the Labour Division had given me a weighty introduction to labour issues. The labour division had also lent me 'for 99 years' a compilation of the latest American collective bargaining agreements. I suspected that Yoshio Ōsawa referred to the same sources, because once we had started our negotiations, he used the same terms and definitions as we did. The communication went smoothly, even without explanations of such unfamiliar terms as 'closed shop' or 'union shop'. I think that with a perfect and lasting collective agreement Yoshio Ōsawa also intended to block the irksome obstructionists from Takarazuka, Tōhō's disagreeable parent company.

Thus our collective bargaining went on, and we were able to draft an agreement like never before. Many companies sent delegates to study it and copy the model. Consequently Yoshio Ōsawa was in high spirits, and had a number of copies printed and handed them out freely.

Yoshio Ōsawa wanted to use the strike as a test case for the establishment of future relations between labour and management, and he delayed the conclusion of the conflict for such a long time that finally I had to ask him what he was up to. He in turn asked me whether we would not like to go on striking for a little longer, and said, 'Come with me, there is something I want to show you.' Then he gave me a handful of telegrams sent by the grey eminence of Takarazuka, Ichizō Kobayashi, who during the war had been Minister of Industry and Trade, which all said something like: 'Finish with the reds at the Tōhō-Kinuta studios, it doesn't matter how long it takes, even if the grass may grow in the studios!' With a smiling face, Yoshio Ōsawa showed us heaps of such messages which he received almost every day. Ichizō Kobayashi was a theatre man, while Yoshio Ōsawa was a film producer, and both men had very divergent opinions. Their attitudes marked two irreconcilable positions within the Tōhō company between which no balance whatsoever could be established.

Having entered into strike action, we would have preferred a speedy settlement, while the management took the position that once the battle had started we should take as much time as necessary in order to develop rational relations between employees and employers. Thus the normal positions were completely reversed. Meanwhile the other companies cheered: 'Fine for us if the Tōhō people continue their strike; while they are busy at it we may as well take over a slice of their business and make a little profit. Yeah, go on with the strike!' Or they said: 'If the people from Tōhō gain something from their strike, we still can jump on the bandwagon.' The people from Daiei were in fact very much afraid that the union might take over the company if they agreed to Nichieien's demand for collective bargaining. They also claimed that Nichieien's action was so rash that it did not leave them enough time to discuss the union's demands sufficiently, and they watched the activities of Nichieien with great suspicion. Those timid underlings were simply not used to a situation in which workers and managers were showing each other their teeth. They acted as if they thought: 'First let's wait and see what the Tōhō people gain from their fight, and whether they can provide a model for us. Then we'll do something here, too.'

Thus Nichieien led a sort of war by proxy with the young company Tōhō, in order to win recognition of its right to collective bargaining, while the other companies were sitting on the fence, waiting to see which way the cookie would crumble.

## The organisational concept of Nichieien as a branch union

In theory our idea was this: apart from being employees of some company, workers in the first place exist as members of a class, i.e. they are craftsmen, actors or technicians. We intended to organise all of them in a union of film and theatre workers with subdivisions according to the industrial federation model. The officials of Nichieien's central committee therefore went to the various companies and explained to their workers: 'You're hired by a film company, and Nichieien will try to reach a collective agreement with the management in the different companies, which will define the conditions offered to you.'

While the companies maintained that Nichieien only pretended to actively promote quality within the film and theatre sector but in reality just wanted to join Sanbetsu Kaigi and instigate a revolution, we insisted that we were a trade union movement of film artists and had no such plans. All we wanted were better working conditions and an improvement of the employees' situation. In the very beginning we had called ourselves an 'employees' union', because at first we somehow did not like the word 'worker'. Every day the directors heatedly debated whether they should call themselves 'employees' or 'workers', and changing our name to 'workers' union' involved endless discussions, with arguments such as that if a school teacher, according to the vocabulary of class theory, was a worker, we were workers, too.

There were some sections within our company for which a confederation of the Tōhō union with the unions from Shōchiku, Daiei, Nichiei News and other companies would have meant that as everyone received the same salary, the agreement on minimum wages would cover them, too. Because this definitely would result in a financial disadvantage for those concerned, they opposed such a confederation. Another problem was the different nature of the work done in different departments; production and marketing people therefore had very diverging opinions. This fact certainly was an obstacle to our goal of creating an industrial federation with subdivisions, and here the first fractures became visible, along which the union was at a later stage to break up. There were quite a number of such inconsistencies which we carried along.

## The symbol of our struggle – Akira Kurosawa's *No Regrets for Our Youth*

Akira Kurosawa's talent had been noted when during the war in 1939 he had written the script for *Silence* (Shizuka nari); having worked for some time as assistant director for Kajirō Yamamoto, he soon grabbed the initiative by making his debut film *Sugata Sanshiro.* Susumu Fujita plays Sanshiro, and in this film Kurosawa showed his novel and very impressive technique for the first time. Cinema-goers and critics alike gave him a standing ovation and heaped generous praise on him. During his time as an assistant director, Kurosawa had sailed in the wake of Kajirō Yamamoto and had managed to learn the art of directing and scriptwriting. His work also gave him a profound understanding of the need to actively promote teamwork with the crew. He loved the simple people working in the studios, and he had the dream of using this atmosphere for creating outstanding works of art.

In October 1946 Akira Kurosawa completed his film *No Regrets for Our Youth* (Waga seishun ni kuinashi). Its subject is the Takigawa incident at Kyoto University. Setsuko Hara, playing the role of the professor's daughter, makes a striking appearance. Susumu Fujita plays the student strike leader. Watching this film, everyone was deeply moved and realised that the war was really over, that Japan had finally changed, that such wonderful films could again be made and that the time in which we lived was a beautiful one.

At the same time Keisuke Kinoshita of Shōchiku presented *Morning for the Osone Family*, which together with Kurosawa's work was praised by the public as one of the highlights of film-making. Hideo Sekigawa who was later ousted from Tōhō and produced *Listen to the Roar of the Ocean* (Kike wadatsumi no koe, 1950) with Tōei, belonged to the same generation as Kurosawa, as did Satsuo Yamamoto, Tadashi Imai and others. *No Regrets for Our Youth* and *Morning for the Osone Family*, two works of art which won world-wide acclaim, became the yardsticks by which their later work was measured. When we joined the October struggles, the old hands as well as the mavericks among the directors all had the same attitude: 'Let the democratic revolution end as it may, we will always fight for the opportunity to produce such films.'

## The open-air event in the Kōrakuen baseball stadium

There is one event connected with the October Struggle which I specifically want to mention here. The October Struggle had started on 15 October, and on 20 October Nichieien mobilised all its forces, rented the Kōrakuen baseball stadium and organised an open-air event. On the spot where the pitcher normally stands, big stages were placed on which everyone who had a name in the Japanese film and theatre world was assembled, among them also were the real stars. About 20,000 people turned out.

At that time Densan, the union of the electrical power workers, was in the middle of a strike. Thus when the event started, it was pitch dark. But then the master of ceremonies told the crowd: 'Densan is striking by cutting the power supply, but I think they will provide electricity for us', and at this very moment bright light replaced the complete darkness. The generators were controlled by the Densan employees, and when they had heard about our event they had simply said, 'OK, let's do it' and had turned on the lights. It was really fabulous. Even a man like the director of the theatre department, Mr Hata, whose real intention for coming was to spy on us, was deeply moved and said: 'This is fantastic!' On this note the big open-air event with dancing and modern theatre (*shingeki*) began. When Yoshi Hijikata, the outstanding *shingeki* actor, took over as chairman of the event, Tomoyoshi Murayama also appeared on stage. Among the actors present were Haruko Sugimura and Jūkichi Uno, accompanied by Kazuo Hasegawa and Isuzu Yamada.

The event was organised under the motto: 'On with our October Struggle!' One could say that this great manifestation was a sort of rehearsal for the general strike on 1 February 1947. We were all in high spirits, and in this mood we started the Second Tōhō Conflict.

## Denjirō Ōkōchi's attempt to split the union

During the second conflict, managing director Yoshio Ōsawa made an energetic attempt to cause a split in the union. It is an iron rule that the management will always try to divide the workers if anything unusual happens within the company, in order to secure its control. Yoshio Ōsawa said: 'Look at India. Only when the British had succeeded in splitting the population along religious lines were they able to exert full authority. The facts are clear: friends who fight each other will never realise who the real rulers are. This principle of divide-and-rule is the fundamental lesson to be learned from the colonial era.' Thus Yoshio Ōsawa's strategy was to bring about a division of the workers' organisation in order to gain control over Tōhō. But although he had meticulously prepared this split, once it was achieved its results went far beyond his expectations.

The first to leave our united front were the employees of the sales department. When the struggle began they immediately formed a second union. As there were twenty salesmen for every prefecture, the department comprised about 800 employees. The salesmen's task is dealing with the cinema owners. Owing to the nature of their work, their working-class identity is not very strong. In fact, lumping all the different groups together and forming a single union with subdivisions turned out to be a doubtful strategy, and they were the first to leave us. Publicly they justified their step by criticising Nichieien for joining Sanbetsu Kaigi. Once the first division had occurred, it happened over and over again until the fourth split occurred in 1948.

The third split, which came on the thirtieth day of the October Struggle, was mainly initiated by the so-called 'Group of the Flag of the Ten'. This group had been formed by Denjirō Ōkōchi; among its members were such stars as Kazuo Hasegawa, Takako Irie, Isuzu Yamada, Setsuko Hara and Hideko Takamine.

This division actually showed a schism within the union between the conservative wing represented by stars such as Ōkōchi and the progressive faction led by Akira Kurosawa, Tadashi Imai and Satsuo Yamamoto, which also comprised Teinosuke Kinugasa, Mikio Naruse, Shirō Toyoda and Toshio Yasumi. If I remember correctly, it was the night of 12 October. At that time only rough paper was available, but when Denjirō Ōkōchi, wet to the skin from an evening shower, knocked on my door, he had a scroll of high-quality paper in his hand. He told me: 'We will never be able to produce films without the support of the company. But even if we could produce them, they still would have to be sold and shown in the cinemas. And if we don't run expensive ads in the papers, no one will turn out to watch them. That's the way it is in the film business, and that's what I'm talking about. If we look at things with some degree of realism,' he continued, 'we have to admit that we cannot live without the company and that it is enough if our economic demands are met. A political struggle isn't really necessary.' The scroll he had brought contained a ten-point manifesto in which he had summarised his views. Ōkōchi told me: 'It is my intention to tell everyone that we will stop striking as of tomorrow.' I replied: 'If you come up with such demands, there is nothing I can do about it. Do as you like, I have nothing more to say.' On these words we parted. It was in fact an attempted coup.

## An extraordinary union meeting which lasted until dawn

Following a demand by about 400 union members led by Denjirō Ōkōchi and the director Kunio Watanabe, an extraordinary union meeting was convened on 17 October 1946. On stage No. 5, the largest in the studios, 800 of the 1,200 union members gathered. The meeting began at exactly 1:00 p.m. and became the climax of the October Struggle.

The first point on the agenda was the election of a chairman. The executive committee proposed me as candidate. After three hours, in the final ballot I was elected with a margin of merely forty votes, thus beating the candidate of the faction advocating the split. In a short introductory speech I pointed out that as chairman I had the right to determine who got the floor, and having admonished everyone to accept the outcome of the votes, I opened the meeting.

My intention was to start by having the members of the dissenting faction speak out one after the other. I invited them to come forward to the platform and gave them the floor. For three hours I permitted them to air their views until they finally had had their say. Next I asked those union officials who had been attacked to engage in self-criticism and encouraged members of the youth department who had become the centre of the strike to give us their point of view. It was already around midnight when in my capacity as chairman I decided that it was time to get some result and presented the following summary. I explained that as the strike had reached its final stage and only a last effort was required we could not agree to a division of the union. I proposed that we reach a solution by re-electing the union leadership. Both sides agreed to this course of action and I was asked to organise the voting. I then called for a break of fifteen minutes. Just when I was about to leave the platform, someone in the audience rose and asked: 'Chairman! Shouldn't we ask Kazuo Kubo [a usually calm and gentle man who was chairman of the control committee] to come up to the platform and have the control committee continue with the meeting in order to avoid another sort of *coup d'état*?' It was Yoshio Miyajima who had spoken, the head of the committee for tactical matters.

However, once this gentle Kazuo Kubo had climbed onto the platform and had started to speak, he grew very excited and started to attack all those who wanted to split the union. The union members responded by shouting 'Yeah, he's right', and the attacks against the dissenters began to get out of hand. Kunio Watanabe, one of the initiators of the movement in favour of dividing the union, later said he had feared for his life. When Shintaro Mimura, known as an excellent scriptwriter (and a very serious person), saw how Kunio Watanabe was shouted down and harassed, he called out, 'This is no way of handling the matter!' and told us he would 'join the other side'. 'The other side' were people such as Kunio Watanabe and Denjirō Ōkōchi who saw themselves as pillars of the company and were convinced that they had gained great merit. They were well-established film artists, surrounded by people such as Kon Ichikawa and someone called 'Palemban' (a nickname given to him because he had served in a suicide commando unit in Sumatra which operated from an army base of that name) who hoped their support for the conservative faction would advance their promotion to directors.

'Our side' were people like Mikio Naruse, Shirō Toyoda and Heinosuke Gosho, who in the mid-1930s had laid the foundations of the Golden Age of the Japanese film but had been discontented with the situation during the war and now wanted to make better films. We had the support of the younger generation represented by Satsuo Yamamoto, Hideo Sekigawa, and most of all by Akira Kurosawa. The division of the union was therefore also a confrontation between this rising group of eager youngsters and the established superstars, who until the day before had been forced by the union to do things they found unpleasant and from now on wanted to produce pure entertainment and be adored by the public. 'Until the day before' the union had made each and everyone – including the big stars such as Kazuo Hasegawa – parade in the streets showing posters and waving flags.

The extraordinary meeting was closed at four o'clock in the morning, but the tumultuous events had not only caused 'the other side' to dig in and make the split inevitable, but had increased the number of their supporters, which grew to about 460 persons. All my attempts as chairman at mediation of this extraordinary meeting had been in vain.

## The founding of Shin-Tōhō

Even Yoshio Ōsawa, the managing director, seemed to have felt that his attempts to split the union had carried him too far. In any case, the collective agreement he was so proud of was also concluded with the newly founded third union, with not a single word changed. This led to an interesting problem. Article 1, Section 1 of our collective agreement specified that 'the company will negotiate exclusively with Nichieien'. Any collective bargaining thus had to involve Nichieien and no other party. Section 2 affirmed that 'the company may not employ persons who are not members of Nichieien. Newly hired employees must apply for union membership within two weeks'. The company was therefore obliged to hire employees on the precondition that they would join the union within fourteen days.

However, those who had enforced the split and formed a new union insisted: 'We want the same conditions. We are not the company's junior partner. We have initiated this division for the sake of the Japanese film and in order to serve the company. They must treat us as a legitimate partner.' And thus they demanded that Yoshio Ōsawa should include Article 1, Sections 1 and 2 in the new contract, but referring to their union instead of Nichieien, which he did. He concluded the same contract with both unions! Had he acted in accordance with these contracts, he would have had to fire all members of one of the unions. For Yoshio Ōsawa, the division of the union had created a serious dilemma. In order to find a way out of this situation, Tōhō founded the Shin-Tōhō company, with Tōhō as the only shareholder. Even though all employees of this new company were union members, the contradiction with the Nichieien contract was resolved, as Shin-Tōhō was a wholly independent company.

This is how Shin-Tōhō was founded. Once this by-product of the labour conflict had been established, the conflict came to an end. The annoying fact was that in effect the labour conflict's main result was the establishment of a new company. But perhaps it had to end like this; perhaps this simply was the fate of the Japanese film industry.

## The meaning of our October Struggle

I want to add that the famous director Teinosuke Kinugasa did not give an inch of ground to the faction advocating the union split. He was a man of great passion, which had caused him to visit the locations where *The Battleship Potemkin* had been shot. In his opinion the position adopted by Nichieien was of no consequence whatsoever. The only thing that really mattered to him was the quality of the Japanese film, and in order to produce films of high quality it was necessary to cooperate with anyone who proved to be cooperative. In this respect our union of film workers was different from other Japanese unions. Our struggle may not have had a great influence on Japanese capitalism, but with regard to the Japanese film it was of considerable importance.

Moreover it should be mentioned that Shōchiku and Daiei, who had simply waited to see how things at Tōhō would develop, officially started collective bargaining procedures with Nichieien once the struggle was over.

## The Golden Age of Japanese film

The collective bargaining agreement which had been the outcome of the Second Labour Conflict called for the establishment of a tripartite management consultative council which brought together artists, crews and representatives of the management (who were called shop stewards). Formerly there had been only two sides: the managing director represented the company, everyone else was a union member. Managing director Yoshio Ōsawa, however, introduced a system of division and department heads, and he also maintained that personnel such as gate-keepers and telephone operators should be regarded as belonging to the company's side and not be union members. His views were accepted and laid down in the collective agreement. Matters concerning production and funding of films were discussed and decided by the three sides – i.e. division and department heads, shop stewards and foremen – within the management consultative council. In 1947 this system was introduced throughout the company. Management consultative councils were also formed in the theatre, marketing and production divisions.

The end of the Second Labour Conflict resulted in a renewed enthusiasm for making films which gave our artistic work a strong impetus. Once the strike was over we all said: 'Oh well, now we're going to make some films! Now there'll be a race with Shin-Tōhō!' The first film made by Akira Kurosawa after the strike was *One Wonderful Sunday* (Subarashiki Nichiyōbi, July 1947). Satsuo Yamamoto and Fumio Kamei started working on *Between War and Peace* (Sensō to Heiwa, June 1947). As I acted as producer for both films, I want to give you some information about them.

In *One Wonderful Sunday* a young couple – played by the actors Chieko Nakakita and Isao Numazaki, who died very young – meet on a Sunday afternoon, and neither of them has any money. Having nothing else to do, they take a walk in the park and spend the day dreaming about what they would do if they had money, and in fact it is not really such a wonderful Sunday for them. It has been said that this film described the life of normal Japanese during the post-war era with great realism.

The story of *Between War and Peace* goes like this: of two young men who went to the war and used to love the same girl, only one returns home. He proposes marriage to her, but she refuses and keeps him waiting for two years. As the other one does not come home, she finally accepts and marries him. Then, however, the other man also returns. Having imagined all the time how he would propose to her, he finds her married already and that she even has a child. He decides not to meet her, and then his personal tragedy begins: he rapidly degenerates, acts as a strike-breaker, commits crimes and finally loses his mind. By showing scenes of a requisitioned ship sinking and of refugees from the mainland aimlessly wandering about to the tune 'Song of the Wanderer' (Rubō no kyoku), the film conveyed a strong feeling of dejection. As a symbol of a new age, it came as quite a shock.

Toshio Yasumi had written the original script for this film, and its planning was supported by Hitoshi Ashida, head of Kenpō Fukyukai (the Constitution Promotion Committee, a government agency). On 3 May of that year the new constitution was proclaimed, and the film was meant to support Article IX, in which the right to conduct war is renounced. Anyway, we were unable to complete it until a couple of days after the constitution had been proclaimed. But then the trouble really started. Normally, a film could be shown in the cinemas as soon as the Civil Information and Education Section (CIE) had given its approval. However, in this case the CIE decided to send it to the department of censorship within GHQ (the CCD). Fumio Kamei, Satsuo Yamamoto and I went to the CCD every day in order to get the film released. But once again Fumio Kamei ran out of luck. The censors went to Brigadier General Willoughby and a heated discussion ensued. When the film was finally released one month later, it had been reduced to ninety minutes. Twenty-four cuts had been made and about 1,000 metres of reel were gone. All scenes which had been cut related to the occupation forces.

Thus the premiere was delayed for one month, but once the film had reached the cinemas, people turned out in great numbers. They seemed to be aware of the fact that the occupation forces had interfered. Moreover, this film was regarded as representing a new era. In the end, 5 million people came to see it.

Subsequently, Senkichi Taniguchi produced *Above the Silver Peaks* (Ginrei no hate, August 1947), and Heinosuke Gosho made *Once More* (Ima hito tabi no, April 1947) based on a book by Jun Takami, which tells the tale of a young man in love who is sent off to war. Next Teinosuke Kinugasa made *The Actress* (Joyū, December 1947). The film depicts the love of Sumako Matsui, played by Isuzu Yamada, a member of the 'Group of the Flag of Ten' who had initially joined Shin-Tōhō but soon found her way back to Tōhō. It is one of Kinugasa's most impressive works and as a result of their working together he married Isuzu Yamada. 'Making films makes matches' – the truth of this saying which had spread when Mikio Naruse married Sachiko Chiba was confirmed once again.

Although only thirteen films were produced that year, six of them led the Top Ten list issued by the film magazine *Kinema Junpo*; these were *One Wonderful Sunday*, *War and Peace*, *Above the Silver Peaks*, *Once More*, *The Actress* and *Four Love Stories* (Yottsu no koi no monogatari, jointly produced by Shirō Toyoda, Mikio Naruse, Teinosuke Kinugasa, and Kajirō Yamamoto). They won awards at international film festivals and laid the foundations for a second Golden Age of Japanese film. New faces dominated the post-war Japanese film world, who thoroughly knew their trade and enjoyed the support of the general public.

These successes gave us the stamina to conduct the Third Labour Conflict during the following year. As *No Regrets for Our Youth* had been the symbol of the second conflict, *Between War and Peace* became the basis of the third, and it was greeted with enthusiasm by the people. This matter is of great importance for a correct understanding of the third conflict which now developed.

## The company prepares a counter-attack

At this stage the occupation policies enforced by GHQ had taken an extremely reactionary, anti-Soviet and anti-Chinese turn. Before the very eyes of the Americans, the Chinese People's Liberation Army was about to drive Chiang Kai Shek away to Taiwan. At home and also in Japan, the Americans mounted a crazed witch-hunt against communist influences.

While this atmosphere increasingly left its mark on the situation in Japan, the labour movement encountered mounting difficulties.

In 1947, Tōhō got a new managing director. Yoshio Ōsawa had led a group of directors who had collaborated with the army during the war, and as a war criminal who in his films had come out in support of the war effort, he had voluntarily gone into retirement in the hope of thus getting an earlier pardon. He was replaced by Katamaru Tanabe, a representative of the marketing department and younger step-brother of Ichizō Kobayashi, managing director of the parent company Tōhō Stock Company and a former Minister of Industry and Trade.

Katamaru Tanabe stuck to the collective agreement which had been reached before his time, but as the months went on he seemed to develop some sort of nervous disability. The reason for his troubles was that the section heads did not do their work properly. As he himself was not in the least interested in making films, his shop stewards' minds also were not on their work. Finally he became totally obsessed with the desire to fire all those section heads he did not like and none of the films, no matter how excellent, found his approval. He seemed to think that if only the marketing side of the business went smoothly, it was not really necessary that Tōhō wasted its energy on producing films. It became ever more evident that he was mainly occupied with licking the boots of his brother Ichizō Kobayashi.

In December 1947, Katamaru Tanabe appointed as managing director Tetsuzo Watanabe, a staunch anti-communist who had been a professor at the faculty of economics of the former Tokyo Imperial University. Although the group of film-makers led by Yoshio Ōsawa had been rehabilitated in the meantime (in contrast to the theatre group), they were ousted from the company and the rumour was spread that Yoshio Ōsawa had been tricked by the union when they had concluded the collective agreement which, to make matters worse, was pro-communist. Then Tetsuzo Watanabe with his hatred of communism was made managing director. In *Twenty Years of Tōhō*, this event is referred to as 'Tanabe's *coup d'état*', as his appointment was actually enforced by unlawful means.

Soon afterwards Takeo Mabuchi, chairman of the First Section of the Central Commission for Labour Relations, was appointed as personnel manager, and Juitsu Kitaoka, also a former professor of the faculty of economics of Tokyo Imperial University and at the same time head of the Fourth Department of the Economic Stabilisation Office, became head of the studios. According to

Tetsuzo Watanabe, the union simply acted as it pleased, and he had been appointed managing director by his friend Tanabe in order to eliminate the 'two red evils', by which he meant the members of the Communist Party and the company's deficit. He also mentioned there were two persons 'I can totally rely on, and these two are Juitsu Kitaoka and Takeo Mabuchi'.

In *Twenty Years of Tōhō*, the collective agreement worked out by Yoshio Ōsawa is criticised as reflecting only the union's interests: all matters of personnel had been subject to the consent of the union, and as the union's approval was needed in the decision on what sort of films were to be made, the rule of the Communist Party had been absolute. However, as I have said before, the agreement made between Yoshio Ōsawa and ourselves was acclaimed far and wide. For instance, Article 29 which covers the issue of 'Employment and Dismissal' clearly states: 'The union recognises the fact that matters of employment and dismissal are subject to the decision of the company.' Moreover, Article 9 which covers the 'Right of Management', says: 'The union confirms that the right of management is the sole responsibility of the company. The union therefore accepts the prerogative of the company in all matters concerning production, distribution and performance of theatre plays and films as well as in management affairs.' What should we think of an eminent economist and professor of the former Tokyo Imperial University who criticised the union without even reading the articles of the collective agreement covering personnel and management matters? Those three gentlemen who had been dispatched to conduct mass dismissals certainly made a shrewd move by pulling the plug on the collective agreement, but distorting its contents was quite unfair. The labour laws categorically forbid the dismissal of employees on the grounds that they are active union members. Watanabe however announced that he had come to 'fire the reds', thereby publicly bleating his dubious intentions and showing an unbelievable degree of ignorance. When it later came to mediation, he defended his measures before the Tokyo Commission for Labour Relations by pretending he had not dismissed anyone for being a communist, but only for showing unwillingness to cooperate with the company. This again was an example of his double-dealing nature.

Thus the Third Labour Conflict was initiated by the company. It must be emphasised that this conflict was grossly unfair, unreasonable, unjustifiable and inhuman. Any claims that the union had started the strike or refused to cooperate must be strongly rejected; the union merely defended itself against unjustified dismissals. The company was lying when it alleged that Tōhō's financial difficulties were caused by Nichieien's illegitimate interference in management affairs: in April when the company announced the dismissals, Akira Kurosawa completed his masterpiece *Drunken Angel* (Yoidore tenshi) on schedule and within the prescribed budget limit, and even after the strike all films whose production had been decided by the consultative council were enthusiastically received by the public and yielded considerable profits. Among these films were *Life of a Woman* (Onna no isshō), *Jakoman and Tetsu* (Jakoman to Tetsu) and *Blue Mountain Range* (Aoi Sanmyaku).

## The announcement of the dismissals

Having thus prepared their move, the management unilaterally announced the first dismissals (of 270 studio employees) on 8 April 1948. Among those dismissed were nearly all of the members of the Communist Party who were union officials or activists. Now the third conflict broke out. The former collective agreement had expired at the end of March and, as the company refused to negotiate, there was no valid contract. One month later further dismissals were announced, first in the head offices and then in the branch offices in Tokyo, Hokkaidō, Kansai, Nagoya, Osaka and Kyūshū. Altogether 1,200 employees were fired. The company had waited until the contract expired at the end of March and then had gone on to the offensive.

## The 'mobilisation tactics'

During the time preceding this strike, Nichieien had been considerably weakened by several internal divisions. The first split had occurred during the second conflict when field service employees of the marketing department had founded their own union. The next split was caused by the establishment of Shin-Tōhō with 460 employees joining the new company. When this strike was over, the theatre people formed their own union. At first it consisted only of the Takarazuka group founded by the clique around Ichizō Kobayashi, but later the Nichigeki dance ensemble joined in. Both groups together comprised about 800 employees who split off in March 1948 and from then on formed the biggest faction. They also adopted the union shop collective agreement of Nichieien without alteration, which stated that only union members could be employed. As everyone who did not join this new union was fired, the theatre people all went over and cooperated with the management.

Nichieien's forces had thus been depleted. Having hitherto enjoyed the support of the general public, we adopted what we called 'mobilisation tactics' in order to gather enough strength to survive the battle: we sent out appeals to democratic groups and the broad masses, asking for their support. We also changed our former strategy by intensively lobbying the Cultural Commission of the parliament and trying to make them listen to our demands. And we asked unions throughout the country to form associations, such as the 'Society for the Protection of Japanese Culture', the 'Society for the Protection of the Japanese Film', or the 'Society for the Protection of Tōhō'.

## The fight intensifies

On 10 April, Katamaru Tanabe, who did not know the first thing about making films, started to interfere by demanding that a budget should be determined for each film production. The production of films which had been planned within the consultative council was allowed to go ahead. These were *Drunken Angel* (Yoidore Tenshi, directed by Akira Kurosawa, April 1948), *Life of a Woman* (Fumio Kamei, July 1949), *White Beast* (Shirōi Yaju, directed by Mikio Naruse, June 1950) and *Blue Mountain Range* (Tadashi Imai, May to July 1949, Parts One and Two). Only *Men of Fire*, which was to have been produced in cooperation with Kokutetsu Sōrengo (National Railway Workers' Union) was cancelled. I would have been the producer of this film; its script was written by Yūsaku Yamagata and Mikio Ōsawa, and we had put all our energy into this project. By adapting the struggle of the railway workers for the screen, we had hoped once again to arouse the same wave of support that the Japanese film *War and Peace* had earlier created. But now we were ordered to cease and desist. When I argued that Yukio Kagayama (the president of the National Railways) himself had okayed the production, Katamaru Tanabe answered: 'I have asked an influential person to make him withdraw his support.' When I asked him whom he meant he replied: 'The under-secretary in charge of transport, Eisaku Satō. He's a friend of mine and has already said he'd go along with my request.'

On 10 April I called together all union members for a general ballot on whether to continue the strike or not. I told them, 'Let's stick to the proper procedure', and in a secret ballot 866 of 965 members voted in support of the strike. However, only 698 of them managed to hold out until the end; the rest gave up. These were all veteran activists who for a long time did not budge, but when the Sanbetsu Mindō movement emerged, an opposition movement within the union which was backed by the occupation forces, they finally surrendered.

While we were still busy implementing our mobilisation tactics, the *Asahi* and *Mainichi* newspapers carried editorials on the strike in which they asked what should become of the Japanese film if the companies only went after quantity but disregarded aspects of quality. Other voices asked the union to consider the dilemma that if all union members were fired, no one would be left to produce good films.

Fourteen directors who had been forced to leave the union because of the new collective agreement published the following declaration: 'As we are artists and not workers, it is perfectly acceptable that we do not have the status of union members. However, we will not cease supporting the union.' This 'United Front for the Protection of the Cinematic Art' which was dominated by the directors completely changed the position of our struggle. It differed greatly from the strikes led by normal unions.

On the one hand we implemented our mobilisation tactics and enjoyed the support of the 'United Front for the Protection of the Cinematic Art', while on the other hand we lodged a complaint against the company with the Tokyo Commission for Labour Relations for discriminating against union officials because of their political views, thereby breaching Article 11 of the labour union law. At that time, the chairman of the Tokyo Commission for Labour Relations was Mr Izutarō Suehiro. In addition, the union on 7 May appealed to the Tokyo Municipal Court calling for an interim order which would guarantee the status quo in the studios and the position of those fired, which in Japan was an unprecedented move. We thereby underlined our willingness to conduct the fight on a legal level as well.

The public generally supported the union. Everyone knew the films which had been produced by Tōhō employees after the war. But our appeals to the Tokyo Commission and the Municipal Court remained unsuccessful. What now happened was an unprecedented lock-out by force which, because of the heavily armed presence of occupation forces and the police, was later described with the words: 'Tanks on the ground; warplanes in the skies; the only thing lacking were the warships!'

## The execution of the interim order

As June turned to July, the patience of the company began to run out. When we augmented our mobilisation tactics with appeals to the Commission for Labour Relations and the Municipal Court, it finally had had enough and initiated the establishment of the Democratisation League (a creature sired by Sanbetsu Mindō) within Nichieien in order to stir up trouble within the union. This was the chief aim of Takeo Mabuchi, and the company organised a discussion meeting of the Democratisation League in the studios. When we tried to intervene, they cried out, 'Nichieien resorts to brutal force', and immediately called in the police. The Democratisation League had increased its membership from an initial 65 persons to 110. It had organised a number of actions such as that of the 'chimney man', who had climbed a chimney on the studio site and stayed there fasting, which we of course considered a provocation.

The union tried to steer clear of any confrontation and asked the members of the Democratisation League to kindly leave the occupied studios. However, these guys started to kick up a row which the management in turn used as a pretext for asking the court for an 'Interim Order for the Protection of Property Rights'. Nearly every day they went to the Municipal Court in order to throw their weight around. They claimed: 'The situation in the studios is dramatic. People who show up for work suffer acts of violence by union members each and every day.' Immediately afterwards a fire broke out in the studios. We suspected arson, but the cause of the fire remained unclear. Nevertheless the management argued: 'Such dangerous incidents occur day by day, and Nichieien is responsible for them.' Using such a strategy of deceit, the management aimed at creating a general feeling of anxiety.

Around 17 or 18 August it was generally expected that the appeal for the Interim Order for the Protection of Property Rights would soon result in the forced expulsion of the first union from the premises. In the early morning of 19 August I heard tanks pass in front of my house which was located near the studios. I called the managing director Katamaru Tanabe and coolly asked him: 'You're getting down to action, aren't you?' Around nine o'clock I received a telephone call from a union member who told me that 2,000 armed policemen together with six armoured personnel carriers were gathering in front of the studios. As rumours said that about 2,000 strikers had occupied the studios and the intention was to arrest all of them, the same number of policemen had been called in. On this particular day, however, only about 400 union members were on the premises.

As chairman of Nichieien I was not directly involved with the union group in the studios, but when three warplanes appeared in the sky and three tanks of the US Army showed up, I thought: 'Now things have gone far enough.' I managed to persuade the union members: 'The court has ordered the execution of its interim order at noon. Wouldn't it be better if you left the studios for the time being and saved your strength?' Although they all boiled with rage, they also feared the whole struggle might end in a flop if they shot their bolts all at once. So, filled with anger, but very calmly, they drew up in formation and in an orderly manner marched out of the studios to the nearby theatre school. There they waited for about three hours and then simply returned to the studios. Thus the day ended.

From the next day onwards the families of the strikers took to the streets in order to focus the attention of the general public on the suppression of the strike. As union groups affiliated with the Tōhō section were active in the cinemas too, and a strike by them would be a severe blow to our adversaries, we asked a number of them to stage a walk-out. Another of our strategies was called the 'parachute strategy'. When a film was over and it still was pitch dark, two actors, such as Hatae Kishi and Hajime Izu for example, would stand and call out, 'Ladies and Gentlemen!', whereupon both were suddenly illuminated by spotlights. Then they greeted the audience with the words: 'We have played in *Between War and Peace* and we thank you for your kind attention', they then delivered a speech and went through the aisles to collect contributions. We continued to use this sort of strategy following 19 August.

## The compromise: voluntary retirement of union officials

On the evening of 17 October, Yoshio Miyajima, head of the association of union groups, and I paid a surprise visit to Mr Tanabe in order to reach a compromise. Our bargaining position was as follows: 'We cannot accept that 270 persons are to be fired from the Tōhō studios. So what if those whom you really want to get rid of left the company of their own accord?' We felt that until that day everybody had stuck together in order to protect us union officials, but that we should not continue to be a burden to them and should therefore voluntarily retire and go on making films without the company. The company drew up a list naming about thirty persons, but we replied that this was far too many and proposed to reduce the number to twenty. They agreed but insisted that Fumio Kamei and Satsuo Yamamoto must be among them. So negotiations continued and we declared: 'According to the new collective agreement, Fumio Kamei and the other directors aren't union members anymore. It's unreasonable to dismiss people who don't even belong to the union.' But Katamaru Tanabe replied: 'I'll only agree if those two leave!' So they were included in the deal and we struck a bargain. Apart from the severance pay, the union received 15 million yen which was used to complete the film *Life of a Woman* which at that time was just being shot. On 19 October the compromise agreement was signed and the conflict was over.

## The fight of the independent producers

Those were the three Tōhō conflicts. By the end of the third one, not only did twenty persons leave the union leadership, but at the same time directors, scriptwriters and producers, including Teinosuke Kinugasa, left Tōhō, became independent and formed various artistic groups. The Tōhō studios were forced to cease making films for a while, and the marketing and presentation departments had to rely on film productions supplied by Shin-Tōhō.

In my function as full-time chairman of Nichieien, I used the funds we had received from Tōhō for our settlement of the conflict to produce Satsuo Yamamoto's *City of Violence* (Bōryoku no machi) as a Nichieien production with actors from many different companies, and had it distributed by Daiei. Akira Kurosawa then made *Rashomon* with Daiei, a film which won some of the most prestigious awards in France and the United States. Slowly but steadily the Japanese film regained its former qualitative level, but still more important the Tōhō struggle had given rise to a new movement and there was a new determination to fight together alongside the public for the survival of the Japanese film. Finally, the quality of the Japanese film again matched international standards.

On leaving Tōhō, we published the following manifesto:

> The promise we made to the public to secure the high quality of the Japanese film could not be kept while working for Tōhō. Therefore we decided to continue our work without Tōhō. This will be the next battle. Nothing is as yet decided. Here and now, a new fight has begun. Whether the Tōhō conflict has ended in a victory or a defeat will be decided in a contest by all film-makers within and without the company which will show who is making the better films!

Implementing this manifesto, however, meant redoubling our efforts. In order to reach a final decision in the sense of this manifesto, Satsuo Yamamoto went on fighting as an independent producer for sixteen years.

During this time he made *The Scout* with which he went to Daiei. As the film was a success, Daiei asked him to do another one. So, by and by, *The Scout* became a series of films. While he produced altogether eight films for Daiei, among them *The Great White Tower* and *Wounded Mountains and Rivers* (Kizu darake no sanga), the Nikkatsu production company got into financial trouble, so Satsuo Yamamoto was able to offer them the plan for his pet project *War and Men* (Sensō to ningen) and to produce it in three parts. When *Annular Solar Eclipse* (Kinkanshoku) which Yamamoto and I did on contract with Shin-Daiei was marketed by Tōhō after twenty-seven years, it became a great success and received very favourable reviews. Then Tōhō asked him whether he would not like to work for them again, and for the first time since the end of the conflict he returned to the company to produce *Wilderness* (Fumō chitai) and recently *The Splendid Clan* (Kareinaru ichizoku).

With hindsight, the most important consequence of the Tōhō conflicts seems to have been that the quality of the Japanese film was secured because the directors did not split into many factions but stuck together. They became the main force dedicated to the protection of the Japanese film at all costs. As a second consequence, the desperate battle which we fought under the most difficult conditions led to our independent productions becoming more popular than those of the big film companies and in the end forming the mainstream of the Japanese cinematic arts.

## Harbinger of the 'red purge'

Finishing my lecture, I want to give you a summary of the Tōhō conflicts. Following Churchill's speech at Fulton which I mentioned earlier, and after the Acheson statement before the Allied Council for Japan, the Cold War was given concrete shape by the formulation of Truman's Policy of Containment in March 1947 (Truman Doctrine, 12 March 1947). As the victory of the Chinese Revolution drew nearer, the anti-communist movement in the United States began to gather momentum. In 1947 Hollywood experienced a red witch-hunt. Forty-five directors, scriptwriters, producers and actors were summoned before the HUAC (House Un-American Activities Committee) and in public hearings which resembled a witch-hunt they were put on trial. Robert Taylor and Adolphe Menjou publicly denounced 'red elements' and kindled the flames, while the others remained silent. The public hearings were repeated every year, and by 1950 more than 300 persons had been interrogated. Ten of them (among them six scriptwriters) were indicted for defaming the investigation committee, and they were all sentenced to a one-year term of imprisonment in 1951. The director David Rosie, Charles Chaplin and the actresses Melina Mercouri and Ingrid Bergmann, decided to return to Europe as the committee continued to harass them.

The Third Tōhō Conflict in August 1948 was in fact a red purge. When, during the forced expulsion from the studios, the US Army appeared at the head of a force of 2,000 policemen and participated in the suppression of the Tōhō employees – a hitherto unprecedented action in Japan – this event was inextricably linked with the movement in the United States which had just started the red witch-hunt in Hollywood.

When the red purge reached Japan, GHQ alerted the government and the entrepreneurs to the fact that they 'should bear in mind that a direct interference by GHQ will not take place'. The appropriate terminology called for the use of words such as 'suggestion' or 'instruction', but everyone knew that these terms carried the meaning of unequivocal orders. The Second Yomiuri Conflict was suppressed by the sending in of 500 policemen. The intention was to force the management into making a decision. The interference of the US Army in the Tōhō conflict was at the same time a warning and an encouragement directed at the Japanese entrepreneurs who had remained passive for too long.

It can hardly be expected that Watanabe and Mabuchi, simply by giving their quick consent to our surprise offer of a compromise entailing the discharge of twenty persons, had rid themselves of the duties assigned to them by GHQ and the government. During the period from 1948 to 1950, Japan experienced a quick turn to the right which was reflected in the cabinet decree No. 201 and the so-called Dodge Line, a new economic policy. The Korean War broke out and, one after another, the unions of the press and the broadcasting sector, of the public employees and finally the union of the electrical power workers were subjected to a purge of alleged left-wing elements. Management took advantage of this situation, and at Tōhō the expected personnel reduction was pushed through within two years through negotiations and without a strike.

On 22 September 1950, the wave of purges reached the film industry. At Shōchiku, Daiei and Nichiei, 106 persons were ousted. Tōhō dismissed only seven employees, but here more than 350 members of the Communist Party of Japan had previously been fired. In the newspaper sector, fifty companies rid themselves of 704 employees, the ministries discharged 1,177 persons and the rest of the public sector 10,978 employees; thus all together 12,859 persons were swept away by this wave. These are data provided by the Ministry of Labour, but there are historians of the labour movement who claim that the real figures were in the range of no less than 30,000.

In the end, the admiration of people in the film business all over the world focused on a group of ten persecuted persons from Hollywood, called 'The Hollywood Ten'.[3] One of them,

Dalton Trumbo, was sixty-six years old when he was first able to write a script for a film under his own name (*Johnny Got his Gun*). This film left a vivid impression everywhere. Trumbo had been forty years old when his name was put on the black list. From then on he was forced to write scripts under an assumed name which he changed every two years. Some heartbreaking stories about other members of the group are also told, and when I think about the movement of independent Japanese film-makers and the Japanese film in general, similar feelings rise in me.

## Notes

1. Nikkeiren: Nihon Keieisha Dantai Renmei, the Japanese Federation of Employer's Associations (JFEA).
2. *Chūshingura*: one of the most famous Japanese historical dramas; it is about forty-seven samurai who take revenge for the death of their master. They are done the favour of being allowed to commit *seppuku* (harakiri) and die an honourable death instead of being executed like common murderers.
3. This group consisted of the following scriptwriters and directors: Albert Maltz, Lester Cole, Samuel Ornitz, Adrian Scott, Alvah Bessie, Edward Dmytryk, Ring Lardner Jr, John Howard Lawson, Herbert Biberman and Dalton Trumbo.

# 4 The Five Labour Conflicts of Tōshiba, 1946–49

*Tadanobu Ishikawa*

**Tadanobu Ishikawa**

1912 Born on 3 August in Akita prefecture
1935 Graduated from Tokyo University of Economics (today Hitotsubashi University) and joined the Shibaura Seisakusho Stock Company which later through a merger became Tōshiba
1938 Drafted for military service and sent to the front (in July)
1945 Demobilised at the end of the war (in September) and rejoined the Tokyo-Shibaura-Denki Company (= Tōshiba)
1949 Voluntary retirement from the company
1950 Founded the Ishikawa Trade Company and acted as its managing director
1959 Liquidation of the Ishikawa Trade Company
1960 Appointed managing director of the Fuji Seiki Stock Company
1964 Due to a merger of this company, transferred to the Denshi Kōgyō Stock Company in the position of managing director
1977 Retired
1996 Died

## Trade union functions

1946 Co-founder of the union in the Tōshiba head offices, spokesman of the workers, later member of the bargaining committee of the Kantō Union Federation and of the management consultative council (in October)
1946 Chairman of the Kantō-regional Union Federation of Tōshiba (in November), resignation at end of the conflict
1947 Renewed appointment as chairman of the Kantō-regional Union Federation of Tōshiba

1948 Chairman of the new Tōshiba Labour Federation (in March)
1950 Resignation from his office as chairman of the Tōshiba Labour Federation

## Publications

'Shūsen chokugono Tōshiba Rōren sōgi' (Chronicle of the Struggle of the Tōshiba Union Federation in the Immediate Post-War Era) in: *Rōdō undō shi kenkyū* (Studies on the History of the Labour Movement) No. 62, Rōdō Junpōsha, 1979
Tōshiba Fūunroku (The Documents of the Tōshiba Struggle), Tōyōkeizai-Shinpōsha, 1986

## I Editor's Overview

During the post-war period of social unrest which lasted for a couple of years, the Tōshiba Rōren (Tōshiba Union Federation), together with the union of the electric power industry, the miners' union and the union of seamen, played a pivotal role in the labour movement of the private sector. Especially during this period when those advocating the principle of industrial unionism formed the mainstream of the labour movement, the Tōshiba Rōren as an organisation of enterprise unions of a company which consisted of several factories, was a major influence, comparable to that of the other leading unions, on social development in Japan. One reason for its influence was the fact that the company had production facilities throughout the country and a large workforce of up to 50,000 employees. Other important factors were the rapid spread of unionisation following the surrender, the employment of many activists, and the continual unfolding of labour conflicts, one following another in rapid succession, during the first four post-war years.

The most important struggles of the Tōshiba Rōren were the so-called Third Conflict in 1946 and the Fifth Conflict in 1949. The Third Conflict, during which the Tōshiba Labour Federation also played a central role in the October Struggle of Sanbetsu Kaigi, aimed at the prevention of mass dismissals planned by the management. At the same time the union supported the persistent and difficult struggle of the Yomiuri employees. The Fifth Conflict is an example of the management counter-offensive type, in which the management succeeded in regaining its entrepreneurial prerogatives by firing union officials.

In all of its conflicts the union demonstrated the extent to which the labour movement of the private sector, even in such difficult times, was able to achieve its objectives. It was a model to workers from other industries, in the sense that it took decisive measures to ensure security of employment, wage rises and other matters of social security, while at the same time restricting the management's authority. On the other hand, the management also offered a model to other companies in private industry by brutally enforcing a plan for restructuring the company and by regaining its prerogatives by means of mass dismissal of union leaders (the red purge). In this respect the Tōshiba labour conflicts marked the beginning of a period of offensive measures directed against the unions (from the First to Fourth Conflict); the final Fifth Conflict then signalled the end of the period of post-war social unrest.

## The First and Second Conflicts, 1945–6

Confronted with a situation of serious deprivation following Japan's surrender, the Tōshiba employees who had established unions in all factories launched a 'struggle for production control' and by the end of 1945 had begun a joint battle with the following objectives: (1) a fivefold increase in wages; (2) recognition of their right to engage in collective bargaining; and (3) establishment of a management consultative council.

The struggle ended with an unqualified victory for the union (29 January 1946). In April of that year, a management consultative council was established and in May a collective agreement was concluded. This agreement gave the union a sweeping say not only with regard to working conditions but also in management affairs. It also included a clause which stipulated that the union's approval was required in cases of dismissals, which clearly meant a considerable limitation of the management's prerogatives by the union.

## The Third Conflict, 1946

The Tōshiba Labour Federation played a central role in the October Struggle of Sanbetsu Kaigi while at the same time it tried to ward off attempts by the management to regain its prerogatives and fire union officials. Therefore the prevention of mass dismissals was the main objective of the three demands put forward, and a conflict ensued which lasted fifty-five days.

During this dispute, there was direct interference by the occupation forces (the so-called Irvin incident, in which union members were forbidden to enter the Horikawachō factory), but finally this conflict, too, ended in a victory for the union, and the management was thwarted in its plans.

## The Fourth Conflict, 1947–8

This conflict was caused by a union demand calling for a minimum wage based on average living costs; the management, however, exploited the struggle and tried to implement far-reaching restructuring within the company. It confronted the union with a plan to determine a minimum wage level according to the economic situation of each factory. The conflict became deadlocked over this issue. After two years in which neither side had gained any significant advantage it ended inconclusively and was immediately followed by the Fifth Conflict.

## The Fifth Conflict, 1949

While the management pressed forward with its plans for restructuring – in which it was supported by a government decree calling for such an adjustment in line with the law of 1947 on removing the excessive concentration of economic power (the deconcentration law) – it made preparations for recapturing its prerogatives by firing union officials, which for a long time had been its chief goal. This move became the spark which set off the struggle.

The underlying intention of the management was to end the period of union offensives throughout the country by eroding the union's capacity to fight. To achieve this goal, it announced the dismissal of 6,228 persons, including nearly all of the leading union officials. The union went on the defensive, but it suffered a serious setback when the Matsukawa incident occurred. Its troubles were compounded by the establishment of a number of new and competing unions, and the struggle ended in a defeat.

In the end, all of those who had resisted their dismissal had to opt for voluntary retirement from the company.

## Results

Even though the union lost its last battle, a number of its proposals were included in the plan for the reconstruction and consolidation of the company. The management expressed its willingness to re-employ some of the dismissed workers and offered favourable conditions to the other retired employees if they wanted to act as salesmen for the company's products. In addition, the Kawagishi factory was transformed into an independent company managed by the union, so to a certain degree one can speak of at least some positive results. Furthermore, in August 1951 the first and the second union reunited.

The defeat of the Tōshiba Labour Federation, which had been regarded as an exceptionally powerful union, resulted in a weakening of the left-wing labour movement led by Sanbetsu Kaigi. The outcome of the Tōshiba struggles boosted the confidence of Japanese managers and enabled them to conduct sweeping rationalisation measures. These measures often coincided with disputes of the management counter-offensive type which were aimed at recapturing management's prerogatives and bringing about the firing of union officials. Such disputes now erupted all over Japan. The end of the Tōshiba struggles marked the beginning of an era in which post-war Japanese labour relations were mainly dominated by management.

## II Lecture by Tadanobu Ishikawa

Following my demobilisation in September 1945, and having exchanged my army uniform for civilian clothes, I returned to my former place of employment in the administrative department of the Shibaura branch office of the Tokyo-Shibaura-Denki Company. Defeat and occupation, burnt-down houses, ruins and ashes, soldiers killed in action and prisoners of war, dismissals and inflation, shortage of housing and foodstuffs, malnourishment and homeless children – I think it will be difficult for today's young people to imagine the extent of the chaos. But in the midst all these problems, there was one thing which gave us hope:

democracy. To me, this word is inextricably linked with my first experiences in the labour union movement.

I was head of the planning section in the administrative department at that time, i.e. I was not a so-called blue-collar worker. Nevertheless, my superior, Mr Motoo Ōtani, the head of the administrative department, called me and said: 'They seem to be establishing unions everywhere, perhaps we should have one, too', and thus my colleague Junkichi Nakahara and I were put in charge of founding a union. Junkichi Nakahara was responsible for the Matsuda branch office located in the Horikawachō district of Kawasaki, and I represented the Shibaura branch office which had its seat in the Tsukamoto building on Shōwadōri Avenue in the Tokyo ward of Nihonbashi. In January of the first year after the surrender, both branch offices formed the union of the company's head offices, and I was elected its spokesman. This basically was the reason for my connection with the union. Now my life as a union official began which lasted for nearly five years until the end of my tenure in March 1950. This period also included the compromise in the so-called 'Struggle Against the Company's Adjustment Measures' of December 1949.

## Establishment of the Tōshiba Roren (Tōshiba Union Federation)

I want to start my lecture by talking about the establishment and structure of the three union federations of Tōshiba.

In December 1945, workers of the newly founded five factory unions in the Kawasaki area (i.e. the unions of the factories of Horikawachō, Yanagimachi, Komukai, Denken and Seiken) who saw themselves confronted with galloping inflation which made life unbearable, presented a list of demands for a fivefold increase of their wages, the establishment of a management consultative council, recognition of their right to collective bargaining and other related matters. They were joined by seven other factory unions, among them that of the Tsurumi factory. On 27 January of the following year this dispute ended with an unqualified victory for the union. This was the First Tōshiba Labour Conflict. The most memorable thing about the victory is Article 7 of the collective agreement which required the consent of the union in case of dismissals or personnel transfers ('The dismissal or transfer of a union member is subject to the prior consent of the union').

Well, only three months later, this fivefold increase in wages had already been eaten up by inflation, and in real terms our wages had even sunk. Therefore the union proposed another wage-hike within the consultative council and on 11 June, when negotiations had shown no results, this proposal was formulated as a demand in which we also called for setting up of a 'fund for solving the hunger crisis'. Thus the Second Tōshiba Labour Conflict began.

Until that time the number of unions in factories located in the provinces had rapidly grown, and on a regional level in the Kantō,[1] Kansai[2] and Tōhoku[3] areas the so-called 'Tōshiba consultation of the three local unions' or Sanrengōkai had been formed. It consisted of fifty-nine unions which represented 48,000 employees. The individual Sanrengōkai member unions confronted the management of their factories with the demands, but the company was able to exploit a lack of coordination on the part of the union and managed to beat down our demand of 5 million yen to 2 million yen plus the issue of 60,000 light bulbs; this was their final offer. In contrast to the first struggle, the second had ended in a complete defeat, and as a consequence the members of the Central Struggle Committee of the Kantō Union Federation resigned to a man. However, what I just said only relates to the unions of the Tōshiba company. As the occupation policies requested the release of political prisoners and called for the establishment of parties and of labour unions as democratic forces in a new Japan, by August 1946 new unions were spreading like mushrooms. On the national level Sanbetsu Kaigi Sōdōmei were created. On a lower level, single enterprise unions were organised in branch organisations.

Once they had reached a consensus, the Tōshiba unions, i.e. the single factory unions (*tan'i kumiai*) which had been founded in the company's factories, joined the union organisation on the next level, the so-called industrial branch federation of enterprise unions or *tansan*. These branch federations were affiliated with either Sanbetsu Kaigi, Sōdōmei or a third, politically neutral organisation; at that time twenty-three of them belonged to Sanbetsu Kaigi and twenty-two to the neutral umbrella organisation. When a confrontation with the Tōshiba company developed, the regional members of Sanrengōkai, i.e. the unions of the Kantō,

Kansai and Tōhoku areas, made joint preparations for the struggle.

## The list of demands

The Third Labour Conflict, also called the October Struggle, occurred in October 1946. At the national level this struggle was meticulously prepared by the Communist Party and Sanbetsu Kaigi, and in my opinion its real aim was the overthrow of the Shigeru Yoshida government. The Kantō Union Federation joined the fight and formulated three demands which on 14 September were presented to the management. They called for:

1. a written promise not to fire any employee;
2. the establishment of a minimum wage system based on average living costs;
3. the immediate holding of a conference covering the whole Tōshiba company and observing democratic principles to discuss the resumption of production.

In my capacity as shop-floor representative of the company's head office employees, I attended the meeting of the central struggle committee at which the decision in favour of this struggle was made. I was surprised at the optimism of the committee members who unanimously adopted the demands. The union federations of the Kantō, Kansai and Tōhoku regions confronted the management with this list and demanded an answer by noon of 21 September. As negotiations stalled, on 1 October Sanrengōkai ordered all employees to go on strike. I was elected a member of the consultation council and of the collective bargaining committee and assisted its chairman, Mr Aketsugu Ryōkai.

The management refused to accept our demands arguing as follows: 'Why does the union ignore the consultation council and go for collective bargaining instead? This conflict is apparently subject to outside control!' The first demand not to announce any dismissals was rejected on the grounds that 'this would mean an appropriation by the union of the management's prerogative in personnel matters'. The second point of the list, which called for the introduction of a system of minimum wages, resulted in a controversy about wage structures. The union argued in favour of minimum wages at least covering living costs in order to secure the workers' livelihood, while the management insisted that wages must not exceed a level the company could afford. In the end the discussions concentrated mainly on figures, i.e. how much would be sufficient and how much the company was able to pay. In view of the extremely high rate of inflation, the union's demand for a minimum payment of 600 yen and an average wage of 1,000 yen was clearly justified, which the company also admitted. But because the wages requested by the union would total 40 million yen per month, while the company's monthly earnings were in the range of 45 million yen, the management claimed that such high labour costs were simply unacceptable. Finally the controversy ended in a discussion which resembled the problem of the chicken and the egg, i.e. which should come first: the union's cooperation in the production effort or the securing of the workers' livelihood?

With regard to our last demand, the holding of a conference on resumption of production, I had the impression that during the meeting of Tōshiba Rōren which drafted the list and at which I had been present, this point had been added somewhat hastily in order to include the main theme of Sanbetsu Kaigi's October Struggle which was 'Re-starting production in the hands of the people'. The management reacted by declaring:

> As this matter directly concerns the company's structure, we cannot agree. Since the end of the war, there has been a considerable degree of democratisation with regard to the company's management, and it should be sufficient to express the relevant positions within the appropriate consultative bodies. Anything which goes beyond this level would constitute a direct interference in the management's prerogatives.

## The Walter incident

The squabble went on for a couple of days, and 1 October, which was the scheduled date for the beginning of the Sanrengōkai (Tōshiba) general strike, drew nearer. One day before strike action started, the so-called Walter incident occurred.

Mr Walter was an employee of the Technical Detachment of the 8th US Army Division stationed in Yokohama. Nobody knew who had authorised him to do so, but he ordered representatives of the union and the company to show up in his office on 30 September at 3:30 p.m. Without even permitting us any questions, he uttered the following threats: 'The strike of tomorrow must be cancelled! If you don't comply we will confiscate the factories and send you to gaol for high treason!' At that time the occupation forces had unlimited powers and people were even more afraid of them than they had been of the Japanese military police during the war. There had already been cases of union officials being deported to Okinawa for disobeying an order of the occupation authorities. The mere thought of suffering the same fate was enough to make the attending union officials break out in a cold sweat.

However, two of them, Tetsujirō Kubo and Makoto Ida, both vice chairmen of the union, managed to turn the tables on Mr Walter by asking: 'Who has sanctioned this order? We want you to give us a document which proves that it has been given! We cannot believe that the occupation authorities have directly issued such an order.' At eight o'clock in the evening of the same day, the chairman of the collective bargaining committee Aketsugu Ryōkai and two others officially met with representatives of the occupation forces, reiterated Tetsujirō Kubo's statement and added they would ask the command staff of MacArthur and the Allied Council for Japan (consisting of representatives of the United States, Great Britain, the Soviet Union and China) to conduct an investigation into the matter.

Mr Walter then relented and the whole matter was simply dropped, but for some time the union members were so frightened by this intervention by the occupation forces that I did not know where it would lead.

## Rejection of the proposal for mediation by the Central Labour Relations Commission

After this incident, the Sanrengōkai went on strike for an unspecified period. Of the sixty-three workshop and enterprise unions which were Sanrengōkai members, fifty-nine joined in the strike, and these comprised about 47,000 of the 50,000 Tōshiba employees.

On 8 October, the eighth day of the strike, the Japanese government, at the request of the occupation authorities, sent a ministerial director of the Ministry for Industry and Trade,[4] Mr

Suzuki. He met with both union and company officials to relay a demand from the American Major General Marquat that the strike end, and to express the wish of the Minister for Social Affairs that the Central Labour Relations Commission act as mediator in the conflict. Management and union were prepared to let the commission try its hand at mediation, and it was decided that Professor Ichirō Nakayama should act as an intermediary.

Concerning the first of our demands, that the company promise in writing not to make any dismissals, the strong support of Ichirō Nakayama narrowed the gap between the parties a bit, but negotiations on the other points – establishment of a system of minimum wages and organisation of a conference on re-starting production – stalled because of the fierce resistance of the management. Nevertheless, Ichirō Nakayama did not give up and energetically continued negotiations with the management.

Meanwhile, I, as a former student colleague of Ichirō Nakayama who was a professor at the Tokyo University of Economics (today Hitutsubashi University, and Yōkichi Yoshida, Second Chairman of the Kantō Labour Federation and himself a former student colleague of Nakayama, complied with a request by Aketsugu Ryōkai and opened a second channel of communication. A couple of times we visited Nakayama late in the evening at his flat in Yoyogi-Uehara, gave him an account of the current state of affairs according to the view of the union, and negotiated details of a mediation proposal which would be acceptable to the union.

On one of these evenings, Ichirō Nakayama, who had belatedly returned from an extraordinary meeting of the Central Labour Relations Commission – we had waited for him in his reception room – showed us his draft of a mediation proposal in order to learn whether it had any chance of being accepted by the union. We looked at it and told him that in view of the protracted strike we would try somehow to gain Aketsugu Ryōkai's approval; then we returned to the struggle headquarters and reported to Aketsugu Ryōkai. Ryōkai took heart and opted for the compromise, and on 27 October he attended a meeting of the mediation committee of the Central Labour Relations Commission. However, the officially presented mediation proposal differed slightly from the one we had shown him, and the amendment was clearly to the advantage of the company's management. When I noticed this, I uttered a silent sigh and thought, 'Oh dear, here we go again!' But Aketsugu Ryōkai kept cool and said that in his position as chairman of the collective bargaining committee he was willing to accept the proposal after he had explained its contents to the audience in the hall, where members of the struggle committee, representatives of subordinate organisations and of the young people's action groups, had gathered.

But when he did so, there where shouts of dismay, especially by members of the Horikawachō union, who cried out: 'Hey you! You really want to accept this trash, you union bigwigs?' Perhaps we had failed to inform them properly about the mediation proposal, or it may have been that the Horikawachō union members who generally sympathised with the Communist Party tried to assert their claim to a leading role in the conflict and to oust Ryōkai – whatever the reason for this chaos, I had no idea what to do. In the midst of this barrage of insults, I simply looked at the profile of Ryōkai who stood there, seemingly unabashed. It was then decided to have the single enterprise and workshop unions discuss the mediation proposal and, following their verdict, take a vote on its acceptance or rejection within the central committee. When the results of the polls of the single unions came in, it became clear that the mediation proposal had been unanimously rejected. On the basis of these results, a meeting of the central committee was held at which the Kantō Union Federation officially dismissed the mediation proposal. Six members (i.e. three unions) voted in favour of the proposal, six abstained from voting, and sixty members who represented twenty-two unions rejected it. Afterwards the Tōhoku and the Kansai Union Federations also rejected the proposal. On 1 November, Aketsugu Ryōkai visited the Central Labour Relations Commission in order to inform it of the rejection, whereupon the Central Commission announced the suspension of negotiations. This meant that the first of the mediation proposals put forward by the Commission had failed.

Thus after more than a month of strike action, the Third Tōshiba Conflict was back to square one. During this month, the situation of the union members had steadily deteriorated. Those with no families, and some of the union members of factories in the country who were able to procure foodstuffs in the villages, were still able to make ends meet. But among the workers in the cities who comprised the majority of the constituency of the Kantō Union Federation's member unions, the willingness to continue the fight began to erode. This gradually led to subtle differences in opinion concerning the appropriate tactics of the struggle.

## I am elected chairman of the central struggle committee of the Kantō Union Federation

After the mediation proposal had failed, the Kantō federation tried to bring the situation back to normal and called a meeting of the central struggle committee, at which the members of the bargaining committee as well as the central struggle committee were newly elected. Representatives of both the right and the left wings attended the meeting on 2 November; on the one hand was the young people's action group of the Komukai union who supported the committee's chairman, Aketsugu Ryōkai, on the other was the action group of the Horikawachō union which intended to force him to resign. Their loud interjections created such a noise that even the strong voice of the chairman, Mr Miyata, could not be heard by the committee members who were seated in the conference hall.

Mr Miyata became so annoyed that he declared his resignation, and the meeting had to begin with the election of a new chairman. As the union of the company's head offices was known for its neutrality, I was elected interim chairman. In a loud voice I had learned to use during my army days, I told the right- and left-wing representatives of the young people's action groups: 'You all go to the back of the room and stay there! And those who disturb the meeting will be kicked out!' This did the trick, and order was restored – which probably was why I then was elected speaker, with Tetsujirō Kubo as my assistant. Next on the agenda was a report by the central committee's chairman, Aketsugu Ryōkai, on his dealings with the Central Commission for Labour Relations. When asked about the chances of solving the problems now that the Commission had suspended its mediation efforts, he replied that he did not think there was any more chance. The meeting had then to vote on Aketsugu Ryōkai's request that it accept his resignation, and accepted it was, with 48 ayes against 19 nays; 5 representatives abstained from voting. Now his successor had to be elected.

The counting of votes received the undivided attention of the delegates, and contrary to my expectations, I received 40 votes while the committee member of the Kawagishi union, Satoshi

Tsujii, got only 34. I already disliked the complexity and the troublesomeness of union affairs, and therefore refused to accept the outcome of the vote. Being elected speaker was the limit to which I was prepared to go, but chairman of the struggle committee? Dear me, no! However, the people from the Horikawachō factory urged me to go along with the vote, and also the group from Yanagimachi and Komukai, which at first had favoured Satoshi Tsujii but then suddenly switched their allegiance and voted for me. As they all now wanted me to do the job they refused to accept my refusal. For more than two hours the meeting remained deadlocked.

Meanwhile I considered: now that the strike had gone on for more than a month and we were in the middle of our struggle, what would be the result if the management became aware of a continuing lack of unity within the union? So I asked the head of the Horikawachō union, Shigeki Katsuhara, to come over to me and told him: 'We have to regain our ability to fight on as soon as possible. Therefore I have no choice but to accept as a sort of interim solution my election as chairman of the struggle committee. Our goal should be to achieve a settlement soon. When I think that the conflict is entering its final stage, I'll seek your advice, and therefore I want your support. If you don't promise to support me, I won't accept the post.' As Shigeki Katsuhara, having carefully thought things over, gave me his promise, I finally took on the job, but with a feeling as if I had jumped off the Kiyomizu ridge.[5] Satoshi Tsujii from Kawagishi and Takashi Kojima from Tsurumi were then elected deputy chairmen.

## The Irvin incident

The collective bargaining of the October Struggle, which was by then back to square one, started on 5 November. The management refused to give an inch, clinging to the line set out by the Nakayama mediation proposal, and the negotiation attempts soon ended in deadlock. As a consequence of their increasingly desperate situation, a feeling of insecurity and unrest began to spread among the workers. In order to find a way out of this impasse, I told the management that as a last resort we would extend the strike action to the special work areas of the Horikawachō factory, the glass production and maintenance department, which until that time had been excluded from the strike. As a result, negotiations were continued on 10 November and went on without interruption for two days until 12 November at two o'clock in the morning. The management expressed its willingness to compromise, and both sides were aiming at a speedy settlement of the conflict.

The zeal of the union members during these overnight negotiations was unbelievable. The hunger strike of the Horikawachō union members, the heavy breathing of the listening workers in the overcrowded room where the negotiations were conducted, the loud battle cries and revolutionary songs chanted by thousands of union members who had surrounded the building, and the flames rising up into the winter skies – this atmosphere marked the mood of the bargaining committee members, and the pace of the negotiations was accelerated by proposals put forward by the union. Finally the positions began to converge even with regard to the second and the third demands, and the compromise expected by the union seemed only a step away.

Suddenly the hall in front of the room in which we negotiated was filled with shouts of angry voices and the sound of stamping feet. The door was opened and an officer of the occupation forces together with a couple of soldiers entered the room. While they levelled their light machine guns at us, they repeatedly shouted orders which meant something like: 'You are laying siege to this building! This is an unlawful act! Disperse immediately!'

In this extremely tense situation I was unable to decide on the spot how to deal with the interruption. I thought that as the negotiations had gone so far we would still reach a settlement even if we interrupted our discussions for a while, and that by all means I had to prevent the angry young union members from provoking a scandal. Therefore I told the managing director, Mr Suzutsugu Satō, who had risen from his chair and was about to take to his heels, that we would reconvene later on: 'Let's take a break right now. At eight o'clock in the morning we'll continue our talk and reach a solution then.' I said the same thing to the union members who were extremely agitated, and I ordered them to disperse.

Lieutenant Irvin took off as well, after he had given us a written order that negotiations between management and union officials must not be conducted by more than ten persons from either side and that the Horikawachō factory must remain closed until the end of the strike and was off-limits to union members. However, on the following day, 13 November, the union chose to ignore this suppressive order. Accompanied by workers carrying a red banner, union leader Shigeki Katsuhara used his own hands to open the locked factory gates to which the written order was attached. Then the workers entered the site. Supported by members of the union federation of the electrical industry which belonged to Sanbetsu Kaigi, they continued to protest against the order with the relevant occupation authorities in Kanagawa, until on 15 November it was revoked.

## The 'House of Madam' incident

The management, however, which had not anticipated the results of such broad-based and bold action by workers who did not even show fear in the face of the absolute power of the occupation forces, broke the agreement to resume collective bargaining on 12 November at eight o'clock in the morning and simply went into hiding. In an attempt to exploit the increasing uncertainty among union members concerning their material situation and the wavering which the protracted struggle had caused within the union, the management adopted a perfidious strategy which aimed at destroying our organisation. Then on 14 November, two days after negotiations had been broken off, the company's directors, whose whereabouts were still unknown, proposed the signing of an agreement they had drafted. It was presented to us by the deputy head of the department of general affairs, Mr Suzuki. The proposal referred only to those issues which had been agreed upon when the negotiations had been interrupted.

Now I really became annoyed. As I immediately rejected the draft, our contact with the management broke off again, and the feeling of uncertainty and confusion among the ranks of the union grew. At this stage the 'House of Madam' incident occurred. The Horikawachō union circulated a defamatory pamphlet within the Kantō Union Federation. Dated 17 November, it claimed that 'the enemies of the workers – those union bigwigs who have drawn out the struggle until this very day – have held a secret meeting in the "House of Madam" in order to cook up a treacherous plan'. It was claimed that the union leaders of Tsurumi, Yanagimachi, Komukai, Fuchū, Fuji, Kawaguchi, the head offices, and other influential unions, had secretly met in the House of Madam in Ichikawa city to discuss how to reach a quick settlement of the conflict.

When Aketsugu Ryōkai, who had been named in the pamphlet, published a refutation, a general mud-slinging contest developed. In his refutation, Ryōkai wrote: 'False allegations are made and we are denounced as union bigwigs. We demand an apology and request that the responsible persons of the Horikawachō union who try to widen the influence of extreme left elements be called to account.'

The strength of a union is solely determined by the degree of its unity. The fact that cracks had started to show only strengthened my resolve to reach a solution as soon as possible. However, I did not want to commit the same mistake Aketsugu Ryōkai had made at the meeting with the Central Labour Relations Commission, and I feared that the Kantō Union Federation might break into pieces if I publicly stated my resolve. Therefore I stayed strictly aloof from the ongoing campaign of mutual slander. Among the energetic members of the young people's action groups, I organised teams which gathered for demonstrations with banners and posters on busy street corners in Tokyo and Kanagawa to catch the attention of the general public. In the meantime I conferred with the Minister for Industry and Trade, Jiro Hoshijima, the cabinet secretary Kanehichi Masuda and the chairman of the Central Labour Relations Commission, Takeo Mabuchi. I pointed out that only the attendance of the missing board of directors at collective bargaining sessions could pave the way for a compromise and the resumption of the company's operation. This move turned out to be effective: in agreement with Article 29 of the old labour law, the Central Labour Relations Commission began its mediation attempts, and on 19 November, one week after the negotiations had been broken off, both sides again met in the offices of the Commission.

## Preventing the defection of the Tsurumi Union

In my opinion, the resumption of collective bargaining offered the only possibility of finding a solution before the union split or fell apart. Even though I realised the danger of repeating the mistake Ryōkai had made earlier, I started negotiations with the firm resolve of reaching a settlement. However, at the appointed time no member of the management showed up. 'How strange. What is this supposed to mean?' Before I had time to think, a couple of guys of the young people's action group came in and reported: 'The directors have jumped out of the window and climbed over the fence near the rear gate. We tried to follow them, but they left in a car!'

Perplexity and dismay – I simply did not know what to make of this situation. They had vanished into thin air again! I was so annoyed, I could have climbed the wall. The only thing to do now was to secure the cohesion of the union for another two days and try to fight against this perfidious strategy of the management. Racking my brains over how to motivate the individual unions, whose impatience with regard to a settlement had become intense, I returned to the struggle headquarters in Kawasaki where I received two disconcerting messages. The chairman of the struggle committee of the Kansai Union Federation, Etsurō Yamamura, had returned to Osaka without leaving a message, and a meeting of the Tsurumi union had been called. The return of Yamamura clearly meant that the Kansai federation would try to reach and sign an independent agreement with the company. The meeting of the Tsurumi union had been called in order to come to a decision on ending the strike.

The Tsurumi union was one of the bigger unions, comprising 3,267 members; their factory was the headquarters of the high-voltage section, one of the two main sections of the company, and at the same time the domain of managing director Suzutsugu Satō, one of the most important protagonists on the management side. The Tsurumi factory was special in the sense that it did the rough work and produced goods on order and with long delivery deadlines. Right from the start it had been difficult to bring them together with the Horikawachō factory, where the work was easier, and light bulbs, vacuum bulbs and other goods were produced for stock. The Tsurumi union members were afraid that a loss of orders due to the protracted strike might bring down production for more than a year, which would inevitably lead to lay-offs. As the management had withdrawn again from the negotiations by fleeing from the building, it was now impossible to allay their fears, and the union leaders had called the meeting determined to put an end to the strike.

The defection of the Tsurumi union would have far-reaching consequences. Not only would the Tsurumi factory end the strike, but all of the other unions of factories belonging to the high-voltage section would follow suit, as well as the whole Kansai Union Federation, whose leader Etsurō Yamamura came from the union of the factory in Mie prefecture, the second main union of the high-voltage section. This in turn should be enough to bring down the Komukai union (the main factory of the communication technology section) and Yanagimachi (machine and tool section), and it could only have the bitter consequence that in the end the Horikawachō union would stand alone.

Gritting my teeth, feeling dejected and lonely, I left for the Tsurumi factory. When I reached the meeting place, a hall which could easily have housed the battleship *Mutsu*, 3,000 union members sat tightly packed on an area roughly a third of the size of the giant Factory No. 9. Around the speaker's stage which had been erected in the control area of the intermediate storey, I saw the Tsurumi union officials sitting in a row. They were just about to take a vote on calling off the strike.

When I mounted the stairs to the intermediate storey, someone called to me: 'This is a meeting of the Tsurumi union! You better go home now!!' I felt like one struck with an axe. In a loud voice so that everybody was able to hear me I shouted: 'I am the chairman of the Kantō Union Federation! At such an important meeting, do you really want to prevent the chairman of the Kantō Union Federation from giving you a situation report?' 'Yeah, he's right! Let him speak out!' the union members on the ground floor shouted in excitement.

Then I stood on the stage. But how should I begin? While I let my eyes wander over the more than 3,000 workers who stared back at me full of expectation, I looked into their faces, trying to speak to them through my eyes. It was a moment of high tension! This is bound to cause some reaction, I thought. Then I started to speak: 'Well, let's go! I'll speak to you as a worker among workers: straight out and no lies!' And in a calm and deliberate voice I told them:

> At the moment, as the Tsurumi union leaders have already explained, the struggle is in an extremely difficult phase. Supported by the great sense of solidarity you have shown, the struggle committee has won a success in the negotiations which were conducted between 10 and 12 November, a success which went well beyond the mediation proposal of the Central Labour Relations Commission. Unfortunately the

> negotiations were interrupted by the interference of the occupation forces. Since then the company's directors have gone into hiding and now are waiting for the union federation to break apart. On 14 November the board of directors, still underground, urged me to sign an agreement they had worked out which would have been tantamount to an unconditional surrender. I refused to do so. This was a mistake, wasn't it?

Enthusiastically, the union members cried: 'No, that was the right thing to do!' I waited until they had calmed down and then continued:

> You have all heard about the incredible behaviour of the managers who yesterday fled from the building of the Central Labour Relations Commission. They will certainly try to stay underground until the moment Tōshiba Rōren collapses. In fact, it causes us a great deal of anxiety that some of the unions, tired of fighting, show their willingness to strike their own bargain with the company. It doesn't matter that much if some of the small and weak unions show the white flag, but if the Tsurumi union leaves the strike front, we're into deep water. If the Tsurumi union goes into retreat, other unions will immediately break down, and the defection of the Tsurumi union would inevitably lead to our defeat after this long strike. Do you really want to be the ones responsible for such a disgrace? I certainly do not want to continue the strike for another week or even ten days. What I want – provided I get your support – is to reach a settlement as soon as the management surfaces again and we can sign a mutual agreement.

And I went on:

> The management is sitting somewhere out there, expecting the Tsurumi union to leave the strike front any moment now. Once they realise that this isn't going to happen, it's their turn to hoist the white flag. Then they'll come creeping to us on their knees, with their tails between their legs. I want you to wait for three more days. During these three days I'll try to reach an agreement which will offer you conditions

> more favourable than what you can expect if you stop now. The workers of Tsurumi who did not retreat even in the face of the occupation forces, who unremittingly fought for fifty days – shouldn't they be strong enough to wait for three more days?

With these words, I left the stage.

The result of the vote showed that they all were in favour of continuing the strike. In desperation and with tears in their eyes the Tsurumi union leaders said: 'That's the end of our factory. After this, it's finished for good!' Again and again I considered the result of my speech, and I returned to the struggle headquarters in Kawasaki with a very heavy heart indeed.

## The four weak spots of Tōshiba Rōren

Right from the very beginning, this struggle was complicated by several union weak spots. These were:

1. an organisational weakness;
2. conflicts between the single workshop unions;
3. material shortages, and
4. qualitative differences between the three demands.

Regarding (1), the organisational weakness was caused by the fact that Tōshiba Rōren comprised more than sixty independent unions scattered throughout the country and grouped in three regional units: the Tōhoku, Kantō and Kansai Union Federations. The complexity of this organisation was a result of the different membership criteria of various unions, differences in their strength, and the multitude of business areas they came from; taken together these differences were just too great. Even one year after the establishment of Tōshiba Rōren there was still no real unity between the three independent union federations which fought a joint battle.

With regard to (2), conflicts between the different workshop unions arose, as became apparent in the case of the 'House of Madam' incident, because in each organisation the influence of the two main wings within the labour movement inevitably led to differences between the most important unions, which were exacerbated by the protracted strike and the confusing course of events.

As to the third point (3), I think it is scarcely necessary to give a detailed account of the material hardship of that time. No houses to live in, no foodstuffs, and so on. Even though the workers were utterly dependent on the meagre wages they received for their toil, these wages were not paid for more than fifty days during the strike. The union members did not have enough money to buy food rations and thus were driven to the brink of starvation.

With regard to (4) what is meant by 'qualitative differences between the three demands' is that although the two demands which called for a renunciation of dismissals and a wage increase reflected urgent economic needs, the demand for the immediate convening of a conference on the resumption of production – that is, for participation in management affairs with the aim of democratising the company – concerned the company's internal policies, which the union should have regarded rather as a long-term goal. The problem with these demands was that there was no real consensus as to what should happen if they were not fulfilled together. Even though a settlement of the first two economic demands seemed possible for some time, the strike went on because no agreement could be reached over the third one, and the whole struggle became tangled. These difficulties were exacerbated by the already mentioned weaknesses, and this suddenly led to a dangerous situation in which a decision to put a hasty end to the strike seemed imminent.

## Secret negotiations with the management

The Tsurumi union meeting aimed at breaking off the strike could have led to a situation in which all the other unions facing the same problems would have been left high and dry. Now, however, the tide had turned and the struggle continued. This started a chain reaction which not only revived the Yanagimachi, Komukai and other important unions, but active parts of smaller unions which had already left the strike front now began initiatives, trying to organise meetings at which the continuation of the struggle should be decided. As the union's fighting power was restored, the delaying tactics employed by the management, which were widely criticised by the general public, turned out to be a stumbling block for the company.

I had successfully used the chance of turning the tables on

them. Having racked my brains for so long over how to regain the initiative, I could now simply sit and wait. I sent members of the struggle committee of the Kantō Union Federation to the most important unions, prepared for the coming battle and eagerly awaited the reaction by the management.

That was a long and hard day. In the afternoon – it was 20 November – vice chairman Satoshi Tsujii came in and whispered into my ear: 'There's a messenger called Kosugi who has been sent by managing director Satō.' 'Go and prepare a plan for the negotiations, but don't tell anyone yet. If things go wrong again, the disappointment would be too much', I replied.

While I felt like I wanted to pray, I eagerly awaited the return of Tsuji. Meanwhile, Satoshi Tsujii was taken by the messenger to somewhere in the vicinity of the Yatsuyama bridge in Shinagawa, but because they were constantly shadowed by members of the young people's action group who since the 'House of Madam' incident had lost all trust in the union officials, the managers again went into hiding and contact was lost. Patiently, I waited for the next attempt. When it came, the message said: 'Let's meet near the Ōmori building in Kanda.' Under the pretext of visiting the Tokyo group of the company's head office union, Satoshi Tsujii and I left Kawasaki by train. We changed to the underground at Shinbashi station and went to Mitsukoshi-mae, where we strolled around near the Ōmori building and also passed the building where the head office union was housed. All the time we were followed by action group members who stayed in contact with the Horikawachō union. As we knew that the managers would not show up as long as we could not get rid of the action group members, we decided to talk about them with the Horikawachō union and therefore returned to Shinbashi.

There, by chance, we met our colleague Tetsujirō Kobu and Mr Hiroaki Hosaka from the Communist Party. I went over to Kubo, briefly explained the situation and told him I had to get rid of our watchers. Tetsujirō Kubo said he understood, went over to the guys from the young people's action group and left the station together with them. Then Satoshi Tsujii and I again rode back to the Ōmori building. Suddenly the messenger Kōsugi was at our side and showed us the way. Looking back at the events now, I recall a moment of surprise when a fantastically beautiful young woman met us at the entrance of a building which seemed to be a tea-house. Then we were kept waiting for a long time. It was already after midnight – about one o'clock in the morning of the following day, 21 November – when managing director Suzutsugu Satō, director Motoharu Kuno and the head of the department of general affairs, Jyunji Hiraga, showed up. They seemed to be relieved that our meeting had the character of a secret round of negotiations, differing so much from the former mass negotiations under the eyes of a large crowd of union members. They started the talk by saying: 'Shouldn't we try to find a settlement along the line of what we agreed upon when we met last time?' 'Even though we were close to an agreement at that time, you have kept us hanging in mid-air since then, therefore what we agreed last time doesn't count anymore', I replied coolly, rejecting their proposal. Difficult negotiations now continued until after five o'clock in the morning, when the dawn of the winter morning cast its grey light into the room.

With regard to our second demand, the wage increase, the management signalled a certain willingness to compromise, but they were not prepared to give up their resistance concerning the other issues. As my mind was on the uncertainty and the wavering which would spread among the union members during my prolonged absence, I finally concluded the talks: 'The already mentioned three demands are the final word of the union. When you are prepared to meet them, you can contact me again!' Then I left. I was tired after the long night and unable to assess the effect this renewed breakdown of negotiations might have, and I was unhappy that in order to get a last chance for a settlement I had to determine the union's position beforehand.

## The last meeting of the struggle committee

In the early hours of 21 November 1946, at about six o'clock in the morning, I returned to the struggle headquarters with an empty stomach. Immediately I called a meeting of the central struggle committee. The news about my return spread like wildfire and the union members gathered in the room eager to hear what results had been gained.

After I had given them a detailed account of what had happened last night, I explained that because of my personal assessment of the situation I had presented the three-point demand as our basis for negotiations, but that the talks had stalled. If the management was interested in finding a solution, they should come up with a proposal for a new round of collective bargaining; if they failed to do this, negotiation would again be off the agenda. I told them that I required a free hand in the talks in order to be able to react according to the needs of the situation. The room was utterly silent; the union members of Horikawachō, Yanagimachi, Komukai, Tsurumi, the company's head offices, and all the others, did not say a single word.

With my eyes closed, I waited for the members of the struggle committee to give their views. Whatever objections they might have, I knew I must push through my proposal. As I had expected, committee member Miyata vehemently objected: 'I disagree!!' Right from the beginning of this struggle, he had played a very influential role. Although he was no communist, he had shown the strongest will to fight. I nodded and said 'Hmm' and waited for the other committee members to speak up. I realised that the silence of the majority expressed their preparedness to go along with my proposal, but at the same time I felt that there had to be a process in which Miyata was persuaded and made to agree with me. Only then would each and every one understand what I really wanted, and for that I had to gain the unanimous support of all those who were attending the meeting. So I told them in a passionate voice:

> Certainly such an end to this struggle is no perfect solution, as our colleague Miyata knows. I myself would love to start from the beginning once again and make things better this time, if this was possible. But we have reached a point at which the condition for continuing the struggle is that the union federations do not break apart in the process. Where is the chairman of the Kansai Union Federation, Etsurō Yamamura? Why isn't he here? Why are the unions from Fuji, Kawaguchi, Fuchū and other members of the Kantō Union Federation not attending this meeting? A glass with a chip broken off the rim is still a glass, but when it's broken into two big pieces, it's not a glass anymore. With a union organisation it's much the same. Whenever there's such a long and difficult struggle as we are conducting now, it's inevitable that some of the unions don't last until the end. In such a big battle we must take that in our stride. But if we gamble away our unity, we can be sure that first the Kansai Union Federation and then other unions of the Kantō federation will

> go their own ways. If that happens, we'll be utterly and totally defeated, and this crack in our union organisation will forever prevent us from launching another united struggle. The most important matter for a union is not whether it wins or loses a certain battle, but is maintaining its unity and cohesion in times of victory and in times of defeat. If these are maintained, another struggle is always possible. And as long as our unity still exists, I want to prepare for a solution. Preparing for a solution now will neither hurt the union federation nor will it mean that Fuji, Fuchū and the others are excluded from the process. If there is someone among you who has the capability and the means of continuing the strike at this point without a settlement, and more still, without destroying the unity of the union, I ask him to relieve me of my post and do the job!

Again the room sank into a gloomy silence, and nobody wanted to take the word. Finally Miyata rose and said: 'OK. We'll do it the way our colleague Tadanobu Ishikawa has proposed.' Immediately a feeling of relief spread among the meeting's participants. Even I felt this relief for a moment, but at the same time I became aware of the fact that from now on I had an even bigger burden of responsibility on my shoulders. In a few words I expressed my gratitude and closed this important meeting of the struggle committee.

## The last round of collective bargaining

During the morning of the same day, the management sent a message proposing a new round of negotiations. At once I asked the chairman of the Horikawachō union, Shigeki Katsuhara, to join me. Katsuhara was a popular colleague, a graduate of Keiō university and member of the Communist Party. 'Katsuhara, you know where we stand. We're about to begin our last negotiations with the management. I want you to be a member of our delegation. This is what I asked you for when I accepted the post of committee chairman', I told him. He went away in order to think about his answer, but soon afterwards told me he would go along with my request.

Then I selected a couple of other colleagues as members of our team and had a short meeting with them. Afterwards we left for Tokyo, again with Kōsugi as our guide. They let us wait for a long time, while we sat there with mixed feelings. I tried to imagine several conditions the management might stipulate. 'The management, too, will be a little confused now that an end of the strike seems imminent. Which strategy will they adopt when they see the members of our union delegation face to face? How will they deal with the three-point demand I presented to them?' Thinking about these matters and others, my spirits rose as if I was about to solve a crossword puzzle.

Evening had already come when finally we were led into the room of the managing directors in the Ōmori building in Kanda. As soon as the members of both groups had gathered, the managers broke their silence and gave their reaction to my three demands:

> Concerning point 1, we'll do as we agreed earlier, with regard to point 2, we'll provide an additional 1 million yen. As to point 3 – the conference without a quorum – the management revises its stance and proposes to form a study group to investigate this issue. Fourth, we'll act as if this settlement and the resumption of work had been achieved on 14 November. The wages for about ten days will be paid and officially declared as funds used for raising production. And fifth, concerning the costs which have been run up during the strike, the management declares its intention to find a special solution.

With this somewhat vague declaration at the end, the statement of the management's position was completed.

During the whole struggle, the management had eyed the activities of the communist cell within the Horikawachō union with great suspicion, but now the presence of Shigeki Katsuhara at the negotiating table seemed to calm them down a bit. Although the managers acted with caution, their comments were comparatively open-hearted. The negotiations proceeded smoothly and in less than an hour they were finalised. Now the results had to be discussed by the members of the various unions. When a ballot was held in which the members could decide on whether to accept or not, all unions gave their consent, except for the unions of Horikawachō, Kawagishi, the Tōshiba Central Research Institute and the Tōshiba Institute for Electronic Research, which all demanded full payment of the October wages.

Thus the strike was officially declared over at a meeting of the central struggle committee, and the state of readiness for action was suspended. On 26 November 1946 both sides signed the agreement, and the historical Third Tōshiba Labour conflict, which had lasted fifty-seven days, was brought to an end.

## Back at work as head of department

During a meeting of the central struggle committee on 24 November I had declared my intention to step down, and my decision had been accepted. I returned to my earlier post as head of the planning section in the business department. Not long afterwards I was appointed head of the product department. My task was to handle the sales of a multitude of electrical appliances, among them the so-called 'three treasures' – electric fans, refrigerators and radio receivers – to the supply unit of the occupation forces as well as on the domestic market. In March 1947, when even in the midst of destruction new demand slowly began to emerge, I was summoned by the general manager for new business ventures who had the following proposal in store: 'The board of directors has decided to establish a department in charge of dealing with labour issues. They are serious in their intention to approach workplace problems, and they want to give you a responsible position in this new department. You'd have a director as main head of department above you, but you would be in charge of all the details. How do you think about this?' I remembered all the trouble I had had during the October Struggle of the year before, and as I did not want to go through such drudgery again – neither for the union nor for the company – I declined the offer out of hand. I promised to do my best to develop new markets for the business department and increase the sales of the company, and finally the general manager relented and accepted my refusal.

## First chairman of Tōshiba Rōren

During the same year – it was in early October 1947 – I was asked by the union, i.e. the Sanrengōkai, to pay them a visit. They had the following matter to discuss: 'We've got the impression that the management intends to have another go at its plan to reduce the workforce, the one it was forced to withdraw during the October Struggle last year. We want to strengthen our position in advance of this conflict. There's a general consensus among our members that only you, Tadanoba Ishikawa, are the right person to do the job of committee chairman. We urge you to accept the post.' 'No way!' I replied, and remained adamant throughout the afternoon. But when the leaders of the struggle committees of all of the unions who one year earlier had gone through the anxieties of the October Struggle with me didn't stop pleading with me, I finally had to give in. Nevertheless, I received their promise to limit my term in office to only six months.

However, each time this six-month period came to an end, we were either just in the middle of a struggle, or no one else was prepared to apply for the post, or there were threats of imminent mass dismissals. In the end I decided to become a full-time union official and remained in this position until my final term in office ended in March 1950.

I will now speak about what we called the 'Struggle Against the Wage System Based on Independent Economic Viability' and the 'Fight for a Consolidation of the Company without Dismissals'.

## Consolidating the structure of Tōshiba Rōren

In the autumn of 1947 when the occupation policies which until then had supported the trade union movement were turned around, I started my first half-year term of office as chairman of the struggle committee. My first goal was to repair the cracks in our organisation which had led to our defeat in the October Struggle of the previous year and then to establish a viable structure. This meant:

1. excluding from Tōshiba Rōren the unions of companies which were only affiliated with Tōshiba and limiting membership to those unions which had been established in Tōshiba factories (March 1948);
2. in view of the increasing complexity of future conflicts, enhancing administrative efficiency by introducing better means of communication between the forty-five unions scattered throughout the country;
3. establishing a union secretariat and departments for propaganda, for conflicts arising in connection with the

consolidation of the company, for wage struggles, legal affairs, public relations, cultural activities and research tasks, each to be headed by a member of the central executive committee to ensure that the decisions of this body were duly carried out;

4. holding regular meetings, and in cases of an emergency, calling extraordinary meetings of the central executive committee to ensure that its members had an equal level of information when decisions had to be made;
5. uniting the former Sanrengōkai which consisted of the Kantō, Kansai and Tōhoku Union Federations as the Tōshiba Rōren (March 1948).[6]

In particular, the measures which gave the secretariat additional authority and put leading union officials in charge of the struggle departments turned out to be successful, as they enhanced the union's ability to act quickly during the later conflicts.

In anticipation of the benefits of a growing unity within the union organisation, I formulated the following goals: (1) promoting a consolidation of the company without a reduction of the workforce; (2) introduction of a system of minimum wages; and (3) improving the system of severance pay – this latter issue was a sort of 'farewell present' left to me by my predecessor, Takehiro Kawanishi.

These goals gave shape to the central issues of dispute in the later three major struggles: (1) the conflict between, on the one hand, a system of basic wages to guarantee the livelihood of the workers as demanded by the union, and on the other, the management's plan for a wage system based on the independent economic viability of each factory in 1947/8; (2) the fight against the company's adjustment measures, i.e. against a decree based on the law on economic deconcentration 1948/9 which called for a reduction of the workforce; and (3) the fight to protect the Tōshiba Rōren from forces intending to break it up during the second half of 1949.

## The meaning of a wage system based on independent economic viability

A wage system based on independent economic viability entailed that, while the single factories were regarded as separate economic units, the whole sum of wages could be freely determined by the management according to the margin of profits or losses and divided up among the workforce according to a special method measuring only the individual performance of each factory.

Accordingly, the wages of workers in factories with inferior conditions of production would inevitably be reduced to a low level, regardless of their individual efforts. On the other hand, the wage differences between these factories and others with better conditions would prevent the union federation from launching a united struggle and even create discord within the single unions. This would seriously weaken the union. The system was therefore designed to pave the way for firing workers and closing production facilities. Accepting the principle of factories as separate economic units and a wage system based on independent economic viability would have been tantamount to selling the workers down the river.

## The draft decree of Mochikabu-Kaisha Seiri Iinkai (the Commission for the Dismantling of Industrial Holdings, CDIH)

During the summer of 1949, the struggle against a wage system based on independent economic viability developed into a conflict which apparently aimed at preventing the consolidation of the company, i.e. a fight against the law on deconcentration, but in reality it focused on the issue of whether Tōshiba Rōren would be kept intact or destroyed.

The first attack by the company's management came on 18 February 1949, when the Commission for the Dismantling of Industrial Holdings sent Tōshiba a draft of a decree based on the law on deconcentration, which completely contradicted the real intention of this law and the occupation policy in general. It recommended that Tōshiba rid itself of twenty-eight smaller and weaker businesses the management regarded as a burden, but unite the two main branches of the company in one body. This measure was not designed to prevent an economic concentration, but on the contrary would have resulted in a very strong concentration in the high-voltage industry. The decree not only caused anxiety among the workers of the twenty-eight small factories, but also among those of the sixteen major factories which would remain part of the company, because in the face of an increasingly harsh stance by management concerning staff reduction, they feared mass dismissals.

The union federation's department for conflicts arising in connection with the consolidation of the company reacted to this draft decree by publishing a paper which outlined the union's position on the matter and in an outspoken manner stated our arguments. They were reinforced by deputy chairman Tomoki Yamashita during a public hearing at which he said:

> Tōshiba cannot be counted among the companies with an excessive concentration of economic power. If, however, the commission includes Tōshiba in its measures to implement the law on deconcentration, this may be because in our country it is the only company active in both heavy and light industry. The plan to rid the company of twenty-eight small and economically insignificant factories is absurd and should be dropped. The company should rather be separated along the lines of heavy and light industry. This would also reflect the historical development of Tōshiba as an amalgamation of companies of the heavy and the light industrial sectors.

Neither the management nor the commission deigned to look at our paper, but on 17 June a decree was issued which corresponded in every detail with the aforementioned draft decree. The management received it with tears of joy and used it as the basis of their plans for consolidating the company. That they failed to take the paper by Tōshiba Rōren seriously, and chose simply to ignore it, turned out to be a big stumbling block for them in a later phase.

## Unilateral breach of the labour agreement

The second attack by the management was launched when they unilaterally declared the collective agreement null and void. This agreement had been made with the Kantō and Kansai Union Federation in the year following Japan's defeat, on 1 May 1946, after the union's victory in the First Tōshiba Conflict. At that time occupation policies still strongly supported the labour movement. As the agreement contained a clause requiring the union's consent in cases of dismissal or personnel transfer, it was a very good protection for union members.

Nevertheless, in December 1948 the management targeted the unions of Kamo, Kawagishi, Nagai and other small and local unions by ordering large numbers of workers to take leave which in fact was tantamount to dismissal. As soon as the union resisted, the factory manager and his deputies went into hiding, and the workers received a letter by registered mail notifying them of their forced leave.

When the union members of the Kamo, Kawagishi, Nagai and other factories went to work as usual and did their job on their own account, i.e. practising production control, the courts interfered and issued interim orders closing the factories. At the same time payment of wages and salaries which had already been delayed, ceased altogether, and the workers who had come to work because they needed the money were evicted from the factories by an executive officer accompanied by a large number of policemen. Such measures were taken in December 1948 while the labour contract was still in force.

Tōshiba Rōren insisted on the validity of Article 22 which stipulated that the existing agreement remained in force until a new contract was signed and appealed to the district court of Yokohama for an interim order. This motion, and one issued by management which claimed that 'as of 18 March there is no valid collective agreement with Tōshiba Rōren', were dealt with jointly by the court, and after a long debate which continued until a new union law eliminating the automatic extension of labour contracts became effective, we were turned down. The management now enjoyed an advantageous position in which no labour contract was in force. As it took us seven years to overcome this situation with no valid contract, everyone will understand how perfidious the management's strategy was.

## Managing director Taizō Ishizaka appears on the scene

The third attack occurred when the new managing director Taizō Ishizaka took over, a man who in financial circles carried the title 'Asaemon[7] of dismissals'. From Mr Kiichirō Satō, president of the Mitsui Bank, he had received the order: 'Whatever the union may do to resist, there will be no agreement! Even if Tōshiba goes by the board: no contract!' In December 1948 Taizō Ishizaka was appointed, and on 6 April 1949 he took over as managing director. At the same time, all leading managers of the company had to sign a formal request for voluntary retirement which put them at Taizō Ishizaka's mercy. Then, one after the other, he implemented all of the plans he had made during the four months before he took up office.

His first measure was a purge of the board of directors, which had been afflicted by serious internal disagreement, and the formation of a new group of directors which would not give him any trouble – he was a newcomer who had joined Tōshiba without any supporters among the company's managers.

Then he motivated his new managers by personally attending negotiations with the union, sitting in the first row; this was quite a contrast to the old management which had always vanished and gone into hiding. Instead of delegating the responsibility for disputes with the workers to subordinates, as his predecessors had done, he dealt with them personally in his capacity as managing director, and made a show of it. By doing so, he reconstructed the internal hierarchy of the company which for some time had been disintegrating. The management, too, had to restore unity within its own ranks before it was ready for battle.

In June, a pamphlet was printed with the title 'Message to All Tōshiba Employees' and handed out to all employees by their superiors. In this pamphlet, Taizō Ishizaka addressed the following issues: (1) the dire situation of the company; (2) his own duties; (3) the decree issued by the Commission for the Dismantling of Industrial Holdings; (4) an immediate staff reduction and the criteria for selecting those who had to leave; (5) conditions for voluntary retirement from the company; and (6) guidelines for a reorganisation of the company after the dismissals. On 16 July, the company began sending out notifications of dismissal. The first to be hit was the strongest enemy, the Horikawachō union, where 1,167 were individually told to leave. In factories which were to remain part of the company, 4,581 workers were fired, while in the facilities the company intended to get rid of, 2,100 persons altogether were dismissed.

## The union busters' intrigue

The fourth attack by the management was the planting of a time bomb. This bomb had already been placed two years earlier in February 1947, when the management infiltrated two union busters, Masahiko Kobori and Toshifumi Tateyama, into the glass production department which was dominated by the strong Horikawachō union (Masahiko Kobori joined the company in February 1947, Toshifumi Tateyama one year later).

Trying to split the workers' organisation when mass dismissals are planned is one of the more traditional management approaches. At Tōshiba, following the October Struggle the management had conducted an in-depth study of the various factions within the union federation and the unions. By pushing through their performance-oriented wage system, they had managed to cause some unions, such as Fuji, Kokura, Gumma and Oshikiri, to leave the union federation, and within the Communist Party-dominated Horikawachō union they had instigated a confrontation between the communist cell and the Mindō faction which had been founded in February 1948. Moreover, again in Horikawachō, they had founded the Tōshiba Workplace Problems Study Group; this group had criticised Tōshiba Rōren for its allegedly extreme left-wing leadership in past labour conflicts. Finally, they had managed to initiate a motion of no confidence against the union leaders which was put to the vote during a meeting of the central committee of the Horikawachō union on 22 October. Their influence was already significant. Three days later at an extraordinary union meeting the motion was voted down by a large majority – 2,057 members supported the union leaders while 1,202 voted against them – but in any case this ballot must have given the management the reassuring impression that the union reputedly strongest within the company was not so strong after all.

The faction of union busters which had lost some of its influence because of this vote regained its strength after 16 July 1949, the day the management announced its plans for mass dismissals. With Toshifumi Tateyama and Masahiko Kobori as their leaders, the faction started a secret campaign in which it collected signatures of workers supporting the establishment of a second union; it helped the management during its lock-out in the glass production department, and its members staged a walk-out during the first meeting of the department's employees. And in the afternoon of 16 July, as soon as the management had announced mass dismissals, the foundation meeting of a second union splitting off from the Horikawachō union with about 4,000 members, was held – what a splendid coincidence!

Gritting my teeth, I witnessed this foundation meeting.

Strangely enough I did not shed any tears of anger but felt only a willingness to fight and to win at any cost grow strong in my breast.

## Announcement of dismissals

The management's fifth attack was to include an exceptionally high percentage of union leaders among those dismissed. However, the union officials of that time, who had been elected because of their popularity and were trusted by the large majority of union members, somehow did not seem to fit the criteria the management laid down for selecting the victims – the 'bad employees' and so on, as it chose to call them. Apart from myself and my two deputies, Tetsujirō Kubo and Tomoki Yamashita, there were a further 16 to 22 persons of lower union ranks who had to go; nearly 70 per cent to be dismissed. At the level of the individual unions, this rose to 90 per cent among the full-time union officials from the Keihin district of Horikawachō, the Matsuda Institute and the Yanagimachi factory! Apparently the selection of victims was designed to get rid of the activists of Tōshiba Rōren and its affiliated unions.

As a consequence, the union federation lodged a complaint with the Central Labour Relations Commission, accusing the management of unfair practices. However, the Commission only debated the case at great length without ever reaching a decision. As late as 16 March 1950, long after the dispute was over, it dismissed the complaint with an utterly absurd argument: 'As the labour conflict is already over, a further investigation into the matter makes no sense.'

The sixth attack was the management's refusal to conduct any collective negotiations. The day the split-off Horikawachō union was founded – 16 July – was also the day when the company first sent out letters of dismissal. From this day onwards the company employed a strategy of declining any proposal to enter into collective bargaining with Tōshiba Rōren made in my name because, as they said, a person not in the company's employ could not be a representative of Tōshiba Rōren. The second Horikawachō union tried to gain influence by adapting to the company's position. They claimed that Tōshiba Rōren had lost its capability to conduct negotiations because it was a union without a leadership, and it would be to the advantage of the workers to join those who could do the job.

This argument was ridiculous! A union is a body formed by the free will of the workers and completely independent of any company. If the management does not like the union's officials and therefore fires them arbitrarily, and afterwards refuses to negotiate on the grounds that the officials are not company employees, a situation is created in which the union's autonomy is completely eroded by the management. I ordered our union office to send every day to the management a document in my name demanding negotiations – regardless of whether this demand was rejected again and again – and to accept only written refusals. When a large number of these refusals had been collected, I handed them over to the Central Labour Relations Commission as proof of unfair management practices. But all of my efforts were in vain and ended with the scandalous decision of 16 March 1950.

## The effect of the Shimoyama, Mitaka and Matsukawa incidents

The consequences of the Shimoyama, Mitaka and Matsukawa incidents can be regarded as a seventh attack.[8] The Shimoyama incident occurred on 5 July 1949, the Mitaka incident on 15 July of the same year, and both came like a cold shower to the railway workers who were fighting against dismissals.

As a reaction to the Matsukawa incident of 17 August – as if they were only waiting for it to happen – the ruling politicians issued communiqués which left the impression that members of the Communist Party had been the real perpetrators. As the mass media generally accepted this explanation, the incident turned out to be extremely useful for the Tōshiba management which was busy firing employees. On the other hand, the Matsukawa incident had a very negative effect on the struggle of Tōshiba Rōren opposing the dismissals, as the Matsukawa factory was in the vicinity of the scene of the incident and its union leader was Saburō Sugiura, a member of the Communist Party.

To make matters worse, on that same 17 August the union federation had called a one-day strike as a signal of protest by unions affected by the closure of factories in response to the decree of the Commission for the Dismantling of Industrial Holdings, among them the Matsukawa union. The *Yomiuri* newspaper carried an article in which the strike proclamation by Tōshiba Rōren was arbitrarily interpreted as a secret order to derail a train, and for some time it seemed as if I, who had ordered the strike, would be arrested as the instigator of the Matsukawa incident. This led me into a bitter confrontation with the chief editor of the column 'Society and Social Affairs', Hasegawa, and on the following day the paper published a minuscule correction which cited the words of chairman Tadanobu Ishikawa. The effect of the first article was softened a bit, but as the whole story was a scoop for the editors of local papers, various rumours were mixed with fantasy and every day a new 'big revelation' was concocted.

On 22 September a large number of people were arrested, and in the end ten railway workers and ten Tōshiba employees were named as the perpetrators, among them my colleague Hajime Satō of the Tsurumi union whom I had sent to Matsukawa in order to organise the fight for the resumption of production there. He was identified as 'the main culprit in a conspiracy together with the railway employees'. The negative effect of this event on Tōshiba Rōren was immeasurable. The second union rejoiced and pointed out that this would be proof of the allegation that the Tōshiba Rōren was a communist union federation. The fighting spirit of rank and file members sank dramatically. Hajime Satō and Saburo Sugiura were sentenced to death by two courts of appeal. However, they were ultimately saved by the fact that they did not cease to protest their innocence. By introducing new evidence which had been suppressed by the police to sustain the fictitious police version of the events, they both were able to produce alibis which defeated the theory of a conspiracy. The case was then referred back to the Sendai Regional Court of Appeal by the Supreme Court.

In the course of these proceedings I met with Judge Monden in order to persuade him of the innocence of Hajime Satō, and gave him a detailed account of what had happened at the time. The verdict 'Not guilty on all counts' was handed down by the Sendai Regional Court on 8 August 1961, and the appeal by the public prosecutor who did not want to give in was quashed by the Supreme Court. But even then it was still two more years until the innocence of all twenty defendants had been established. Counting from the day of the arrests in September 1949, the whole matter had gone on for fourteen years until it was finally settled in 1963! During the whole of this time Tōshiba Rōren was unable to get rid of its reputation as a red organisation, and those accused of being the culprits of the Matsukawa incident were made to fear for their lives.

## Counter-attack of Tōshiba Rōren

Apart from the above-mentioned seven attacks by the management, two other factors impeded the fight of Tōshiba Rōren against the measures aiming at a consolidation of the company: first there were the minimum wages which were determined solely on the basis of the economic strength of each factory – the Central Labour Relations Commission had refused to act on this issue – and second was the management's successful request for an interim order for a lock-out of the union.

These wide-ranging waves of attack continued unrelentingly, leaving us in a state of shock in which we repeatedly asked ourselves: 'Oh Lord, and what comes next?' They clearly aimed at destroying Tōshiba Rōren as an organisation. We were actually being pushed to the point where it became highly doubtful whether the union federation would be able to maintain its fighting power at all and whether the union's autonomy could be preserved.

Faced with this barrage of attacks which threatened to paralyse the organisation, Tōshiba Rōren adopted a new strategy. First, a comprehensive defence system was organised, and then the union itself went on the attack. This attack focused on several issues.

The first counter-attack was directed at some inconsistencies of the expected decree based on the law on deconcentration. On 17 June 1949 the management had received a decree which was identical to the former draft and acted quickly in preparing a plan for consolidation of the company along the lines of this decree. The union federation on the other hand had intensively lobbied for hearings on the law in the Upper House, in the Lower House Committee on Cabinet Affairs, and in the Committee on Matters of Economic Stabilisation. However, our efforts had been in vain, and the decree had been passed. On 16 July we sent a letter to the Prime Minister, Mr Shigeru Yoshida, in which we expressed our protest against the way things had been handled. This letter outlined the standpoint of Tōshiba Rōren, which accepted the necessity of a consolidation of the company, but only if it did not victimise the workers, and which contained a sharp protest that the decree reflected only the interests of the capitalists. As a result, the original plan presented to parliament was considerably mitigated with regard to those factories Tōshiba wanted to get rid of. Moreover, the sum of extraordinary losses designated in the decree was increased to a level the union had proposed. This thwarted the management's intention of doubling the company's capital in advance of getting approval for implementing its consolidation plan, and there were fears that this might antagonise the shareholders. As the Central Labour Relations Commission, which had been the addressee of our letter of protest, now promised a thorough investigation of the matter, the management's schedule for implementing its plan became uncertain, and it became obvious that Tōshiba would suffer a serious competitive disadvantage compared to firms such as Hitachi, Mitsubishi and other companies.

Unions normally find it very difficult to enter into such tiresome legal disputes, and the management had counted on an unconditional surrender by Tōshiba Rōren. But we had meticulously prepared our case and skilfully focused attention on the company's mistakes and incorrect implementation of the decree of the Commission for the Dismantling of Industrial Holdings.

All this caused managing director Taizō Ishizaka a great deal of trouble, and he bitterly complained about 'the insolence of those greenhorns in the Commission'. However, these remarks won him no new friends among the Commission members, and only served to complicate the situation. Now the management was forced to find some sort of compromise with the union federation, and it became clear that our strategy of endurance and of widening the scope of the conflict had been successful.

## The management's attack breaks down

The second counter-attack aimed at turning the tables on the management's refusal to conduct collective bargaining and at winning a battle in our struggle for wage rises. The Tōshiba Rōren members who had been utterly exhausted by the several attacks of the management in 1949, suddenly got their second wind when on 22 August the union called for wage negotiations and the management was unable to decline the request any longer.

After some preparatory negotiations, the union federation presented a preliminary proposal to the management. The wage levels outlined in this proposal were not really satisfactory, but the former 50:50 ratio between basic wage and bonus payments was changed to a 60:40 ratio which reflected the union federation's long-standing demand. After some rounds of negotiations, the wage level of 8,000 yen offered by the management, which was based on the system of independent economic viability, was raised by part of the amount the union had demanded to 'cover actual living costs' to 8,573 yen.

Unsatisfied with this result and in an attempt to challenge Tōshiba Rōren, the second union continued its struggle for higher wages and staged some unnecessary actions. This lost it the goodwill it had earned from the management because of its reputation as a 'yellow union'. The Tōshiba Rōren members, although they got only a small increase in wages, had forced the management to make some concessions and this strengthened their trust in their union leaders, who they promised to support and follow in the coming struggles.

The more the members' trust in their union leaders grew, the more we were able to limit the influence of the second union. This was the third counter-attack. The rift within Tōshiba Rōren which went back to the 1946 October Struggle had become deeper with each of the many strikes, and during the fight against the wage system based on independent economic viability in 1948 it had led to a confrontation with the unions of Fuji, Kokura and Gumma, which left the federation. During the subsequent fight against the consolidation of the company, union busters had moved in on the unions of Adachi, Ōsaka, Kamo, Yanagimachi and Kōfu, and in all of these factories a second union had split off and won the support of part of the workforce. Nevertheless, the number of workers who joined the second unions never exceeded a sixth of the strength of the first unions and stagnated at about 3,000 members. The second union federation, trying to bring together these unions, had been forced to postpone its planned foundation meeting until 4 November. Among the 3,000 members, many had chosen to change sides because they feared being fired. When the waves of dismissals eased in July, the tide was turned and many returned to us. Suddenly nobody wanted to join the second unions any more. In the end, management hopes of establishing a second union federation and bringing about the decline of the first Tōshiba Rōren were shattered. This was also noticed by the Central Labour Relations Commission, Nikkeiren and the Chūō Keizai Saiken Seibi Iinkai (Central Commission for Economic Reconstruction and Consolidation).

A fourth factor which underpinned our preparedness to launch a counter-attack was the fifth re-election of the chairman of Tōshiba Rōren and his two deputies. In spite of the dismissals announced by the management and its subsequent refusal to negotiate, the broad majority of union members supported me and my deputy Tetsujiro Kubo by re-electing us for a fifth and the second deputy chairman Tomoki Yamashita for a third term in office. The management, which had secretly anticipated our defeat in these elections and banked on our failure, must have been deeply disappointed. It was like having a big whale already secured in the net when it suddenly breaks through the mesh and serenely swims out into the ocean.

The conflicts launched by the unions of the Kamo and Kawagishi factories, which the management had expected to put down in no time, were still unsettled after nearly a year, and when the management resorted to lock-outs, the struggle spread like wildfire to factories throughout the country and the heroic fight staged by Tōshiba Rōren won great popular support. This was our fifth counter-attack.

Union members of both the Kamo and the Kawagishi factories who had lost their jobs and then the capability of implementing production control because of the lock-out, suddenly became aware of the real nature of their struggle when they encountered extremely brutal suppression by the police force. While the management was convinced that the union, in the face of these measures, would turn tail and give up, the workers did exactly the opposite. They formed a sort of story-tellers' group and travelled through Japan, telling the people about the brutal treatment they had suffered from the police and the extent to which the company was linked with the public authorities, that is, with the courts of law, the police force and so forth. By doing so, they became exceptionally aware workers indeed.

As a sixth counter-attack, we – the members of the central executive committee of Tōshiba Rōren – held a meeting in the house of committee member Kitamura in the Ōmiyachō district of Kawasaki. This social gathering which lasted the whole day enabled us to regain a harmonious relationship after the heated discussions during meetings of the central executive committee.

It was only natural that differences would arise between those executive committee members who had been elected for only a half-year term in office and the committee chairman and his deputies who had already been re-appointed for a third or a fifth term. Such differences concerned the evaluation of subtle changes in the company's position and also the question of how to react to them. The social gatherings which we organised during the couple of months after the summer of 1949 were a very effective way of defusing internal disputes, and by settling our differences of opinion we were able to bring the last step of our long struggle to a successful conclusion.

## Steps towards a settlement

After the systematic and far-reaching attacks by the management had come to an end in October, during one of the aforementioned social gatherings all members of the central executive committee came to a joint evaluation of the situation. Their analysis was as follows:

> Unfortunately the mass dismissals have, like a spring tide, swept away thousands of union members, and our resistance against these measures was to no avail. Let's call a spade a spade and admit our failure. But the motto 'Consolidation of the company without sacrificing the workers!' leads to further problems. The workers in the factories which will be separated from the company as well as those in the sixteen facilities which will remain with it and who have not been fired, haven't they endured and put their trust in us despite the massive attacks and the pressure by the second unions which denounced them as members of unions belonging to a federation devoid of a real leadership? We must not betray their trust and hand over the struggle organisation of our federation to these unions of union busters! Now as the plans for a consolidation of the company and the decree based on the law of deconcentration are clear and a massive personnel reduction has been enforced, we who oppose dismissals must use all our strength for the task of maintaining the struggle capacity of Tōshiba Rōren.

I myself made the following remarks:

> No matter how strongly one may emphasise the importance of a fighting organisation, its real importance will only be fully understood by those who now oppose the dismissals and enjoy the trust of the masses, and possibly by others close to them. But the more than 10,000 workers threatened by dismissals are tired from the strain of this long fight and desire to get some rest. If we who at this stage still strongly oppose any dismissals continue the struggle, it could lead to the misunderstanding that we are only fighting for our own return to our former workplace. Especially now that our counter-attacks show signs of success it is important that we avoid such a misunderstanding and reach a compromise with the company in order to guarantee the future existence of the union federation.

To union leaders, the principle of justice is very important when it comes to starting a fight, but it is even more important for them to know when the struggle is nearing its end. In this fight against the consolidation of the company, we were the injured party and the management or, if you like, the capitalists, had created the reason for the conflict. If our side now backed down and ended the conflict, it would give our adversary the impression that he could push us around at will.

I was looking for the right occasion to make my views public. Around the end of October deputy chairman Tetsujiro Kubo came back to the house where we gathered and told us: 'When I just went to the company, the light was burning only in the offices of the department of personnel affairs, so I went in. They all sat there, making long faces'. When I asked him, 'Did you speak with them?' he replied: 'Yes, we chatted a bit about how best to run the world, but the department head, Tadashi Hagio, made a grave face and asked me about the union leadership's position. In my mind, the time has come for some serious talking.'

To get another opinion, I asked deputy chairman Tomoki Yamashita for his views. Again I considered the circumstances: the effect of our letter of protest which had been written by Tomoki Yamashita's department for conflicts arising in connection with the consolidation of the company; the sudden development of our struggle for wage rises, for which I was responsible; and the information Tetsujiro Kubo had given us about the number of workers active in the second unions. Having digested these, I was certain that the time for a settlement had finally come. Therefore I decided to send both of my deputies, Tomoki Yamashita and Tetsujiro Kubo, to enter into preliminary negotiations on behalf of the union federation.

Not wanting to lose face, the company's management had refused to give an inch so far. Now, business manager Tsunesuke Takahashi and main department head Tadashi Hagio did not conceal their satisfaction that things had finally started moving again. The preliminary negotiations continued for a couple of days. Although the time seemed to be ripe, and up to a point good progress had been made, the negotiations suddenly stalled on the issue of a fund for the labour conflict. Both of my deputies were certain that the matter would not be clarified by further negotiations at the present level and told me that the time had come for me to negotiate directly with managing director Taizō Ishizaka. As Tomoki Yamashita put it, in view of the effect of the letter of protest, a prolonged struggle against dismissals might drive the capitalists to despair and the company might actually go bankrupt.

## Secret talks with managing director Taizō Ishizaka

On 9 November 1949, one month after our re-election as union leaders, I left my home and went on foot to the estate of Taizō Ishizaka which was well within walking distance. Barely had he recognised my face, when he said, 'This time it really looks as if you will succeed in destroying the company!' He was a man who did not hold back his opinion, and as I knew his character well, I understood that the union federation's strategy must indeed have been very effective.

'If we really wanted to ruin the company, we wouldn't have received such strong support from the union members. A little while ago, deputy chairmen Yamashita and Kubo held talks with business manager Tsunesuke Takahashi on the conditions for a settlement, but as the management, with a rather strange stubbornness, refused to discuss a point of minor importance, there were problems. As you must know by now how efficient our strategy is, my colleague Yamashita thought that I should ask for your opinion. Thus here I am.' When I had said this, Mr Ishizaka's face suddenly brightened and he replied: 'I want to thank you for this. I haven't received a report from Takahashi yet, but your conditions are quite difficult to meet, aren't they?' I was surprised because I had not expected the managing director not to be informed of every detail. 'The company has exerted severe pressure on Tōshiba Rōren for a long time. At this moment we are not demanding any settlement but we're waiting for our strategy of attacking the management at its weakest spot to work. I cannot believe that Mr Takahashi isn't aware of the consequences. However, you, Mr Ishizaka, who have a good understanding of financial matters, will fully comprehend what is going to happen now that we've hit the company at its Achilles heel and lodged a formal complaint against the plans of the management. This is what we all think. Why doesn't Mr Takahashi give you all the relevant information?' Managing director Ishizaka gave me a somewhat forced smile and then told me straight away: 'I don't know what Takahashi's intentions are, but my time is running out and I am really getting worried.'

I replied: 'As far as the union federation is concerned, I have entrusted my two deputies with the negotiations, therefore I don't know every detail. But as you seem to be in a hurry, let's meet again tomorrow in the Tsukamoto building. It might be the best if you came alone, thus avoiding any disagreement on your own side.' He agreed, and on the following day, 10 November, managing director Taizō Ishizaka and we three union officials met for further talks.

On this occasion the union federation presented Ishizaka with a document which became the basis for the later agreement, and my deputy Yamashita explained it in great detail. The most important condition for a settlement was the demand that those who had rejected their dismissal – among them the three of us – consented to voluntary retirement from the company. In return for this consent we demanded a clause which protected Tōshiba Rōren from further destructive attacks by the management. Managing director Ishizaka replied: 'I agree with that; as far as I am concerned, that's okay. But I'll have to get approval from above.' Then, point by point, Ishizaka gave his own views, which generally favoured a settlement and showed his willingness to go along with the union's ideas about an agreement.

At ten o'clock on the morning of 16 November, official collective bargaining began in the conference room of the Tsukamoto building. The company's delegation consisted of ten persons led by managing director Taizō Ishizaka, and Tōshiba Rōren was represented by ten union officials under my leadership. After much discussion, a preliminary agreement was signed by both sides at ten past seven in the evening. Because the representatives of the union federation had to seek the approval of the National Committee, at this stage the agreement was still a preliminary one.

## The agreement – voluntary retirement from the company

From that evening until confirmation of the agreement during a conference of the National Committee, the management must have been greatly concerned that the strength of the union federation might be insufficient to push through the settlement of this long conflict. In fact, a settlement which called for the voluntary retirement of those who had so strongly resisted their dismissal and had not ceased fighting for three years gave me, who had vowed to fight together with them until the end, a feeling of having sacrificed the 343 persons concerned. From whatever angle I looked at it, it was an extremely sad matter and a very difficult step to take.

Nevertheless, now that all obstacles had been overcome and the plans of our adversary to shake the union federation to its very foundation had been thwarted; now that the masses of workers who would not be fired had regained their fighting spirit because of the tenacious struggle of those who opposed dismissals; now as we felt that we enjoyed the trust of more than 10,000 union members; now that the impatience of the managers had become plainly visible; now that the management together with union leaders of the supposedly 'leaderless' Tōshiba Rōren had retracted the already announced dismissals of those who had refused to accept them, allowing them to retire voluntarily from the company; now that the management had withdrawn the disciplinary dismissals at the Kamo, Kawagishi and Niigata factories and had corrected mistakes regarding the planned reorganisation and consolidation of the company in our favour and even was prepared to pay the costs of the labour conflict: it is not exaggeration to say that now the union federation as a whole, apart from those who still opposed their dismissal, had the feeling they had won a great victory. In spite of the strong doubts I had felt, all union members who had fought against their firings unanimously gave their unreserved consent to my proposal.

However, looking back now after thirty years have come and gone and asking myself whether the settlement really reflected our demand for a 'consolidation of the company without sacrificing workers', I cannot help but feel a burning shame deep inside me.

Now, thirty years later, I ask myself whether all those colleagues who had struggled so hard against being fired and who in the end, with me, chose to leave Tōshiba, really approved of my decision without reservations . . .? [Here the speaker's voice fails . . .]

## The end

Until the conclusion of my final term in office at the end of March 1950, I held the important post of chairman of the central executive committee of Tōshiba Rōren. Afterwards I never walked through Tōshiba Rōren's gates again. According to the book The History of our Union Movement published by Tōshiba Rōren in 1963, 'all of those who had ardently fought against their dismissals' chose to retire voluntarily from the company, and following a purge of members of the Communist Party (the red purge) in October 1950, a conscientious and politically neutral wing became the mainstay of the union and managed to strengthen the federation's organisation. Following a joint struggle with the second union, on 26 August 1951 a conference was held in Horikawachō at which both unions reunited. This is proof that the union split during the mass dismissals had really been part of a scheme planned by the management. To my mind Tōshiba Rōren could be proud of the fact that it managed to hand over to the younger generation a struggle organisation which was six times as strong as that of the unions which had split off.

The main clauses of the agreement of 16 November 1949 which concluded the 'fight for the consolidation of the company' are as follows:

*Article I*
The management retracts the dismissals of persons belonging to the union federation and who at this point resist their dismissal, and converts them into 'voluntary retirement from the company'.
*Article II*
When hiring new employees in those factories which will remain part of the company, the management will preferably hire those persons who now are leaving the company. In this case the management will not resort to any discriminatory practices against those persons who at the moment resist their dismissal.
*Article III*
The management will help all those persons who are affected by the personnel reduction and until now have not been otherwise re-employed, to find new employment. The union federation will support the management's effort.
*Article IV*
To the limit of its capabilities, the management will grant those persons who are affected by the personnel reduction and until now have not been otherwise re-employed favourable conditions concerning the sale, etc., of products of the company.
*Article X*
The management will settle on a separate basis the problems of the Niigata production facility as follows:

(a) The management retracts the dismissals of fourteen persons.
(b) The management pays each of the mentioned fourteen persons severance pay and acts according to the principle of 'voluntary retirement from the company'. The total amount to be paid to the mentioned fourteen persons will be 50,000 yen.

*Article XI*
The management will settle on a separate basis the problems of the Kamo production facility as follows:

(a) The management retracts the disciplinary dismissals of four persons.
(b) Those persons who at the moment resist their dismissal, inclusive of the four persons mentioned above, will be treated as stated in Article I.

(c) The company will employ twenty-five members of the Kamo factory union (in the following referred to as 'the first union') in the Kamo production facility.

*Article XII*

The management will settle on a separate basis the problems of the Kawagishi production facility as follows:

(a) The management retracts the disciplinary dismissals of four persons.

(b) Those persons who at the moment resist their dismissal, inclusive of the four persons mentioned above, will be treated as stated in Article I.

(c) In line with the proposals of the union and provided that the Kawagishi factory union lifts the siege of the Kawagishi production facility, the management will sell machinery and tools, the type and number of which being deemed sufficient by the management for 120 persons to produce electrical clocks, to those persons mentioned in Article XII (b), at a fixed price which is stated in the implementing regulations of the plan for the reconstruction and consolidation of the company.

(d) The management will to the limit of its capabilities lend its support to the production of electrical clocks, etc., as mentioned in Article XII (c).

## Notes

1. Kantō: in the Tokyo area.
2. Kansai: in the Osaka area.
3. Tōhoku: in the northeastern area of the main island of Honshu.
4. In 1949, this ministry was renamed and reorganised as the Ministry of International Trade and Industry (MITI).
5. Kiyomizu: a temple in the ancient city of Kyoto which is built on a ledge 150 feet above the ground.
6. From this time onwards one can actually speak of a Tōshiba enterprise union as a federation of unions of the various Tōshiba factories; its official name was 'Tōshiba Rōdō Kumiai Rengōkai', abbreviated to 'Tōshiba Rōren'.
7. Asaemon was an executioner of the Edo era.
8. Accounts of these three incidents may be found in Chapter 5.

# 5 The Planned General Strike of 1 February 1947 and the Fight Against the Law on Personnel Levels in the Public Sector of Kokurō, 1949

*Ichizō Suzuki*

**Ichizō Suzuki**

1910 Born on 25 March in Kanagawa prefecture
1923 Finished elementary school education; apprentice in the construction company of his father
1934 Employed by the National Railways
1941 Training as engine driver at the Railway School (equal to advanced professional training of today's School of the National Railways)
1942 Finished training
1943 Assistant in the passenger train department at Shinagawa station (Tokyo)

Trade union functions

1946 Vice chairman of the central struggle committee of Kokutetsu Sōrengō (the Union Federation of the National Railways, UFNR) (in November)
1948 Vice chairman of the central executive committee of Kokutetsu Rōdō Kumiai, or Kokurō (the National Railway Workers' Union, NRWU) in May
1949 Representative of the chairman of the central struggle committee of Kokurō
1949 Dismissed by the National Railways; resigned from his union posts

## Other functions

1950 Member of the standing committee of the Communist Party of Japan (extraordinary member of the central leadership)
1955 Member of the central committee of the Communist Party of Japan (Head of the Union Policy Section)
1958 Member of the executive committee of the central committee of the Communist Party of Japan
1962 Delegate to the Upper House (nation-wide)
1964 Expelled from the Communist Party of Japan

## Publications

*Shigunaru wa kiezu* (The Signal Isn't Extinguished), Gogatsu Shobō, 1949
*Ni-ichi Suto* (The General Strike of 1 February 1947), Aki Shobō, 1979
*Shimoyama-jiken zengo* (Before and After the Shimoyama Incident), Aki Shobō, 1981

## I Editor's Overview

During the immediate post-war era, Kokurō (the National Railway Workers' Union) and Zentei (JPWU) played a leading role in the labour movement of the public sector. The strikes of Kokurō were of particular importance, as the railways were the only means of mass transport linking the whole country. This fact enabled the railway workers' union to overcome the differences between the union movement of the private and the public sectors and become the linchpin of a general strike which covered all industrial sectors. This planned, but later cancelled general strike of 1 February 1947 was strongly influenced by Kokurō's distinctive features. During the preparations for the strike, workers of all other industrial sectors followed Kokurō's lead and acted according to the slogan 'Let's hang on to the railway workers'.

As the labour movement of the railway services was so conspicuous, it was only natural that the attacks by GHQ and the government should concentrate on it. During the years 1948-9 in particular, when the structures of the Cold War between the United States and the Soviet Union became visible and the outbreak of the Korean War was imminent, the attacks on Kokurō intensified. The political goals of GHQ had shifted and now aimed at transforming Japan into a 'bulwark against communism in Asia' (speech of the US Secretary of the Army, Kenneth C. Royal, on 6 January 1948). One element of this new political strategy was a document signed by General MacArthur which formed the basis for Cabinet Decree No. 201 (issued on 31 July of the same year). This decree robbed the employees of the public sector of their right to strike and limited their right to collective bargaining. Another element was Teiin Hō (the Law on Personnel Levels in the Administrative Organs) which was forced through parliament in May 1949. This law led to the announcement of the dismissal of 95,000 employees of the National Railways and 26,500 postal workers. The unions offered resistance, but their efforts failed in the aftermath of the Shimoyama, Mitaka and Matsukawa incidents (acts of murder and sabotage, described in more detail below). Now mass dismissals were enforced which also included a purge of the red union officials of Kokurō.

The defeat of Kokurō resulted in a serious weakening of the Japanese labour movement in general, which was almost totally destroyed by a 'purge against communists' conducted in all industrial sectors in 1950. The rise and decline of the labour movement of the National Railways during the five-year-long 'period of unrest' thus typifies the Japanese labour movement's rise and decline in the immediate post-war era.

## The labour dispute of 15 September 1946

In July 1946, the administration of the National Railways announced its intention to fire 75,000 employees because of a surplus of personnel. These dismissals were mostly of women and young workers. During the war, male employees who had been drafted for military service were replaced by young men and women who worked as engine operators, engineers, conductors, pointsmen and lorry drivers. Kokutetsu Sōrengō (The Union Federation of the National Railways) launched a struggle against these dismissals in which women and young workers took the lead, and decided to go on strike as of 15 September. Because of internal disagreements over matters of strategy, a split occurred between the western regional union federations (Nagoya and the areas to the west) which wanted to seek an arrangement with the railway administration, and the eastern federations which favoured a course of uncompromising resistance. Before the eastern regional federations, which had continued their preparations for a nation-wide strike, actually began their offensive, the railway administration gave up and withdrew its plans for personnel reduction (on 13 September).

The dispute then developed into a joint struggle with Kaiin Kumiai which at the same time faced the dismissal of 43,000 of its members and the second Yomiuri struggle against the firing of union officials. Now that the unions of railway workers and seamen had won a decisive victory, the labour movement in general received a fresh impetus, which led to the October Struggle of Sanbetsu Kaigi in the autumn of the same year.

## The general strike of 1 February 1947

During its Third Extraordinary Plenary Meeting on 29 September 1946 in Togura, Kokutetsu Sōrengō, which had been reunified after the dispute of 15 September, adopted demands for a system of minimum wages and for several other changes which aimed at improving the dismal living conditions of the union members. These demands were said to constitute a 'Fight for the Right to a Minimal Livelihood' and were thus presented to the National Railways' administration.

So in parallel with the October Struggle of Sanbetsu Kaigi organised by unions of private enterprises, the employees of the public sector began a fight for the basic conditions of existence by establishing a minimum wage system and on 26 November 1946 founded Zenkankō (the Committee of Joint Struggle of Government and Public Corporations Workers' Unions). Kokutetsu Sōrengō' Union now took the lead, and its fight for the right to a minimal livelihood was a move in preparation for the planned general strike of 1 February 1947 in whose preparations the unions of the public sector played a dominant role.

On 15 January 1947, Zentō, (the National Committee for Joint Strike Action) was established, through the cooperation of Zenkankō a number of unions of private enterprises, the national umbrella organisations Sanbetsu Kaigi, Sōdōmei and Nichirō Kaigi, the Communist Party, the Socialist Party and several other organisations. During the conference at which Zentō was founded, a declaration was adopted which called for joint preparation of a general strike on 1 February. The preparations for the general strike, far from concentrating merely on economic matters, began to assume the shape of a revolutionary struggle seeking to overthrow the Shigeru Yoshida cabinet and promoting the establishment of a democratic people's government. All unions participated in this movement which was headed by Kokutetsu Sōrengō. On 31 January, one day before the start of the general strike, GHQ, which had all along tried to get a grip on the movement, published a declaration by General MacArthur in which he ordered the cancellation of the general strike. Zentō chairman Yashirō Ii was left with no choice but to go to the National Japanese Broadcasting Service (NHK) and call off the strike on the radio. With tears in his eyes, Ii closed his radio speech with the words: 'One step back, two steps forward.' Thus the general strike had failed. Nevertheless, the government was willing to compromise regarding the demands for a system of minimum wages, and agreed to a settlement of the dispute which was advantageous to the unions.

## The fight against Teiin Hō (the Law on Personnel Levels), 1949

Teiin Hō (The Law on Personnel Levels in the Administrative Organs) was ostensibly to regulate personnel levels in the public sector, but actually provided a legal instrument for firing active members of the public sector unions, especially that of the National Railways, and for weakening the unions' capacity to fight. The law demanded a reduction of National Railways' staff to 506,734 employees and gave the company's president the right to 'demote and discharge employees without their consent'. Moreover, it suspended the right to collective bargaining in disputes as specified by Kōrō Hō (the Law on Labour Relations in Public Enterprises). In the final analysis, it allowed the administration to legally fire active union members at will while at the same time it completely divested the workers of their right to protest against such measures. Supported by this law, in July 1949 the government announced the dismissal of 95,000 railway employees and 26,500 postal workers. Following the MacArthur document, the Cabinet Decree No. 201 and the Law on Personnel

Levels, this was the last phase of a repressive policy aimed at the destruction of the labour movement in the public sector.

Kokurō intensified its resistance to these measures by launching a 'fight by leaving the workplace' which was initiated by the National Independence Action Groups,[1] as well as other shop-floor disputes such as the running of the so-called Jinmin Densha (People's City Railway) in the area around Sakuragichō station in Yokohama. However, a confrontation developed between left and right wings within the executive committee of the union, which in the end became so intense that agreement on a joint strategy could no longer be reached. Soon afterwards the first wave of dismissals (37,000 employees) was announced, and immediately afterwards the Shimoyama incident occurred. After the second wave of dismissals (63,000 employees) the Mitaka incident happened, and one month later the Matsukawa incident. Because the mass media managed to manipulate public opinion and portrayed the incidents as a union conspiracy, Kokurō suffered a crushing defeat without being able to offer any resistance. Exploiting this situation, the administration enforced the firing of seventeen left-wing members of the union's central struggle committee. The right-wing Mindō faction then published a so-called 'Decree No. 0' which sanctioned this measure, thus trying to gain supremacy over the union – a move which is still widely regarded as a bitter disgrace for the Japanese labour movement.

## II Lecture by Ichizō Suzuki

The Japanese labour movement has reached an impasse. The number of strikes or labour conflicts is decreasing. 'The times of hardship are gone for good', is an oft-heard statement from union officials, and opinion polls indicate that about 90 per cent of the people regard themselves as members of the middle classes. The union movement of such a middle-class society is exhorted to refrain from launching labour conflicts and to promote a cooperative relationship between capital and labour.

In my opinion, claiming that 'the times of hardship are gone' is a serious mistake. With America taking the lead, the unemployment figures in the developed capitalist nations of Europe and the United States are steadily rising. At the moment, the total number of unemployed in the major capitalist societies is higher than 35 million. In these times when new hardships are in store for us, the Japanese labour movement, with its history of magnificent battles, has undergone a complete change. The situation has deteriorated to such a degree that using the term 'labour movement' in the workplace is regarded as shameful, and the term 'working class' has all but disappeared from the Japanese language during the past couple of years. I therefore want to express my respect for you who in such a time try to rediscover the history of the labour movement and to understand the true nature of this movement.

## The labour movement fights to preserve human dignity

As someone who has been personally involved in the battles of the four tempestuous years of the post-war labour movement, I want to tell you about my own experiences. Being able to speak on this occasion about the history of the labour movement is splendid and marvellous for me. The labour movement is like a magnificent tapestry, with both victories and defeats woven together into the fabric: there are times when workers raise their voices out of a situation of utter despair, and sometimes they succeed, but sometimes they fail. The lives of millions of male and female workers together form a maelstrom, and no other movement in history has involved so many people and at the same time created such a dynamic force.

There is one common denominator of the whole labour movement. It is the fight to preserve human dignity, the demand for human happiness. In my mind, the history of the labour movement is an ongoing fight for the preservation of human dignity and for the abolition of misery and poverty. For four stormy years, I personally took part in this fight. In order to give you a better understanding of these eventful years, I could say that this period saw a change as great as the difference between heaven and earth; a change from an era when the labour movement seethed and simmered and which may well be described as a time of revolutionary upswing, to a completely reversed situation of defeat and failure.

As to the first half of this revolutionary era, I think that people who have not experienced these tumultuous events are actually lacking something. As I will make clear to you in my account of the events, in such stormy times the blood of the people starts to boil. Only in such times does the way people think undergo any real changes, so their cultural and their political awareness makes tremendous progress. Those who have personally experienced this era can consider themselves lucky, and I believe that within themselves they possess something of great value. The first half of the four years during which the labour movement developed into a dynamic and electrifying force meant such a thing to us. The later two years were a time of failure and defeat into which we were dragged against our will. I now will speak to you about the matters which took shape during these four years.

## The fight of 15 September: the female workers rise

Even today, when I hear the words 'National Railways' it still is as if someone were calling my name, and a feeling of excitement takes hold of me. In 1934, I started working for the National Railways as an apprentice in the passenger train section at Shinagawa. My wage was 1 yen per day. One part of our job at the end of the war was saving the dining cars and the personal train of the Emperor from destruction. The dining cars were all hooked up to a train and driven to a place which was safe from air-raids. In the area around Tokyo, the marshalling yards of Asakawa and Haramachida were used for this evacuation. During the rest of their working hours, the apprentices dug air-raid shelters in the station of Shinagawa in order to save their own lives.

When, after the war, a union was established, I was elected the first chairman of the passenger-train-section union of Shinagawa (which had about 2,200 members). Then we joined Kokutetsu Sōrengō, and on 15 September we started the fight against dismissals. This marked the beginning of the first phase of the struggles of the National Railways which lasted for two years.

The war was over in 1945, and already during the following years the National Railways announced plans for a rationalisation. When a personnel reduction is announced today, there are hardly any real dismissals, but at that time 75,000 railway employees were actually told to leave. To Kokutetsu Sōrengō, which had just been established, the news came like a bolt out of the blue. Representatives of the National Railways administration came to the union's central headquarters in Harajuku, and when they told us straight away of their plans, we were really shocked. We had no idea how we should organise our resistance in order to prevent them from giving 75,000 of our colleagues the sack. None of us had any previous experience in running a trade union.

But – perhaps one may speak of an instinct – workers know their strength as soon as they have been on strike. I know how their eyes start shining with enthusiasm when they have once experienced a strike. Anyway, at that time we thought about simply suspending all train services, and that was the beginning of our fight against the dismissals which mostly were of female and young workers. In this struggle the women played a leading role.

Shortly before the end of the war, women worked as conductors and engine operators on the Yamanote, the Chūō and the Yokosuka lines. During the last weeks of the war, American Grumman fighter planes based on aircraft carriers used to fly over the burnt-down city of Tokyo and fire from the air on anything which moved below. Well, the only thing which moved within this desert of ruins were the trains driven by the female workers. Now they could not believe that they would be fired simply because the war was over, and therefore they became the main force in our struggle against the dismissals.

When women comprise the main force in any battle, they tend to be extremely tough. But the male workers too joined in and fought for the preservation of the women's jobs. One thing the war had brought about was that the women had developed a strong sense of justice. The National Railways administration had made a serious mistake by under-rating their determination and targeting female workers for the planned dismissals.

## The union's split

However, you must not think that the union conducted its struggle in a united and straightforward fashion. In this conflict we experienced for the first time the problems created by internal disagreement. The union was split into two groups of diverging opinions: one thought that we should try to reduce the number of dismissals by negotiating with the company, while the other wouldn't accept them at any price and argued that we must mobilise our total energy to prevent them. As we experienced such a situation for the first time, a bitter argument ensued which finally led to a split.

This split actually was quite a strange affair: geographically, the borderline between both groups lay in the vicinity of Nagoya city. The unions west of Nagoya wanted to conduct a struggle on the basis of negotiations, while those east of the city advocated strike action. These were the two halves into which the union was divided. The reason the western union groups supported a settlement by negotiation was their anti-communist orientation. Exploiting this split, the administration launched an anti-communist attack by accusing the union groups of the east of being manipulated by the Communist Party. The fact that anti-communism was the ideological basis for the split was a new experience, too.

In order to reconcile both factions, we organised an extraordinary union conference in Ujiyamada. In the Imperial School of the main shrine of Ujiyamada, i.e. in the hall of a school where Shintō priests were trained, a plenary meeting of the union took place! These really were strange times! However, I do not think that anyone actually visited the Ise shrine. To my mind, the knowledge that nothing gets done if you simply rely on divine intervention was one type of awareness the workers who participated in the labour movement had quite naturally developed. However, the conference only resulted in the final split between the western and the eastern unions. The way this split occurred and the theoretical dispute was a prototypical case for the later division of the entire Japanese labour movement into right-wing and left-wing camps.

## The initial success

In contrast with the situation today, interrupting the train services was a matter of life and death in those days. The train was an indispensable means of transport when it came to procuring foodstuffs, and every time passenger or freight trains of the National Railways departed, the carriages were crowded by huge numbers of people who went to the villages to buy food. If you did not return at least with some potatoes, food became scarce and your family starved. Such was the situation. For this reason the suspension of train services was a frightening thing. But because of the determination of the workers in the eastern regions who wanted to fight at any price and to go on strike, the administration was forced to give in and withdraw the dismissals when the situation became serious. We had triumphed.

I believe this victory was too great. It was not a victory won by the union alone. The American troops which had occupied Japan adopted a sort of let's-wait-and-see attitude and watched the strike with benevolent neutrality. This attitude was the background of our strike and one of the main reasons for our success. Had they interfered and told us that a strike was out of the question, it would have been impossible to go on strike, no matter how much we wanted to. At that time, I believe, one of the occupation policy guidelines advocated the strengthening of the Japanese union movement. And as far as the government was concerned, it had lost its confidence because of Japan's defeat and appeared to be paralysed. The government was in no position to resist when the workers stood up and a situation developed in which a strike seemed imminent. This gave us sufficient strength to force the railway administration to renounce its plans of firing 75,000 employees.

When taking a historical perspective on the post-war Japanese labour movement, it becomes evident that of all conflicts in which major unions were involved, this struggle of the railway employees was actually the only one which ended in an unqualified victory for the workers. All of the later conflicts resulted in the defeat of the union. The railway workers' strike of 15 September was the only case in which the post-war labour movement achieved a great and unparalleled success. For the first time we had directly experienced just how massive a force the labour movement can be, recognising that the power created by a workers' association is immense and that workers can be winners when they join forces.

In any case, never had the workers felt such a joy as when the union had won and the dismissals were off the agenda. In the passenger train section at Shinagawa we had a big party. Faces radiant with joy, the workers celebrated their victory for one whole day. Even two musicians – heaven knows who had invited them – honoured us with their presence at our party; they were the two famous ballad singers Koume Akasaka and Katsutarō Tamagawa. Both joined us in our workplace celebration and supported us with their performance. I was fascinated when I heard Katsutarō Tamagawa sing his ballad 'Tenpo-suikoden'. Then suddenly a couple of soldiers of the occupation forces turned up and wanted to know what was going on, and when we explained to them that we had a workplace party in order to celebrate a victory by the workers, they gave us oranges which were loaded in some freight carriages – a strange situation, isn't it? – and also foodstuffs, sugar, coffee, etc., from their own rations.

## Two problems at the same time

Another problem which occurred for the first time during our struggle of 15 September concerned the relationship between workers and political parties. The Communist Party supported and promoted the struggle of those railway workers who had opted for strike action. This fact cannot be denied. On the other hand, the Socialist Party favoured those who wanted to proceed on the path of negotiations. Both parties have really contributed to the success of the railway workers, but concerning matters of tactics they were at odds with each other. Because the strike faction of the railway workers had won, the influence of the Communist Party on the workers was considerably enhanced. They all thought: 'Let's join the Communist Party. The Communist Party is the party of the workers.' But looking at the events with some hindsight, the union as a mass organisation had to maintain its independence, even when it enjoyed the cooperative support of the parties. I believe that at that time we had not yet fully understood the importance of this point.

The second problem was that of leading a joint struggle while at the same time maintaining the union's independence. I want to explain what I mean. Once the railway workers had successfully pushed through their demand for a withdrawal of the dismissals, we immediately retreated. However, other unions who had supported us and were associated with Sanbetsu Kaigi, such as the unions of miners, seamen, electrical workers and machine workers, now wanted to present their own demands and proceed with the October Struggle of Sanbetsu Kaigi with the railway workers as its main force. But this was difficult for us because we had just won our fight and had withdrawn our troops. Nevertheless, the principle of a joint battle required that the railway workers should participate, and we were faced with the demand that we should go on strike again. This we could not accept. Therefore the question of how to maintain one's own independence even during a joint struggle together with other unions was presented to us for the first time.

## The aftermath of the success

After the victory, the unions of the western wing decided to return to Kokutetsu Sōrengō. We told them: 'Come back and join the union again, but don't ask for any concessions.' They replied: 'Okay, let's do it!' And thus they all returned to us.

The divided union reunited and this reconciliation strengthened the authority of the left-wing Japanese labour movement. One of the administration officials of the National Railways, Masaru Kawamura, who today holds a seat in the Lower House for the Democratic Socialist Party, once remarked that the railway union, because of its victory, had played a fundamental role in strengthening the post-war labour movement; it had been a serious mistake not to subdue the union at that time, regardless of what the cost might have been. These words are a clear indication of the influence our struggle has had on the post-war labour movement. Unfortunately only a few people have correctly assessed the relative importance of our struggle of 15 September, and only a limited number of historians and critics have appreciated its magnitude, a matter which to my mind is quite deplorable.

At that time, the chairman of our executive committee was a navvy called Seiichi Suzuki. Suzuki, a platelayer from the Kawasaki line maintenance yard, was the one who signed the agreement which finalised our victory with a print of the thumb of his calloused hand. Until this very day I have a clear recollection of the fingerprint of his labourer's hand on the document. His counterpart was the now deceased former prime minister Eisaku Satō, who then held the position of state secretary of the railway section within the Ministry of Transport and Traffic.

In 1977 NHK broadcast a dramatised television documentary called 'Japan after the war – before and after the strike of 1 February 1947', which included an episode in which Yashirō Ii (leader of the action department of Kokutetsu Sōrengō) goes to the apartment of Eisaku Satō and tells him: 'Withdraw the dismissals, or else a strike cannot be prevented any longer!' Eisaku Satō replies: 'Okay, I agree with you' and retracts the dismissals. Takashi Katsura, who at the time of the strike was a member of Kōrōi (the Committee of Public Sector Labour Relations), has left a short note documenting this episode, but the story actually cannot be true. It is absolutely impossible, given the chronological order of events and other relevant circumstances, that Yashirō Ii in the midst of the conflict secretly went to the struggle headquarters, drove to Eisaku Satō in Kyūichi Tokuda's car and had such a discussion with him. I want to take this opportunity to put the matter straight and tell you that this documentary by NHK contains some errors. I have written a letter of protest to NHK and asked them to correct their account of the events. Whenever there is a major battle, fictitious accounts of this sort are created. I believe that Takashi Katsura's fantasy has been retold time and again; perhaps he would have preferred the event to have happened that way and then offered his fiction for fact.

## The fight for the right to a minimal livelihood

As a consequence of the victorious conclusion of the 15 September struggle, our colleagues from the western union federations returned and the spirit of the railway workers rose steadily. Unfortunately the October Struggle of Sanbetsu Kaigi was a failure and achieved no results. This was because of the general strike in the news media industry. The Sanbetsu Kaigi chairman, Katsumi Kikunami, was a very competent journalist of the *Asahi* newspaper, but he was seriously mistaken when he thought that just because he held the post of chairman, all unions would have to obey his commands without reservation. In the final analysis, his attitude had the effect that the October Struggle ended without any real results. Seen from a historical perspective, the struggle can well be regarded as a defeat. Nevertheless the fighting spirit of the railway workers continued to rise, and in order to consolidate the position we had gained, we developed our concept of a fight for the right to a minimal livelihood. What was this supposed to mean? Living conditions immediately after the war were dismal, and during this time demands for the three bare necessities – food, clothing and shelter – were paramount. We urgently needed wages high enough to overcome hunger and therefore demanded a minimum wage sufficient for survival. Thus we began what I have termed the 'Fight for the Right to a Minimal Livelihood'. Our movement, which had begun as a fight against dismissals, now began to develop into a struggle for securing the bare necessities of life.

## The meeting at Togura

To prepare for our struggle, we held a union meeting in Togura, in Nagano prefecture. It was the first meeting of the National Railway workers in preparation of the general strike of 1 February 1947, and it took place in the gymnasium of an elementary school we had rented for this occasion. Today, union conferences are held in great halls or suchlike, fitted up with seats, a situation unimaginable to us at that time. The meeting had to be held at a location able to accommodate some thousands of workers and where it was possible to get some food for them. Fortunately Togura was a hot spring resort which had not suffered from air-raids and all of its guest accommodation was still intact. This is why we rented the gymnasium of the local elementary school. However, by November Togura is quite a cold place, and as sitting on the bare wooden floor was enough to make you shiver, we went to farmers in the nearby villages and borrowed hundreds of straw mats from them. These we spread out on the floor, and then the conference could go ahead.

The salutary speech by the representative of the schoolteacher's union left a very strong impression on the audience. The teachers had been the first to demand higher wages in advance of the general strike of 1 February. It was a very modest demand, and the representative of the teachers' union had come to ask us whether we would not like to join forces with them. He had the following story to tell: the director of an elementary school had stolen the lunch packets of his pupils, taken them home and cooked a vegetable stew for his family. When he was caught, he was called to account for his unbelievable behaviour and finally committed suicide. This story came as a shock to us. We all felt numb, nobody was able to say a word. 'This cannot go on any longer, we must do something!' was the general feeling, and almost unanimously we adopted a demand for a wage increase – the fight for the right to a minimal livelihood had begun! It really was a very moving speech.

There is another impression I recall: on our way back from the gymnasium to the hot springs and our accommodation in Togura we walked along Chikumagawa river. There was no street lighting in those days and, as you may know, the uniforms of the National Railways workers are black. Whenever a group of railway workers came along, people used to call out: 'The crows! The crows are coming!' As this pitch-black group of workers walked through the dark night on the banks of Chikumagawa, they suddenly started to sing. In this moment I felt that singing songs is something which comes naturally to workers who are engaged in mass action. Suddenly more and more voices joined in; you could not see where they came from. The hymn of the railway workers has always been the 'Song of the Red Flag'. It is right what some people say: the workers of the National Railways are simple people . . .

A journalist whom I knew only by sight once visited me in those days and told me: 'Suzuki-san, you railway workers will go on forever singing the "Song of the Red Flag", won't you? Listen to the guys from Densan they are singing the "Internationale!"' It was just as if he intended to say, the difference between them and you is that the electrical power workers have a higher educational background, while the railway workers are only simple navvies. 'What's this guy talking about?' I thought, but actually he was not that far off the mark.

This group of black-clad workers was in high spirits at Togura when they adopted their demands. From now on the railway workers were firmly on a path which eventually led to the general strike of 1 February. As news got around that the railway workers were prepared for battle, the union organised a conference together with civil servants and employees of public enterprises in order to form a joint front.

## The establishment of Zenkankō and Zentō

At this conference for the establishment of the Zenkankō, Kokutetsu Sōrengō was represented by our colleague Yashirō Ii who was the leader of the action department. Because he was the representative of the powerful Railway Workers' Union, he was elected chairman of Zenkankō. Other participants were such pioneers and leaders of the post-war labour movement as Kazuyoshi Dobashi of Zentei and Hideo Urabe of Jichirō (the All-Japan Prefectural and Municipal Workers' Union). In my opinion, the establishment of Zentō was one of the outstanding achievements of the movement preparing the general strike of 1 February. At this time a united union front was created. The formation of a united working-class front has two important aspects to it: on the one hand it requires the unification of different union movements, and on the other hand the several political fronts of the working class must unite. Only if both of these things happen is there a real united front of the working class, which then is immensely powerful. The unification must therefore move forward on both levels – it is like a coach with two wheels. One of the two aspects, the formation of a united union front, was successfully achieved. Sanbetsu Kaigi, Sōdōmei, Zenkankō and almost every organisation which called itself a union came together in Zentō. The Japanese unions had managed to achieve unity to such a degree that the greatest alliance which had ever existed now became reality. This actually happened not so long ago, only thirty years have passed since then. I would be happy if you would keep this in mind.

At the same time, unification on the political level made progress too. A united political front of the working class means in simple terms the political cooperation of both the Communist and the Socialist Parties. The political condition for a revolution is that communists and socialists manage to form a united political front. Kyūichi Tokuda and Ritsu Ito were the leaders of the Communist Party who promoted this association, while the socialists were represented by Kanjū Katō, Mosaburō Suzuki and Kanson Arahata. These friends, who belonged to the left wing of the Socialist Party, actively promoted the creation of a united front with the communists. The fact that both forces got together led to the establishment of an action committee which aimed at overthrowing the Yoshida cabinet. Behind the scenes the chairman of the Sōdōmei secretariat, Minoru Takano, and the vice administrative head of Sanbetsu Kaigi, Matsuta Hosoya, pulled the strings. When you look at the persons involved, you will realise that actually all leading personalities of the progressive political and union movement were taking part in the organisation of the general strike of 1 February.

## From an economic to a political struggle

Suddenly the fight for the right to a minimal livelihood had turned into a political struggle. As the title 'fight for the right to a minimal livelihood' indicates, the general strike of 1 February started from economic demands which aimed at overcoming the hunger crisis and at obtaining minimum wages which would cover the bare necessities of life. But during the general strike preparations, in which more than 1 million workers took part, a situation was created in which all unions got together, the political front united and an action committee was established with the goal of overthrowing the government. This sudden development towards an inherently political struggle is justification enough for regarding the general strike of 1 February as a revolutionary struggle.

The most threatening thing about this strike was that although we did set a date for its beginning, 1 February 1947, we never said when it would end. A fight with a beginning but no apparent end is something apt to cause great concern. 'As long as our demands are not fulfilled, we will not cease fighting', was what we publicly announced.

In the country, action units were formed which included the peasants, something which we called an 'alliance of peasants and workers'. Today, farmers are independent small-scale entrepreneurs and the main pillar of support for the Liberal Democratic Party. But in the context of class struggle, a united front of peasants and workers is an extremely powerful force. Many workers who participated in this great movement actually had high hopes that on the very next day they would be able to form a people's government. The great hall on the second floor of the Prime Minister's residence was in fact under siege by masses of workers singing the 'Internationale'. And the big hall of the eight-storey building of the National Railways central administration near Tokyo station was occupied by the workers who had come to join the general strike. About 3,000 members of the youth action groups slept there. The mass movement took on such proportions that the union urged all workers who wanted to take part in the action to bring food rations which would last at least three days.

A situation developed in which the workers were actually on the brink of toppling the very foundations of the state; their superiors were frightened and did not know what to do. Police headquarters and the National Railways central administration alike – the whole power structure seemed paralysed from its lowest level to the very top. When such a situation occurs, a worker's ideological and political awareness is suddenly expanded in one great leap. Yesterday still a common labourer, he all of a sudden turns into a worker who cries out: 'Hurrah for the establishment of a people's government!!' This change really happens suddenly, and it constitutes the rise of a mass movement in revolutionary times.

## MacArthur's order to cancel the general strike

Thus the movement grew bigger and bigger with ever more forces joining in, and just when it had reached its peak, MacArthur ordered the general strike to be cancelled. His order was issued on 31 January 1947. The main statements he made in his order can be summarised much as follows: 'Don't the Japanese people suffer from food shortages because Japan has lost the war? The Allies and in particular the United States are trying everything to help, but the workers sabotage the process of reconstruction by organising a general strike. This is unacceptable!' These words meant the end of the general strike.

At that time I was the leader of the central struggle committee of Kokutetsu Sōrengō. To me, the news came as no surprise. Things had happened as they had been bound to happen, I thought. Right from the beginning I had doubted very much whether the occupation forces would permit the general strike to go ahead and simply look the other way. During the whole period, from the struggle of 15 September until the general strike, I had never been in any awe of the Japanese government because I was certain that once we mustered all of our strength we would be able to form our own government the next day. But because the occupation forces were a power in their own right, I was always wary of how they would react. Now they interfered illegally and there were many signs that under the circumstances they might even resort to military intervention in order to suppress our movement.

Just to give you one example, we used to write our slogans on the sides of the passenger and freight carriages and had them circulating around the lines. In the beginning this drew such comment as, 'Interesting, isn't it? The carriages themselves are a rolling promotion of the goals of the railway workers.' However, some days later we were ordered to stop it. 'We'll not let you use the carriages as a sort of advertisement for your goals', we were told. Moreover they told us that the trains serving the occupation forces had to run strictly on time, and that even minor delays would lead to the punishment of the responsible person. Because of these and other signs I already had a hunch that the occupation forces would not simply turn a blind eye to what we did.

I already knew that the general strike would be called off one day before the order was issued. As the formation of a united political front had successfully been achieved, the alliance of the Communist and Socialist Party leadership had held a conference to discuss how to proceed after the general strike. It has often been said that during these talks even the cabinet members of a new government to be formed after the successful conclusion of the strike were selected, but as far as I know this is not true.

I still remember the night of 30 January 1947. A last meeting was scheduled before the beginning of the general strike, and the members of Zentō as well as the representatives of the Communist and the Socialist Parties all gathered in a room on the fourth floor of the Kangyō Bank at Hibiya, one of the few buildings remaining intact in the city of Tokyo. Apart from myself as the representative of the National Railway workers, there were Kyūichi Tokuda and Ritsu Itō of the Communist Party, Mosaburō Suzuki, Kanjū Katō and Kanson Arahata of the Socialist Party, and the delegate to Zentō from Zentei, Kazuyoshi Dobashi. I believe that Kōzō Mizuguchi, the chairman of Zen'nōrin (the Union of Forest and Agricultural Workers) was also present.

It was a cold night with sleety rain. Suddenly the door opened and Shizue Katō, the wife of Kanjū Katō entered the room. She wore a Western-style coat over her Japanese clothes and carried a colourful Japanese umbrella with a ring pattern. She came in, shook off the raindrops, went over to her husband and simply said: 'The whole thing is off.' Until recently, Shizue Katō was a Socialist Party delegate to the Upper House. A very intelligent woman who had attended the Gakushūin School, she had studied at an American university before the war; her English was excellent. Shizue Katō had gone to some informed officer of the occupation forces and asked him: 'What's going to happen with regard to the general strike two days from now? Are the occupation forces going to call it off or anything?' Thus she had put out her feelers. I believe that she did not have direct access to MacArthur himself, but she somehow met someone in charge who told her, 'MacArthur will issue a declaration and order the strike to be cancelled.' So now she said, 'The whole thing is off!' Immediately the mood of all participants changed. I remember that there was a conversation on how to find a solution, but it ended inconclusively. They all then left the room in small groups and vanished into the dark city night. Thus I knew already one day before MacArthur's order that the situation had turned around. The left wing of the Socialist Party then promptly left the united front. To my mind this was the very moment when the united front of the political forces fell apart. Everybody now had to re-check the orders he had given; perhaps they would give it another try later on.

On the evening of 31 January at 9:10 p.m., the chairman of Zentō, Yashirō Ii, went on the air and in an NHK broadcast read a declaration which stated that the general strike was called off. In a dramatised NHK documentary ('Japan after the War – Before and After the Strike of 1 February') which also describes this event, Yashirō Ii arrives in the lobby of the NHK building and runs into Kyūichi Tokuda who tells him: 'The declaration that the strike is off will be broadcast.' Now Yashirō Ii, who seems to abruptly awake from a dream, decides on the spot to read the declaration himself. In his book (*Looking Back on the Strike of 1 February 1947*, Shin-Nihon-Shuppansha, 1977) Yashirō Ii himself has given this account of the episode, but I think this is simply a piece of fiction, and that the reality was quite different.

The facts which caused Shizue Katō to make her statement on the evening of 30 January were also known to the government. Although the Yoshida cabinet was utterly shocked by the extent of the planned general strike and in such a tight corner that the dissolution of the cabinet was regarded only as a question of time, on the evening of 30 January the ministers suddenly showed a very relaxed attitude. They knew about the forthcoming ban of the strike by MacArthur. Kyūichi Tokuda at once realised what was going on. He too had heard Shizue Katō's remark. So he immediately asked Yashirō Ii to meet him near the moat of the Imperial Palace and told him that the situation had developed to a point where it would be better to resort to the strategy of 'One step back, two steps forward.' He in fact used those very words, and there is someone still alive who can confirm this, that is, the driver of Kyūichi Tokuda, who was Secretary General of the Communist Party, a man called Seiichi Kaneyoshi who at present is the chairman of Zenjikō (National Federation of Automobile Transport Workers' Unions) based at Harajuku. It was he who met Yashirō Ii in front of the building which housed Zentō and brought him to the dark and deserted moat of the Imperial Palace. He overheard the conversation of both men. Together they assessed the situation and arrived at the conclusion that there was nothing to be done but to obey MacArthur's order and call off the general strike. These are the historical facts, as far as I know.

What may have caused Yashirō Ii to invent his story – that he met Kyūichi Tokuda by chance in the lobby of the NHK building, that he was then told a declaration calling off the strike would be broadcast and that he decided to do it himself – remains a mystery. Our colleague Yashirō Ii and Mr Kyūichi Tokuda died some years ago. There is no one left who could give a truthful account of the event, but one thing is remarkable: Yashirō Ii did not tell his story until eight years had passed. Mr Kyūichi Tokuda died in Beijing in 1953, and only after his death did Yashirō Ii publish his account for the first time in the magazine *Chūō Kōron.* Why he did so remains one of the big mysteries. I believe it is important to clear up the matter some day in order to get a better understanding of the Japanese history after 1945.

## The aftermath of the general strike

This was the way the general strike of 1 February broke down. I now want to address three outcomes of those events.

First of all, what became of our demands? We had adopted them in the context of our fight for the right to a minimal livelihood, and then our members had participated in the preparations for the general strike. Despite the failure of the strike, we managed to push through about 90 per cent of our demands for a wage increase. To me, this was a miracle. The government's reaction was extremely positive and they fulfilled nearly all of our wishes. I could not help but wonder whether we could not have reached our goals solely by negotiating a compromise, without having to organise a general strike and fail in the process – what a strange thought!

I suspect that the positive answer we received was determined by the following factors: When MacArthur banned the general strike, this was a serious blow to his career. To my mind there can be no doubt that an American commander who had advocated democracy so strongly, and especially MacArthur whose ambitions to become a presidential candidate were well known, ended up with a lot of egg on his face when he used his authority to ban a strike of the workers. Therefore, although he did ban the strike, he could not help but advocate the almost complete fulfilment of our demands. According to my personal experiences, gathered in many labour conflicts, there is no way that the other side will take the initiative and happily fulfil the workers' demands if there is not some sort of concrete pressure put on them. Consequently I have to conclude that in this case our demands were met because it was impossible to resist the force of a united front which comprised more than 6 million workers.

Second, ever since these events, the differences between the left and the right wings of the labour movement have been a dominant factor. Shortly after the planned general strike of 1 February, an anti-communist alliance was formed within Kokutetsu Sōrengō. It later developed into the 'Mindō wing'. Such a group, which openly declared itself to be an anti-communist alliance, established itself within our union and later within the labour movement in general. But at the same time the development from the struggle of 15 September to the general strike also led to the formation of a left wing within the labour movement. The whole movement thus was divided along political lines into a left and a right wing. This polarisation reached its peak during the general strike.

Third, the date of the general strike also marked the beginning of the alliance of the conservative forces in Japan. During the mobilisation phase of the strike, Prime Minister Shigeru Yoshida publicly denounced the workers involved as 'lawless scum'. This caused a tremendous uproar among the workers and was one of the factors which later led to the downfall of the Yoshida cabinet.

But Yoshida certainly exhibited a huge measure of self-confidence when he dared to describe as 'lawless scum' over 6 million members of an organised labour movement who had shown their courage during the strike. However, this was certainly the type of personality necessary for someone who was to become the leader of the Japanese conservative forces, and his remark became a rallying cry for the right-wing political spectrum of post-war Japan. At the centre of a group of high-ranking civil servants who went over to Shigeru Yoshida were Eisaku Satō, then state secretary in charge of the National Railways in the Ministry of Transport and Traffic, and Hayato Ikeda, a state secretary in the Ministry of Finance and later to become prime minister. The so-called 'Yoshida School', which today is recognised as the mainstream of the Liberal Democratic Party, has its roots in those days. The two main factions on the Japanese political scene – on the one hand the progressive forces of the Communist and the Socialist Parties which had tried to create a revolutionary situation in Japan by forming a united front, and on the other the high-ranking bureaucrats who wanted a reconstruction of the country under the leadership of a conservative party yet to be established – both took on their distinctive shape, and again 1 February can be regarded as the peak of this development. By examining these facts, we are able to understand how the major struggles of the workers changed the face of the country and how they became the driving force for the creation of new historical conditions.

## Cabinet Decree No. 201

More than a month had passed since the cancellation of the general strike of 1 February. Kokutetsu Sōrengō held a conference at Iizaka Onsen in Fukushima prefecture to assess the situation. During the conference, we were unexpectedly visited by a lieutenant colonel of the occupation army. This was an extraordinary event, and I immediately smelt a rat. He informed us that on 12 March of that year the United States of America had issued an anti-Soviet declaration which constituted the rationale for the Cold War, the so-called 'Truman doctrine'. Afterwards the policy implemented by the occupation army underwent a drastic change and now aimed at suppression of the workers and progressive forces. From then on the labour movement went through a long and difficult period in which it had to operate under the conditions of the Cold War between the United States and the Soviet Union.

On 22 July of the following year, 1948, the occupation administration presented a letter from MacArthur to the then Prime Minister Hitoshi Ashida. This letter called for measures to deprive all public employees of their right to strike and to restrict their basic labour rights. This was an extremely serious matter! All employees of the public sector were robbed of their right to go on strike. The only right left to them was to form coalitions. To cut a long story short, they were still permitted to found unions, but had neither the right to strike nor the right to engage in collective bargaining. All of the rights and labour agreements the unions had fought for and cherished were made null and void by this incredible and criminal act, and we were pushed back to square one again. The fact that employees of public enterprises today have no right to strike goes back to those days. It also affects Kōrōkyō, i.e. today's Kokurō and in the same way Zentei and all of the others.

In this situation the public sector workers rose in opposition against the letter from MacArthur. They were again led by the employees of the National Railways. Coinciding with the publication of the MacArthur letter, the Hitoshi Ashida cabinet issued Cabinet Decree No. 201 (31 July 1948). In order to punish the workers who opposed the MacArthur letter, they enacted this deplorable and suppressive law in the form of a cabinet decree.

At the time the decree was issued, the National Railways experienced a wave of workplace struggles. During the course of these disputes, workers who served on locomotives on a line through the Shintoku tunnel which, near Karikachi Pass on Hokkaidō, has a particularly dangerous section, went on strike. In the long tunnel of Karikachi Pass there are several sloping sections where the engine operator and the engineer who had to supply the engine with coal continually suffered from serious oxygen deficiency. The workers therefore demanded that the net weight of the carriages used on this line be limited and that their working hours be reduced. However, their struggle was set back by Cabinet Decree No. 201. The angry workers organised a workplace meeting and began a so-called 'workplace struggle'.

Now the Asahikawa police force brutally intervened and tried to suppress them, saying that their action violated Cabinet Decree No. 201. The even more enraged workers left their workplace, publicly denounced the oppressive policy of the occupation forces and began touring the whole country. This form of dispute was termed a 'fight by leaving the workplace'. However, it would probably be more correct to speak of 'active propaganda groups trying to regain the right to strike'. From Shintoku tunnel they went to Yūbari, Oiwake and then to Furano and Hakodate on Hokkaidō. Then they hid in the lower decks of the Seikan ferry and made their way from Hokkaidō to the main island of Honshu. They visited Aomori and continued their travels until they reached Moji on Kyushu. Wherever they went, the group of 1,500 young workers from the engine department protested against their violent suppression. They formed small propaganda groups which publicly announced their complaints, even in the smaller villages. At this time, the so-called 'action groups for the independence of the Japanese people' were formed for the first time. The song 'Preserve the Freedom of the People, Rise, Workers of the Fatherland' also dates back to this period.

Their action made it more difficult for the government to deprive the workers of the National Railways, the postal services and public employees in general, of their right to strike. They changed their tactics and, although they did not restore the right to strike, they conceded to the unions of the National Railways and the postal workers the right to engage in collective bargaining. On 1 July 1949 the new labour law for public and state enterprises came into effect.

Of course, the 'fight by leaving the workplace' strategy had been effective. Nevertheless, 800 workers who had taken part in it were indicted and lost their jobs as a disciplinary punishment. Thus this dispute ended with a defeat as well. As I have told the current workers of the National Railways time and again: the participants in this 'fight by leaving the workplace' were fired and to this very day the regulations on union support for victims of strike action have not been fully applied to them. Not even their honour has been restored. I keep telling them: you who are always speaking about regaining the right to strike for the National Railway workers, first restore the rights of these workers, and do it in the name of all railway employees at a regular union conference. These workers took a great personal risk when they left their workplace, travelled the whole country, protested against the injustice of the American occupation forces and raised the banner of national independence. To this very day I have not ceased to urge the union to act, but they have failed to fulfil my wish. I find this a very sad matter indeed.

## Teiin Hō (The Law on Personnel Levels in the Administrative Organs)

Following these events, the occupation forces adopted the so-called Dodge Line (7 March 1949), a catalogue of nine principles which were to lay the foundation for the recovery of the economy and which also aimed at curbing post-war inflation. This plan, too, was pushed through by force. MacArthur published a declaration which stated that all persons who opposed the implementation of these nine principles would be suppressed. There would be no pardon for people who offered any resistance nor for those who criticised the measures. The Dodge Line became the basis for personnel cuts, enterprise rationalisations and dismissals. The nine principles were used as a way to attack the workers who belonged to Zenkankō, especially those of the National Railways who, now that they had lost their right to strike were like a crab without its claws, by threatening mass dismissals. In fact it was a law on dismissals which came in the guise of a law on personnel levels. It carried the inconspicuous title of Gyōsei Kikan Shyokuin Teiin Hō ('Law on Personnel Levels in the Administrative Organs') and limited the number of employees in government offices and administrative bodies. This, in fact, was all. Nevertheless the law was used as a tool for enforcing the dismissal of about 100,000 employees of the National Railways and 26,500 postal workers. This did not mean early retirement or natural personnel fluctuation within the companies. The workers were fired while they were in the midst of their professional lives.

This law, Teiin Hō, having gone through parliament, went into force on 30 May 1949. Until this date we did our utmost to prevent it. As MacArthur had taken from us the right to strike, we put all our energy into fighting the bill in parliament. Today this may seem incredible, but we even spent our nights in the parliament building. We brought in a mimeograph and distributed a struggle newspaper. Today one would not even dream of doing such a thing, but in those days this sort of campaign was still possible.

In the Upper House, the ante-room of the Socialist Party became our struggle headquarters, while in the Lower House we used that of the Communist Party. At that time Eisaku Satō headed the Committee on Political Questions of the Democratic

Liberal Party.[2] When I asked him: 'Would you let me go to your party and make a speech against Teiin Hō?' he replied, 'Okay, why not?' Although the DLP was about to use Teiin Hō as a basis for their government policies, they agreed to listen to a polemical speech by a union representative. This sort of magnanimity still existed in those days.

Then there was the chairman of the Committee on Cabinet Affairs in the Upper House, Yahichi Kawai. This committee actually adopted the bill by a margin of only one vote. Although the bill would not have passed the Upper House if Yahichi Kawai had voted against it, he told me afterwards: 'Suzuki, when I listened to your speech I really felt that you were right. On the other hand, as chairman of the committee I was in no position to agree with you.' He voted in favour of passing Teiin Hō, and thus the bill passed the Committee of Cabinet Affairs in the Upper House. There were quite a number of similar incidents, and we pursued our fight within the parliament with all our energy. Nevertheless, the law went through and later came into effect.

## Transforming the National Railways into a public enterprise (Kōrō Hō, the Law on Labour Relations in Public Enterprises)

The next bill to be passed was the law on matters of employment in the public enterprises, and the National Railways were transformed into such a public enterprise. The present status of the company thus goes back to those days. Until then it had been a state enterprise under state administration. Now it is still fully owned by the state, but is under public, not state administration. It is quite important to understand just *why* the National Railways were transformed into a public enterprise. The government said that it was unreasonable to put the blue-collar workers of the National Railways on the same level as other mostly white-collar public employees and to deprive them of their right to strike. Therefore it was necessary to give them at least the right to engage in collective bargaining, even though the right to strike would still not be granted. Because in the case of state-owned enterprises under state administration the preconditions for conducting necessary personnel cuts and other adjustments are quite stringent, transforming the National Railways into a public enterprise benefited the government. This point is of great importance. There was not a single economic reason for giving the National Railways the status of a public enterprise, but the execution of personnel cuts and other adjustment measures was greatly facilitated by this step. These considerations were at the heart of the matter, while economic aspects were of minor importance. It is necessary to know this, otherwise one will come to ask inadequate questions and draw wrong conclusions.

This was the way a public enterprise was created. The relevant American law on employment matters was transferred to Japan with no alterations and here became Kōrō Hō, the Law on Labour Relations in Public Enterprises – a bill whose text appears to have been translated in full. In America, the law was passed after the great economic crisis of 1929, when under President Roosevelt construction work in the Tennessee Valley and other big public projects was started as part of the New Deal policy. A law conceived and applied in the United States was thus simply translated and became Kōrō Hō serving as a tool for transforming the National Railways into a public enterprise.

I would like you to try to imagine the situation which is created by the dismissal of 100,000 workers. First there was the change in status of the National Railways, and on top of that 100,000 employees were fired! These events of June and July 1949 were a dreadful blow to us. The resulting confusion was as if a volcano eruption on Miyakejima Island had been followed by a great earthquake and a hurricane had hit the coast.

In fact, the dismissals were mentioned only in an appendix to the law on personnel levels, while the main text contained no word of them. Concerning this matter, Article 2 of the appendix said that the right to engage in collective bargaining would not be recognised in connection with dismissals. In short, the law on personnel levels was a law on discharges which did not provide for any dialogue or negotiations.

The Minister of Transport in those days, Shinzō Ōya, was at the same time managing director of Teijin, a major textile company. He died some years ago. When I went to him to speak about the dismissals, he simply told me: 'Listen, the whole matter does not even merit a talk over a cup of tea!' and thus refused to conduct any collective negotiations. As the appendix to the law did not require such collective bargaining, Ōya expressed his attitude by claiming that the whole conversation had the same relevance as tea-time talk. This most serious problem of firing 100,000 workers in the midst of their professional lives, and the question of what should become of the livelihood of – counting in the family dependants – about 400,000 people, was only tea-time talk to him!

This sort of attitude assumed by the mighty and powerful violates the principle of equality among men. In the beginning of my lecture I claimed that the protection of human dignity is the starting point of the labour movement, and by these words I meant [protection against] exactly this type of contemptuous, discriminating behaviour of those in power. Therefore to this very day I cannot accept this remark about 'tea-time talk' by the Minister of Transport.

## Before and after the Shimoyama incident

During the dispute, our direct adversaries were the president of the National Railways, Mr Sadanori Shimoyama, and his deputy Yukio Kagayama, as well as all of the leading managers. The company's president, Sadanori Shimoyama, was actually a mere figurehead with no power at all. The headquarters of Kokurō were located in the main building of the company at Marunouchi in Tokyo. We occupied two rooms on the fourth floor. On the next floor was the president's office. It was a place never too far away for the paying of an unwelcome visit. The general picture of the negotiations was as follows: tables were positioned in such a way that there was absolutely no room left between the representatives of the administration and the union, not even an ant would have fitted in between us. The room was divided into two exact halves in such a way that you could not get onto the other side without jumping over the tables. On the other side sat the president and representatives of the administration, the door behind them opened, and facing them directly was our delegation with myself sitting in the middle of it.

Let us go one step back in time. The chairman of Kokurō was a man called Etsuo Katō, and I was his deputy. Just when the dismissals were imminent and we started our battle against the law on personnel levels in parliament, chairman Katō decided to travel to Europe. The head of the labour commission at GHQ, R.T. Amis, had invited him on this journey under the pretext that he should attend a world conference of the International Labour

Organisation at Geneva. The chairman of a union leaves Japan while under his very eyes the discharge of 100,000 members of his own union is being prepared and a fight against this measure threatening every fifth employee is in progress! And he goes to London to discuss with representatives of GHQ the establishment of the national union centre, Sōhyō!

In 1949 the labour movement experienced a world-wide division. After America had announced its Marshall Plan (on 5 June 1947) with the aim of exploiting the support for economic reconstruction to bring Europe under its control, European unions fell out with each other over the pros and cons of the Marshall Plan and the World Federation of Trade Unions fell apart. The forces supporting the position of the United States then founded the International Confederation of Free Trade Unions (at a conference held from 28 November to 5 December 1949) as a counterpart to the World Federation of Trade Unions. The chairman of Kokurō, Etsuo Katō, was invited to London for discussions on the establishment of the national centre, Sōhyō, which was to be the Japanese bridgehead of the International Confederation of Free Trade Unions. In accordance with the statutes of our union, I, as the deputy chairman, automatically became the responsible union official for the ongoing dispute.

But whatever was said in the negotiations, my counterpart Sadanori Shimoyama sat there with averted eyes and did not utter a single word. For two days I persistently spoke to him, but he never opened his mouth. Among the administration representatives, only the head of personnel, Satoshi Isozaki (later the president of the National Railways) deigned to speak to us: 'The dismissal of 100,000 workers is absolutely necessary. For the reconstruction of the National Railways, this staff reduction is unavoidable.' He was the only one to get down to business and talk with us while all of the others remained silent; they seemed to have lost their confidence.

## The Shimoyama incident – murder or suicide?

At this stage, the event which is publicly known as the 'Shimoyama incident' occurred. On 5 July, the dreadfully mangled body of Sadanori Shimoyama, who earlier had been reported missing, was found on a railway track. His death provoked many theories, some assuming that he was murdered, others speaking of suicide. There even was a film with the title *The Shimoyama Murder* (Director: Kei Kumai). This film endorses the murder theory based on material collected by an ex-journalist of the *Asahi* newspaper. The former defendant in the trial arising out of the Matsukawa incident, Hajime Satō, speaks of suicide (Hajime Satō: *A Verdict on the Shimoyama Incident*, published by Jiji Tsūshinsha in 1976). The famous writer Seichō Matsumoto on the other hand supports the murder theory (Seichō Matsumoto: *Dark Fog over Japan – An Investigation into the Shimoyama Incident*, published by Bungeisyunjūsha in 1960). Relying solely on such sources, it is impossible to decide whether Sadanori Shimoyama committed suicide or not. I personally believe that Sadanori Shimoyama was murdered. I do not think there was any reason for him to commit suicide.

Regardless of these still unresolved questions, the simple fact that the president of the National Railways was run over by a train and found dead on the tracks was an enormous shock. Everywhere in Japan demagogues spread the rumour that the railway workers had killed Sadanori Shimoyama. It was claimed that embittered workers had taken revenge on Sadanori Shimoyama as the person responsible for the dismissals. The rumour that the railway workers were murderers spread like wildfire throughout the country, and the situation became so tense that it was dangerous to carry our uniforms or even our caps in public. I personally received many threatening letters: '*You* are going to be the next! You may as well say your prayers and prepare for death!'

The first wave of dismissals was thus conducted while the public was in the grip of mass hysteria. In order not to compound the troubles we experienced after the Shimoyama incident, and to avoid any further discouragement of the already despairing workers, we tried everything to regain our capacity to fight. But then, during the night of 15 July – only ten days had passed – the so-called Mitaka incident occurred, in which an unmanned train started to move by itself. This train then drove through the Chuō line station of Mitaka in Tokyo where it broke through a buffer and ran into an apartment block on the other side of a railway crossing, killing seven persons. Again, one month later on 17 August the Matsukawa incident took place. On the Tōhoku Line in the northeast of Japan, near the city of Matsukawa, a locomotive was derailed, killing the engine driver and his engineer.

These three incidents happened within little more than a month, and because of them the struggle of the railway workers' union suffered a complete defeat. By the time of the Shimoyama incident we had not yet gathered enough strength to stand up and fight. The Mitaka incident was a serious blow, but we still were able to resist. The Matsukawa incident, however, really finished us off. These three darkest events of the Japanese post-war era, which are generally recognised to have changed the course of history, were all directed against Kokurō.

## The confrontation with the anti-communist Mindō movement

The confrontation with the Mindō movement which had established itself in the National Railways was a bitter and troublesome matter. The Mindō movement opposed all active measures of the union during the struggle. Finally they resorted to leaving the central struggle committee. As this opposition group had many followers, the struggle committee was unable to continue the fight because less than two-thirds of its members, the quorum prescribed by our statutes, were attending its meetings. No directives could now be issued. Nevertheless we persisted; we simply had to do something. But leading the struggle became a very difficult affair.

I believe that you can imagine just how difficult our position was. In addition to the internal disputes, the Shimoyama, Mitaka and Matsukawa incidents had occurred. The government, the Democratic Liberal Party and the mass media all attacked us and raved: 'The violent revolution of the Communist Party has begun!' A wave of hysteria swept the country. Only three hours after the Mitaka incident, the *Asahi* newspaper had brought out an extra edition with a headline screaming: 'Conspiracy of the Communist Party!!'

As you may know, the result of the ensuing trial was that no conspiracy ever had occurred. The claims made by the police were proved to be wrong, and all of those who had any connection with the Communist Party were acquitted. Only one person, Keisuke Takeuchi, an engine operator on the Mitaka line and a father of five children, was found guilty as a single offender and sentenced to death. The death penalty was not enforced, but he died in prison. I feel deeply sorry for him. Keisuke Takeuchi was the only victim of the attacks by those in power during the struggles of the railway workers who actually died in prison. I still believe in his innocence. I must admit that I have no proof whatsoever of who was the perpetrator, but it rarely happens that workers destroy the things they have produced. Because I have a very deep understanding of how the railway workers felt, I find it hard to believe that any of them would set in motion an unmanned train.

## 100,000 victims of a purge

After the Mitaka incident, a disastrous anti-communist propaganda attack was launched. It was a thoroughly anti-communist campaign which focused on accusing the Communist Party of preparing a new attempt at violent revolution. Caricatures of a raving Kyūichi Tokuda crunching a train between his teeth were attached to telegraph poles, and throughout the country the 3 million members of the voluntary fire brigade were mobilised and put on the alert. In a cabinet meeting, Cabinet Secretary Kanehichi Masuda said that one should be wary of the Communist Party's plans, and the situation became so tense that even a man such as Mosaburō Suzuki of the Socialist Party in Ōsaka announced that his party would seek a confrontation with the communists. Helplessly fighting back our tears, we had to retreat from our fight against the dismissal of 100,000 workers.

Although I was the responsible leader of this fight, I had no idea of how to help these 100,000 workers and their families. Unable to hold out any longer, we had to give up. I felt extremely depressed. But history knows no compassion. In its essence, the dismissal of 100,000 workers was a purge of left-wing elements. Those who were fired were mainly union activists, members and sympathisers of the Communist Party and of a group called 'Kakushin dōshikai' which existed only in the National Railways and was made up of people who had formed a united front of Communists and other political groupings. The magnificent struggle launched by Kokurō thus ended with a total defeat.

## The end

In my opinion, the defeat the railway workers suffered in this fight was brought about by the emerging global structure of the Cold War between the United States and the Soviet Union. We were not defeated by the Japanese government, I believe. We were defeated by the American occupation forces. In short, they took repressive measures against those who opposed the American occupation policies in Japan. It was necessary for the United States to push its policies through in order to transform Japan into a nation completely under its control. This was the power which put us down – the power of the United States which, with Japan as one element of its global strategy, with the Korean War of 1950, and with the separate peace treaty of 1951, was trying to push ahead an anti-Soviet policy.

## Notes

1. National Independence Action Group: by adopting this name, the members of such a group intended to state that they sought to resist any interference on the part of the US occupation forces with the Japanese economy and the Japanese labour movement. The demand for national independence was put forward by the Communist Party of Japan when the occupation policies took a sharp turn to the right.
2. Democratic Liberal Party (DLP): one of the predecessor organisations of the Liberal Democratic Party (LDP).

# 6 The Labour Conflict of the Ōmi-Kenshi Silk Mills, 1954

*Minoru Takita*

**Minoru Takita**

1912 Born in Toyama prefecture on 15 December
1931 Graduated from Takaoka Technical College as electrical engineer; employed by the company Nisshin Bōseki

## Trade union functions

1948 Chairman of the Nisshin Bōseki Union, chairman of Zensen Dōmei (the Japanese Federation of Textile Workers' Unions, JFTWU)
1954 Chairman of Zenrō Kaigi (the All-Japan Labour Union Congress, AJLUC)
1960 Chairman of the Regional Congress of Asian Textile workers
1965 Vice chairman of the International Confederation of Free Trade Unions (until 1972)
1967 Chairman of the Asian Regional Organisation of the International Confederation of Free Trade Unions
1968 Chairman of Dōmei (the Japanese Confederation of Labour, JCL)
1971 Resigned as chairman of Zensen Dōmei; since then its adviser and honorary chairman
1972 Resigned as chairman of Domei; since then its adviser
1983 Awarded the First Class Great Cordon of the Order of the Rising Sun

## Present functions

Chairman of the Institute for Social Problems of Asia, chief adviser to Nihon Seisansei Honbu (the Japan Productivity Centre).

## Publications

*Kyokō no seisan – rōdō sensen tōitsu e no shuppatsu* (Removal of a Fiction – Setting Out for a United Union Front), Japanese Federation of Textile, Garment, Chemical, Mercantile, Food and Allied Industries Workers' Unions, 1971
*Waga kaisō – rōdō undō hitosuji ni* (Retrospections – for a Joint Course for the Labour Movement), Yomiuri Shinbunsha, 1972
*Watashi no rirekishō* (My Life), Nihon Keizai Shinbunsha, 1973
*Rōdō kumiai e no teigen* (Proposals to the Unions), Nihon Hyōronsha, 1978

## I Editor's Overview

In 1954, shortly before Japan entered a period of high economic growth, a labour dispute lasting 106 days occurred at the Ōmi-Kenshi Silk Mills.

This dispute was regarded as unusual. One reason was that the strike had the character of a 'fight for human rights'. In contrast to most other post-war labour conflicts which started as struggles for economic demands and then turned into political ones, this fight for human rights concerned a controversial issue between management and labour which was generally perceived to have been already settled: the company's president tried to prevent the founding of a union and refused to respect even fundamental human rights. The strike occurred immediately after the establishment of Zenrō Kaigi, (which later became Dōmei, established on 22 April 1954 with Minoru Takita as its chairman) and became a struggle in which the whole energy of this new organisation and of Zensen Dōmei was concentrated. Shortly after Sōhyō had taken a turn to the left with its 'Four Principles for Peace' and the 'Thesis on the Forces of Peace' and after the failure of strikes in the coal mining industry and the energy supply sector, the Japanese Federation of Textile Workers' Unions, Kaiin Kumiai and other conservative labour organisations had left Sōhyō and founded Zenrō Kaigi. The division within the labour movement into left-wing and right-wing camps had entered a new phase, and this was the first struggle to be led by the conservative forces.

As the strike received the undivided support of foreign and domestic unions, and because the public showed an overwhelming solidarity with the strikers, the dispute ended in an unqualified victory for the workers. It also focused attention on the ignorance of many bosses of small and medium-sized companies in which feudal labour relations, such as those of the Ōmi-Kenshi Silk Mills, were still the order of the day, and – last but not least – it had a lasting effect which went beyond the modernisation of labour relations.

## Background

The Japanese cotton milling industry is led by an association of ten big firms founded during the Meiji era which is known as 'The Ten Giants'. In comparison to these companies, Ōmi-Kenshi Silk Mills is a late-comer. It was founded in 1916 by the late Kumajirō Natsukawa with an original capital of 500,000 yen. During the war, its business activities widened due to an intensive collaboration with the armed forces, and by the end of the war its capital had grown to 8 million yen. This growth continued during the post-war era because of the boom in demand created by the Korean war, and by 1953 the firm's capital stock had grown to 1 billion yen, it employed about 14,000 labourers and had risen to the top of the 'New Giants', a group of companies competing with the original 'Ten Giants'.

The secret of this quick growth was the despotic family-style management practices of the Natsukawa clan and the firm's feudal labour relations, which were so backward that the Natsukawas were outcasts even in industrial circles. For instance, all employees had to convert to Buddhism, their letters were opened, their personal belongings were searched and they had to obey a strict curfew. Breaches of the law on labour standards occurred daily, among them overtime and holiday work without extra pay and night shifts which were called 'owl service'. In view of these malpractices, Zensen Dōmei launched a 'fight for democratisation', but it was not yet strong enough to resist the pressure exerted by the management, and a further five years came and went before a union could be established.

## Development

On 25 May 1954, Zensen Dōmei finally managed to establish a union in the head offices of the company and presented a list of twenty-two demands to the management. This was the signal for the founding of unions in two business locations and seven production sites, and the fight for democratisation spread like wildfire through all parts of the company. The management reacted by confining the workers to their quarters, closing all canteens, and hiring thugs who beat up union members; it tried its utmost to intimidate the protesting workers. The conflict thus developed into an all-out battle, with the union of the Ōmi-Kenshi Silk Mills and Zensen Dōmei with a combined membership of about 320,000 on the one side and a single company on the other.

In contrast to the management, however, which did not enjoy the support of its peers, the union had the full backing of Zenrō Kaigi, while Kaiin Kumiai organised a transport boycott of all products of the company, and this group of supporters was augmented by Sōhyō and its affiliated unions, such as the Teachers' Union (Nikkyōso), Kokurō and the Union of the national transport company (Zennitsū), and further non-affiliated unions. Even the International Confederation of Free Trade Unions and a number of foreign textile workers' unions expressed their solidarity, and the news media openly declared their sympathy with the goals of the union. The management was thus attacked from all sides, but as it still rejected all demands for collective bargaining, the strike developed into a drawn-out struggle.

While the conflict intensified, it also became a problem affecting society in general. Minister of Labour Zentarō Kosaka tried to reach a solution behind the scenes and went to the company's creditor banks, asking for their help. But although the mediators did their utmost to find a solution, their efforts were in vain.

This failure exacerbated the tensions between both sides in the conflict, and now the Central Labour Relations Commission appeared on the scene. Led by its former chairman, Ichirō Nakayama, an attempt was made to work out a mediation proposal by including all three parties in the negotiation process. However, when the company rejected the first and then another proposal, the union broke off the negotiations, demanding the resignation of the company's president Kakuji Natsukawa and his clan. The Central Commission then suspended its mediation attempts.

As all efforts to bring the situation under control had failed, the fight between management and employees became even more dangerous. There were frequent reports of violent acts; suicides occurred; workers were injured and suffered nervous breakdowns. The five main shareholders of the company, among them Mitsubishi and Sumitomo, could no longer stand on the sidelines and asked the Central Labour Relations Commission again to negotiate a settlement. Chairman Ichirō Nakayama then presented a third mediation proposal. It contained all the union propositions and was accepted by Zensen Dōmei which, after 106 days, declared the strike at last to be over.

The contract was sealed in the offices of the Central Commission, and in the presence of all parties President Natsukawa and the chairman of the Japanese Federation of Textile Workers' Unions, Minoru Takita, signed the agreement. The union had won a great victory.

## Results

This outstanding conflict paradigmatically showed that 'the support of the public decides victory or defeat' (Minoru Takita). It also became a model for the desirable relationship between the leading organisation and the individual unions within a strike. In this conflict, which started with the establishment of a new union, Zensen Dōmei paid all costs of the strike and living expenses of the union members as the Union of the Ōmi-Kenshi Silk Mills had no funds of its own. Zensen Dōmei asked each of its members to contribute 480 yen per month (at that time, the wage paid by the big mills to a mill worker aged fifteen was 4,760 yen) raising a sum of 154 million yen.

## The list of twenty-two demands

1. Immediate recognition of the Union of the Ōmi-Kenshi Silk Mills.
2. Immediate dissolution of the yellow union loyal to the management.
3. Retraction of all regulations concerning the nomination of workers' representatives by the management.

4. A guarantee limiting working hours to eight hours per day.
5. Immediate re-introduction of devices for measuring working hours, payment of overtime pay, creation of a wage system.
6. Determination of acceptable severance pay, travel-cost reimbursement and extra pay for night shifts.
7. Guarantee of paid holidays and one additional monthly holiday for women (menstruation day).
8. Enlargement of the canteens, installation of locker-rooms, improvement and enlargement of living accommodation, improvement of social facilities.
9. Installation of night watch rooms, immediate employment of watchmen, cleaning and kitchen personnel for all living accommodation.
10. Complete abolition of the obligation to convert to Buddhism.
11. Permission to attend evening classes and recognition of the right to additional education.
12. Recognition of the right to marry. No forced separation of spouses.
13. Full recognition of the freedom to enjoy cultural activities such as hiking, music, picture shows, etc.
14. Abolition of all sorts of 'contests' enforcing higher work efficiency.
15. Immediate discontinuation of all measures violating human rights, such as the opening of personal letters or the searching of personal property.
16. Abolition of the obligation to spy on each other, of bonus payments for informers and of the practice of shadowing employees.
17. Permission to leave the company sites.
18. Abolition of the regular monthly dismissals conducted by the factory manager.
19. Immediate reinforcement in all departments of the necessary minimal personnel levels.
20. Prohibition of behaviour on the part of superiors which offends against human dignity and abolition of the practice of forcing workers to submit written apologies.
21. Abolition of the obligation to live on the factory sites for

company drivers and the provision of suitable accommodation outside the sites.

22. Immediate insurance coverage against damages resulting from traffic accidents.

## II Lecture by Minoru Takita

From the time immediately after the war until the present day I have been actively involved in the Japanese and the international labour movements, especially that of Asia, sometimes at risk to my life. I was chairman not only of Dōmei, but also of the Asian Regional Organisation of the International Confederation of Free Trade Unions; moreover, I was vice chairman of the ICFTU. While in my lecture I concentrate on the events connected with the labour conflict of the Ōmi-Kenshi Silk Mills, I also refer to my own experiences as a worker in the textile industry and to my activities in the domestic as well as the international labour movement.

In 1931 I was first employed by a spinning mill. It was a big company called Nisshin Bōseki. The female workers received 40 sen[1] per day, and I got 95 sen because I had attended school.

The conditions in the living accommodation of the Ōmi-Kenshi Silk Mills were actually exactly the same as those which I had seen in my own company when I was a foreman. At five o'clock in the morning the machines in the factory were switched on, but in the morning after a holiday many of the female workers did not show up. They had used the little money they had on drinking too much ice water and eating too much *udon*[2] the previous day. On such days I, as the person in charge, had to go to their quarters and cry out in a loud voice 'All of you who have no medical certificate, get up!', and even if I had to tear them from their *futons*[3] by force, I got them ready for work.

When, later, after the war, I became an active participant in the labour movement, I was overcome by a feeling of shame every time I remembered my former experiences; in that respect they turned out to be very useful. There are many possibilities for a leading union official: he may become a member of parliament or an important manager of some company. But to me, all this means nothing. The only thing that counts for me is not to leave the straight path. In my opinion, a union official's role is more relevant to society than that of a member of parliament or a manager.

The pain I felt when I witnessed how badly the female workers were treated during the period from the beginning of the Shōwa era until the end of the war has become the main motivation for my continuing involvement in the labour movement.

## The situation of female workers

Historically speaking, to my mind female workers have been the main victims of oppression under Japanese capitalism. At the beginning of the Meiji period, spinning mills were founded everywhere in Japan. They formed the basis for the development of Japanese capitalism. The Japanese textile industry has been built on the exploitation and misery of country people and female workers. On a smaller scale, this fact became apparent during the strike at the Ōmi-Kenshi Silk Mills.

Because the name of the company was 'Ōmi Kenshi', the strike is often referred to as the Kinken[4] strike. At the beginning of the strike, I personally invented this name. But when the events unfolded and the attention of the whole nation focused on this dispute, the newspapers called it a 'fight for human rights' because it differed from normal labour disputes and was not merely a strike for economic ends. Normally, unions try to achieve an improvement of labour conditions with economic goals as their main objective. But the Kinken strike was no conflict over economic matters, it did not occur because of dismissals or demands for a wage increase. It really had the character of a fight for human rights. I think I must tell you more about the background of this conflict. The Ōmi-Kenshi Silk Mills had been founded in 1916 with an original capital of 500,000 yen, but when the conflict erupted, their stock capital had grown to 1 billion yen! According to official sources, the company employed 11,753 persons at that time. Its headquarters were in Ōsaka. The company had production facilities at Hikone, Ōgaki, Tsu, Nakatsukawa, Nakahama, Fujinomiya and Kishiwada; as the name 'Ōmi' tells you, they were mostly located in Shiga[5] prefecture.

The company reputedly had plans to hire 4,000 new employees each year. But the actual number of newly employed was about 3,500. However, because working conditions were extremely bad, most of them soon took to their heels. In spinning mills it was normal practice that someone packed his bundle and climbed over the fence, making a face as if he just intended to take a stroll. But at the Ōmi-Kenshi Silk Mills conditions were so dismal that within one year of 3,500 newcomers 3,000 left the company or simply vanished into the night. The fluctuation in the workforce is a clear indicator of just how poor working conditions were at the Ōmi-Kenshi Silk Mills, a fact which became quite prominent during the strike.

## The antiquated attitude of managers with regard to their workers

When I am giving a lecture, people often ask me to say something about the problems of personnel management. My standard answer is that the relationship between workers and managers is like a mirror image. If the boss thinks about one of his subordinates, 'My God, what a fool!' the latter will be inclined to think the same about his boss. During the time after the war it often happened that some company boss came to me and told me he had a problem because a union had been founded in his company. He then came to ask for my advice: 'Can't we just somehow get rid of the union again?' he would ask me. And when I asked him whether a union was such a bad thing, he would answer: 'No, I don't think unions are bad, but I had never thought there'd be one in *my* company. How on earth can I get rid of it again?' I often had to deal with such questions, and I used to tell these people: 'You know, the most important thing about labour relations within a company is that the employees are treated as human beings and that they get a fair share in the company's profits. When working conditions are good, the employees will stick with the company, but if they are bad, they'll simply leave, even though their boss may think that they will not dare to give up their jobs. It is the duty and the responsibility of any real entrepreneur to create good working conditions for his employees and to show his sympathy towards them. That is the right way of dealing with people, and it will automatically put an end to a high rate of personnel fluctuation.' It is a clear indication of incompetence on part of an entrepreneur if he acts differently.

Kakuji Natsukawa, the boss of the Ōmi-Kenshi Silk Mills, turned out to be a man not devoid of any charm once the strike was over, but he was not easy to handle. In April 1954, the average wage of a male worker at five other spinning mills roughly the same size as the Ōmi-Kenshi Silk Mills was 18,711 yen, while a female worker received 7,837. The difference was because the men's period of employment was usually longer and they had received a better education. But the Ōmi-Kenshi Silk Mills paid only 5,981 yen to men and 4,909 to women, which was less than half the pay they would get in other companies of the industry. Moreover, at Ōmi-Kenshi they had to do night shifts, and employees were obliged to work overtime. Consequently, the standard of working conditions was less than half as good as in other companies. President Kakuji Natsukawa once wrote in an article which was published by the magazine *Kaizō* (August 1954): 'If you do not put the workers on the same level as pigs or cows, you cannot make any profit.' Therefore he exploited the female workers in every conceivable way. On the other hand, he used to invite *geishas* to his house and then he would throw a big party. That is the way most of them behaved, those company bosses of the pre-war type.

When I joined my company in 1931, the situation was just as that shown in the TV series *Oshin*[6]. The country girls who were a financial burden on their families were sold as prostitutes to the brothels or sent off to the spinning mills to earn some money. When the strike broke out in 1954, the American magazine *Time* published an article on the subject, in which it was said: 'The Ōmi-Kenshi Silk Mills, a company which only seven years ago had a value of only about $30,000 dollars, has managed to raise its value to about $3 million dollars today. The reason for this growth is simple: it is the management practices of its President Natsukawa who violates each and every labour law.' Before the war such practices were not restricted to the Ōmi-Kenshi Silk Mills but were usual in this industry. However, after the war, the big companies changed their ways, and only the Ōmi-Kenshi Silk Mills refused to accept the sign of the times. If you compared the Ōmi-Kenshi Silk Mill with a wooden post in a stream, the strike was the water which finally swept it away.

## A model case of a dispute led by a democratic labour movement

In 1954 Japan was just at the beginning of a period of high economic growth. Japan was not yet an affluent country. In the years 1952 and 1953 there was a series of big strikes in the key industries, for example the labour disputes in the coal mining and the energy supply industry which continued for a long time. These strikes mainly concerned economic demands or were launched as resistance against rationalisation measures which would eventually lead to dismissals. However, they were guided by the spirit of class struggle. It was a generally accepted notion among labour leaders that problems between workers and entrepreneurs could only be resolved by force and that the capitalist system had to be changed. The strikes were actually encumbered with revolutionary theory. The Communist Party of Japan resorted to an illegal strategy, and the unions in important industrial sectors were guided by Marxist and Leninist ideas.

I want to give you a somewhat broader picture. In 1950 the union federation Sōhyō, which still exists today, was established. In February of the previous year the International Confederation of Free Trade Unions had been founded. This is an international organisation of labour unions of free countries. Because the World Federation of Trade Unions which had been established in 1945 had come under the domination of the Soviet Union, the labour unions of the free countries left it and formed their own organisation.

When Sōhyō was founded, it was expected to join the International Confederation of Free Trade Unions. But as only four years after its establishment Sōhyō took a sharp turn to the left, a split occurred and Zenrō Kaigi (today's Dōmei) was founded. I was elected its chairman. Precisely at that time the labour conflict of the Ōmi-Kenshi Silk Mills broke out. After so many strikes which had been guided by the theories of class struggle, now for the first time there was a labour dispute which was led by a free and democratic labour movement. But although this fight for human rights had, as it were, the character of a premodern struggle the left-wing labour movement would have loved to lead, our approach to this dispute of the Ōmi-Kenshi Silk Mills was fundamentally different from that of the labour disputes which were influenced by left-wing ideology.

Of course, during the strike many bitter confrontations occurred, in that respect it was in no way inferior to the struggles guided by left-wing theories. I myself was twice almost killed. One day when I was in the office of the Central Labour Relations Commission and was having a chat with someone, suddenly a black-clad guy entered the room with a dagger in his hand and asked 'Is Chairman Takita around?' I kept my head and answered him, 'Yeah, he just left through that door over there', and off he went. The other time I was in Osaka during the strike. A waitress in a restaurant by chance overheard a conversation of some members of the extreme right: 'This time we'll give Takita the bullet. As soon as he's finished, the strike will be over.' She contacted me and told me what she had heard. There were also quite a number of cases in which striking workers committed suicide or suffered a nervous breakdown. You will realise just how violent a struggle it was by taking into account what I, as its highest-ranking leader, had to go through.

In those days there were many bosses of small and medium-sized companies who did not treat their workers as human beings. There will still be some of those around. I believe that the Ōmi-Kenshi Silk Mills can serve as a representative example. Therefore I was convinced that if we fought with all our energy and managed to achieve a victory, our struggle would have a lasting effect on Japanese labour relations in general. Because of this conviction, my sole aim in leading the strike was to achieve a victory. Nearly all labour conflicts in which left-wing ideology had played a major role had ended in a defeat. The strikers had not been able to push through their demands, or their organisation had gone to pieces so that nobody wanted to take part in such a conflict again. Right from the very beginning of the strike until the ultimate settlement, I was fully aware of the fact that we wanted to conduct a labour conflict based on a democratic labour movement and totally free of the hitherto dominating class-struggle ideology. When the settlement had finally been sealed, I called all the leading members of the Ōmi-Kenshi union together and told them: 'Tomorrow you'll get back to work. And nobody should be late, not even by a single minute! And you should work even harder than before the strike.' They all were drunk because they had celebrated the end of the strike, and there were some who protested, 'Take it easy, we can't switch back to normal just like that!' But I replied: 'You can, and you will. Your demands have been fulfilled, and now you must show your solidarity with each other on the job!' And I made them 'switch back'.

During the strike it often happened that angry strikers came to me and urged me to 'get down to some real action!' Others made remarks such as 'The only proper place for Kakuji Natsukawa to be is six feet under the ground!' But even when there were suicides and cases of nervous breakdown, I firmly rejected and prevented any violent actions on the part of the strikers and kept them on the straight path.

## The antecedents of the strike

The establishment of the Union of the Ōmi-Kenshi Silk Mills occurred on 25 May 1954 when a local group of Zensen Dōmei was founded in the company's head offices. This was a matter of life and death: immediately after the management had been notified of the union's founding, its members were fired and attacked by hired thugs.

But of course this was not the only reason for the strike to break out. Zensen Dōmei had already been trying to gain a foothold in the company for six or seven years. Nobody has kept a record of how many times they formally appealed to the management for permission to organise a union in the normal fashion. They also tried to talk with employees outside the company's premises or exchange letters with people inside, but all of their attempts were thwarted. If the person concerned was not to be influenced either by soothing words or by intimidation, the company tried to have his parents convince him not to cooperate with the union. Six or seven years passed until the situation had become so tense that the founding of a union in the head offices of the company would automatically lead to an uprising of the workers in all production facilities. When all preparations had been made with due consideration given to the mood in the workplace, the working conditions, the president's behaviour, the intensive surveillance of the workers and other factors, a union was founded in the head offices of the company. On the following day, union groups were formed in all production sites.

I believe that at this point in time the employees simply had had enough. The company was violating all legal regulations. Between 1948 and 1954, the year the union was founded, the company committed 147 registered offences against the labour laws alone. After the war I was a member of the commission which drew up the law on labour standards. The supervisory authority often warned the company, but the management never heeded these warnings. If you add up the number of legal offences and criminal cases which occurred during the strike alone, there were fifty-four lawsuits filed against the company. In all cases the courts judged in favour of the union. But even this did not help. To sum it up: the strike was caused by the inhuman treatment of the workers by President Kakuji Natsukawa, and this is why the strike became a fight for human rights.

## Public support

The whole labour dispute can be divided up into three phases. During the first phase, the demands were on the table and both sides fought a grim battle against each other. In the second phase, the Central Labour Relations Commission tried to find a solution to the dispute, while at the same time the fight continued on a legal level in the courts. In the case of the Ōmi-Kenshi strike, there were even attempts to end the conflict by issuing a cabinet decree. Political pressure was put on the company. Against this background, the Central Commission was preparing plans for a settlement, while on the other hand a fight against the company's legal offences was launched. Of course, the confrontation between both sides continued unabated. During the third and final phase the big question was which factor would in the end decide our victory or defeat in this struggle. In my opinion, this decisive factor was the public support which we enjoyed. Because the *Yomiuri* newspaper wanted to publish an account of the events, on the same day the conflict was settled I sat down and made some notes on them. I remember that I wrote: 'The determining factor in this struggle was public opinion. It was the common sense of the people which in the end carried the day.'

History has seen a number of great labour conflicts, but in all cases the factor determining defeat or victory was whether the demands were rational or not. And here public opinion comes in: does the union stand alone with its demands, or do they appear just to everybody? In my opinion, the unions intrinsically have a 'correct standpoint': as one worker alone is too weak, he enters into an association with other workers which is called a union. The desire for justice and fairness is the basis of union activities, and this must be explained to the public. To give you some examples: the magazine *Shūkan Asahi* carried an interview between me and Musei Tokugawa about the strike. Because of his character, my interviewer had no sympathy for the strike, but nevertheless he told me: 'Mr Takita, I really hope that you will win.' Also Mr Shinnosuke Abe, at that time the head of NHK, the Japanese broadcasting service, and the commentator on economic affairs, Mr Ritoku Obama, shook my hand and told me with tears in their eyes: 'Whatever some may say, Mr Takita, this is a just fight, and you must win it'. And Shinnosuke Abe added: 'I am not a rich man, but I would like to contribute a little, Mr Takita, if it only helps you to win. But apart from President Kakuji Natsukawa, there's another one whose downfall I pray for. It's Shigeru Yoshida[7] and his cabinet that we of the press want to see brought down'.

## Securing the livelihood of the strikers

The only major labour dispute which can be compared with the Ōmi-Kenshi strike is the Mitsui-Miike struggle. Well, it resembles the Ōmi-Kenshi strike in that it also concerned wage raises and dismissals, but the strike leadership followed a different course which was guided by the attitude: 'Even if because of this strike the coal mines and the company go bankrupt, we still have gained a victory.' I had a different opinion: 'If we don't ask ourselves how we can save the coal mining industry, then in the final analysis the workers will lose, although they apparently may have won the class struggle.' This was because even if the strikers won their battle, crude oil would replace coal as an energy source. If new applications for oil and other energy sources were developed, the coal mining industry would not survive. If this happened, the victory of the workers would only be temporary and there would be no guarantee that they would be able to enjoy its fruits also in the future.

In a documentary on the strike at the Ōmi-Kenshi Silk Mills ('The Revolt of the Female Workers') there is one scene in which female workers are shown eating *o-nigiri*.[8] Workers supporting the strike each had brought one *o-nigiri* as emergency food aid for the female workers. The company had closed down all canteens and the female workers were deprived of their normal rations. The hungry women were therefore fed by their male colleagues. Whenever workers watch this scene, some of them break out in tears. I encouraged such action because I believed: 'When I am the responsible leader of a strike, I have to find a way of securing the livelihood of the strikers during their battle. If I cannot do that, I must not call a strike.' For the whole 106 days the livelihood of those involved in strike action was secured by the donations of other organised workers. Each of these workers gave approximately 60 per cent of his wage to the strikers.

During the Mitsui-Miike struggle, there were groups of supporters who came and agitated, but they did not help a bit in securing the strikers' livelihood. When the strike was over, the union members had all accumulated high debts. At that time I first realised that donations by organised workers and financial relief for those involved in a strike are important factors for achieving a victory in a long-term conflict. Therefore during the Ōmi-Kenshi dispute I collected money among the organised workers so that the female workers could go on strike without having to worry about their financial situation. I think that even years later this labour conflict still served as a model of how to organise support in a major dispute.

## The reaction of entrepreneurs

In contrast to the union, President Kakuji Natsukawa not only antagonised the unions but in the end was at odds with his colleagues in the leading companies as well. A short while ago there was a party given in commemoration of the publication of the book *Hidden Post-War History* by Mr Nobutaka Shikauchi, the President of Fuji Television and the *Sankei* newspaper. In his book he says: 'If today Japan is an affluent country, there are two factors which brought this about: the common and high level of education, and the good Japanese labour relations.' A major labour dispute must have a rationale which wins the support of public opinion, which goes beyond economic demands; it must not be seen merely as a clash between two sides. This is one reason why President Natsukawa did not receive the support of business circles.

Apart from the attempts by the Central Labour Relations Commission, there were quite a number of initiatives by business people and politicians which aimed at a speedy settlement of the conflict. But Natsukawa was unwilling to listen to anyone. We therefore developed a strategy which concentrated on destroying the life-support system of the company by cutting the capital supply from the banks. However, we did not only think of money but also made an effort to interrupt the supply and transport of raw materials and finished goods. The unions of companies which transported these raw materials and goods decided to boycott Ōmi-Kenshi. Whenever the Ōmi-Kenshi Silk Mills now tried to sell their products in order to make some money, they found it impossible to get them shipped. Even when they resorted to hiring groups of thugs to do the job, they still could not get the dock workers to load the products on to ships. At our instigation, products to be sold in foreign countries were no longer accepted. At that time I had a leading function in the International Confederation of Free Trade Unions, and I went to the American and European unions for help. Thus at home as well as abroad, the company was totally isolated.

When even these measures had no effect, we decided to put pressure on the banks. Zentarō Kosaka was then Minister of Labour, and as he was a friend of mine, I asked him to lend a hand, and he spoke with representatives of the banks. First the president of the Sumitomo Bank, then the president of the Mitsubishi Bank and afterwards other influential members of financial circles tried to persuade Mr Kakuji Natsukawa to give in. However, all their efforts were in vain. When the president of the Sumitomo Bank, Shōzō Hotta, asked me for a meeting, we met secretly in Osaka. After our talks, Mr Hotta went to President Natsukawa and told him: 'If you don't fulfil the demands of Zensen Dōmei, the Sumitomo Bank will cease all business contacts with your company.'

Earlier when the banks were still reluctant to help us, we had cooked up a devious strategy. We asked all 320,000 members of the textile workers' unions to withdraw their savings. These amounted to 2 billion yen at that time. And in order to put additional pressure on President Kakuji Natsukawa and to give the banks some more trouble, we resorted to another trick: you went to the bank with 1 yen. This 1 yen you paid into your bank account. Then the next union member went in and withdrew 1 yen from his account. When a couple of hundred persons played the game, the banks became extremely busy, but they were unable to resist. We went on with this wicked game until the bank people told us: 'If the whole federation of textile workers does this to us, we may as well close down for good!' But they never regarded us as their enemies, and I think this was because our demands were supported by the public.

## Conditions for success or defeat in a strike

I have spent my whole life serving the labour movement. A leader of a strike or a union must choose his steps with great care when planning his strategy in a labour conflict. There are some criteria for measuring the success or failure of a labour dispute. First, after a major strike you have to look back and see whether the demands were actually fulfilled. There have been many strikes which did not achieve their goals. A second consideration is whether the organisation was strengthened by the conflict or not. Many labour conflicts have resulted in a division of the union involved or even its destruction. And, third, you must ask yourself whether or not the strike has encouraged workers to think: 'Wow, why don't we do something like that here, too?' This is the so-called 'radiation effect'. But a reaction such as 'Oh god, we're really fed up with such a strike' is disastrous.

After the Ōmi-Kenshi dispute, many other unions were encouraged by the Ōmi-Kenshi strike to adopt the same demands. In nearly all small and medium-sized enterprises the workers won their battles. And the entrepreneurs feared, 'If they repeat with us what they have done at Ōmi-Kenshi, we're in deep water.' They arrived at the conclusion, 'If we continue with management practices which are unacceptable to the workers, they'll do to us what they did at Ōmi-Kenshi!' And they said: 'Beware of another Ōmi-Kenshi strike.' The result of the labour conflict at the Ōmi-Kenshi Silk Mills was that the workers gained courage and the bosses had to reconsider their practices. This was really a great success which went far beyond our expectations.

## Review

We have conducted a survey of the changes which the strike has brought to the company and its employees. Previously, within six months of their employment many of them suffered from loss of appetite and other diseases and left the company. Today they tend to stick with the company, they do not lose their appetite and stay healthy. The female workers have experienced an improvement of their financial and living conditions even in areas which were not concerned with the demands.

The current president of the Ōmi-Kenshi Silk Mills, Tetsunosuke Natsukawa, is the younger brother of the former president, Kakuji Natsukawa. Sometimes I meet him, but we do not talk about what happened during the strike. To my mind, once the fight is over, arms must be laid down. His behaviour towards me is very polite.

When the end of the strike drew near, the most important point of the mediation proposal put forward by the Central Labour Relations Commission was a clause by which the company accepted the closed-shop principle. This principle requires every new employee of the company to join the union established by Zensen Dōmei. Until that time the company had tried its utmost to prevent the founding of any union. Now they were even prepared to agree to the closed-shop clause.

Zensen Dōmei had to raise about 154 million yen. The union members organised by the Federation first paid a monthly contribution for the strike of 100 yen, later this amount rose to 170 yen. All additional costs of the strike were paid by the Federation. Furthermore we received donations from various sympathetic groups and unions. During the Mitsui-Miike strike it sometimes happened that people from Sōhyō arrived carrying bags full of money, but later I learned that they had received it from the banks as a loan raised by the Mitsui-Miike union. We on the other hand did not burden the Ōmi-Kenshi union with a single sen of debt. The receipts which prove this are still available.

When the mediation proposal had finally been accepted, we, the representatives of Zensen Dōmei and of the Union of the Ōmi-Kenshi Silk Mills ran outside, threw our arms into the air and shouted '*Banzai!!*' This was a success which really gave the workers a feeling of having won a great victory.

## Peculiarities of the leadership in the strike

I now want to remark on a number of points which we observed during this strike. First of all, no persons who were not members of Zensen Dōmei were allowed to take a leading role in the strike. Of course it was a conflict in which outside organisations were also involved; when Zensen Dōmei is engaged in a labour dispute, there are always many political groups who want to join in as supporters. However, if they are given an actual say, outside pressure will grow too strong. If a union engaged in a strike is dragged into such a quagmire, it may lose its independence for good. In such a case it often happens that in the end nobody really knows any more what the strike is all about and who is the responsible leader. I use to call this an 'encircled strike'. It is characterised by the fact that people gather only to form agitation groups which have no real responsibility, and once a settlement is at hand, serious problems may arise. During the Ōmi-Kenshi strike we managed to avoid such a situation and the independence of Zensen Dōmei was maintained throughout, which led to positive results.

And one further point: the Ōmi-Kenshi strike mainly involved female workers, and we took great care to identify the best way of leading women in a strike – how they must be organised. I have been involved in many strikes, and I have to admit that when the going gets tough, women are stronger than men. In the beginning, the men show a great deal of energy too, but they tend to go to the wall too soon. In drawn-out conflicts especially, married men with families have a hard time. During the strike they do not receive their wages, and when their wives start nagging at them and keep saying, 'You've got to put an end to this, we're running out of money!' they tend to give in. In later conflicts we often fought for minimum wages for female workers, but the first to turn tail were always their male colleagues. They have a big mouth alright, the men, haven't they? But women are more liable to act on the spur of the moment, and once they have made up their minds they are awfully hard to discourage. This was exactly what happened in the Ōmi-Kenshi strike.

## The problems of poverty, unemployment and nuclear weapons

Finally I would like to comment on some of the problems the labour movement encounters today. In June and July of this year [1983] I attended a conference of the International Confederation of Free Trade Unions in Oslo, Norway. I was invited as one of three honorary members of the international labour movement since 1949. The conference focused on the question of what were today's most serious global problems. The list was topped by the problems of poverty and unemployment, and nuclear disarmament took the second place. The third issue regarded as a serious problem was union rights.

The first issue concerns industrial nations and developing countries alike. Poverty is a major problem in developing countries, especially those in Asia, Africa and Latin America. In some remote areas poverty is so severe that people cannot even light a fire. They have to survive on a diet of raw fruits. India can be seen as the focus of the world's problems. Class discrimination and religious conflicts are the bane of this country. With regard to the second problem, nuclear weapons and disarmament, the conflict between the two superpowers, the United States and the Soviet Union, has shaped world affairs in many respects. All nations publicly declare their opposition to nuclear weapons and warfare, but actual programmes solving the question of how to achieve disarmament and how to use the money which can be saved in the process are yet to be worked out.

An Englishman once told me that although there was no scientific basis for it, there was a figure termed the 'misery index'. Today the three major problems of unemployment, inflation and low economic growth create a very difficult global situation. The severity of this situation could be calculated as an index. West Germany and Japan would have the most favourable score, some also would add Australia. In my opinion, Australia has a great potential for development. But anyway, the highlights were West Germany and Japan. However, in recent times West German industry has experienced a serious decline. That is something which must not happen to Japan!

## The disease of the industrialised nations

During the last two years [1981–2], the Institute for Social Problems of Asia, which I actively support, has carried out an opinion poll which included 2,000 Japanese and the same number of German workers, and we have conducted a comparative study into the most prominent problems. When asked, 'Are you unsatisfied with the current economic and political situation?' workers of both countries answered 'Yes'. But when asked, 'What is the cause of this situation?' the majority of the Japanese answered,

'The politicians are bad', while Germans mostly put the blame on the entrepreneurs. This is evidence of a difference in perspective.

In Japan, the conservative party has led the country without interruption for a long time, and it is increasingly corrupt and generally on the decline. The opposition parties, knowing that they will never get the chance of forming a government, have made themselves comfortable and limit their activities to simply saying 'no' all the time. In a country without a chance of a shift in power, neither politics nor the economy nor society will show satisfactory development, because there is no pressure on the politicians to keep a clean house.

Germany, on the other hand, has seen a number of changes in government, but the opinion poll clearly showed that labour relations are characterised by class distinctions. Moreover, in Germany all matters concerning employment within a company are regulated by contracts. In Japan there is a system of lifetime employment and automatic promotion according to length of employment. There is hardly anyone who would simply drop the work he is doing and go home when normal working hours are over. Also more than 90 per cent of Japanese employees approve of technical innovations. In Germany the number of those who oppose such innovation is extremely high. As in Germany, wages are determined separately for each occupational group; education is also profession-oriented. Therefore workers are extremely annoyed if the introduction of new machines devalues their professional qualifications.

German workers thus have reason to regard industrial and technical development with strong suspicion. As wage rises have for some time slightly exceeded the country's economic capabilities, investment in plant and equipment has become impossible. This has resulted in a stagnation of economic development. Willingness to work has also sharply declined. Of the 365 days in a year, German workers work only 54 per cent. The remaining 46 per cent of these are public or other holidays. German figures for the so-called magic quadrangle, i.e. solid growth, low prices, stable employment and an equable balance of trade, are all showing signs of deterioration. Therefore Japan now has become the only country in the world with brilliant economic performance.

However, there are some factors which throw a shadow over Japan's future development. One of the most critical is a shift in values which changes the way people think. We often hear the question of what would make life worth living. As long as the majority of a country's population is convinced that it is work that makes life meaningful, the country still has a real potential for economic development. However, if more than 50 per cent hold the view that only leisure makes life worth living, it can be expected that the country's economy will show a tendency towards stagnation.

Twenty years ago, the overwhelming majority of West Germans perceived work as the meaning of life, but today the figures have turned around, and most of them see leisure as the most important thing in life. Leisure is one of the human necessities, but it is only natural that a people which makes leisure its highest value cannot expect further economic growth. In order to correct this, education of the people in the right values is of extreme importance, and this education will also have a strong impact on labour relations. This is a most important aspect to keep in mind if Japan is not also to be infected with the disease of industrialised nations.

## Unemployment and disarmament

Unemployment has become the most serious problem on a global scale, and Japan too has not been left untouched by it. Between 1950 and 1975, the working population of the world has increased by approximately 22 million people per annum. But between 1975 and the end of the century, this figure will rise to 40 million each year. Today, the working population each day grows by 100,000–120,000 people. But there is no corresponding economic development which would provide jobs for them, no container, as it were, in which they can find room. There are some who propose to shorten working hours and divide up work by so-called 'work sharing'. But if that does not go along with increased productivity, this measure will lead only to inflation.

When thinking about suitable measures on a global scale, one must focus on the issue of how the money which today is spent on armaments could be used for solving the world's problems. Today, the average percentage of net social product spent on armaments world-wide is in the region of 6–7 per cent. Even countries such as neutral Switzerland or Sweden, with their comprehensive social security systems, have large military budgets.

According to a calculation of the Stockholm Institute for Peace Studies, $700 billion were spent on arms in 1983 alone. A reduction of this amount by only 10 per cent would mean that $70 billion could be saved. If a change in the way of thinking took place and this amount was used for reviving the global economy, we would be one step closer to a solution to the unemployment problem.

However, these issues cannot be solved by politicians alone. People of all social strata and from all walks of life have to participate in finding a solution. In order to overcome poverty and unemployment, affluent countries such as the United States, Japan and West Germany must pool their forces. I myself have a number of proposals as to how to use the money saved by disarmament for the revival of the global economy. In Asia, for instance, the ice caps of the Himalaya mountain range could be used for producing hydroelectric power. The ancient Silk Road could be re-developed, a second Panama canal be built, the tidal currents of oceans be used as an energy source. Other projects could be the development of solar power or the irrigation of Africa's vast deserts. In many Latin American countries, for instance in Brazil, conditions for hydroelectric power production are excellent. If not within ten years, let us do it within twenty – this is the way the money saved by disarmament should be spent on long-term projects.

## The unity of the trade union front

At the moment, there are 70,000 trade unions in Japan, comprising almost 12.5 million workers. The proportion of organised workers is approximately 30 per cent. Between July and September of this year, my Institute for Social Problems of Asia conducted research into the amount of money workers spend as union dues. On average, each member pays 1.7 per cent of his monthly wage as union dues. If the annual dues of all Japanese unions are totalled, you get an amount of 500 billion yen.

Although the Japanese unions are such wealthy organisations, their social influence is only marginal, and they do not have the power to change current policies. The Japanese labour union movement is stagnating. The reason for its lamentable situation is its fragmentation into 74,000 enterprise or workplace unions. Moreover, the national umbrella organisations are divided. In order to revive the union movement, the democratic unions have to gain strength and formulate practical policies. They can gain strength by forming a united labour union front, and their practical policies must aim at improving working conditions within the framework of the existing economic situation. I advocated such measures as long as twenty years ago. Although the workers' demands and proposals may be justified beyond any doubt, as long as they do not have sufficient strength they will not succeed in pushing them through. We need a movement which unites first the unions of the private sector and later those of the public sector also. This movement was started with the establishment of Zenmin Rōkyō in December 1982.[9]

## Cooperative activities of the unions

Furthermore, the unions which receive such a large amount of money must improve the service they provide for their members. They must not limit their activities only to such matters as wage hikes, extra pay and union elections, but perhaps make a little contribution to the pension of a retired ex-member who for more than twenty years has faithfully paid his dues.

In comparison with unions of other countries, as far as cooperative activities are concerned the Japanese unions are lagging far behind. When I was in Switzerland, I met a union member who wore a golden badge on his shirt. I asked him, 'Everyone here has a silver badge, why do you have a golden one?' He answered, 'That's because I have paid union dues for 25 years.' I was surprised: 'What's so special about that?' He replied: 'If you have paid your dues for 25 years, after your retirement the union will pay you a maximum of 50 per cent of your pension. The golden badge shows that I have a right to such a pension.' In foreign countries, the unions are giving something in return to members who have paid their dues. This is of course only one example. But as union members have to worry about unemployment, illness and old age, it is quite important that the unions they belong to develop such cooperative activities. Otherwise, ordinary members will turn their backs on the unions, and they will lose their appeal.

## Final remarks

At the moment, only 60,000–70,000 of all Japanese union members belong to the Socialist Party of Japan. A further 70,000 are members of the Democratic Socialist Party. In Great Britain, with only half the population of Japan, the Labour Party has 6 million members, and the Social Democrats of West Germany count more than 1 million members. The Japanese progressive parties apparently are in no state to entice union members into contributing their money. Therefore the day on which the progressive parties will take over the government of Japan is still in the distant future. In order to change the current situation, the parties will have to regroup.

Recently an organisation called Zenmin Rōkyō has been established. This is a new movement which aims at strengthening and uniting the unions of the private sector. Under the motto 'Strength and Practical Policies', it is at the moment engaged in the process of bringing together 5 million members. Soon it will have the capacity to influence and change the political scene. But strength is a double-edged weapon. A movement without common sense, which tries to impose its will by force, should not be part of any government.

In recent times, the demands put forward by unions have changed from merely asking for higher wages to requests for secure employment. In my opinion, the Japanese unions will in the near future be less concerned with wage matters and increasingly confronted with the issue of unemployment. The union movement therefore must gain new strength and work out political proposals as a reaction to the breathtaking advance of technological development. And it must not forget to make an international contribution commensurate with Japan's role in the world.

## Notes

1. sen = a hundredth of a yen.
2. *Udon*: Japanese soup with buckwheat noodles.
3. *Futon*: Japanese mattress.
4. Chinese characters used in Japan usually have at least two pronunciations: a Japanese one (called the *kun* reading) and one borrowed from the Chinese original (*on* reading). The *on* reading of the first character 'Ō' of 'Ōmi' is 'kin'. The word '*kinken*' is made up of the

first character of 'Ōmi' and the first character of the word '*kenshi*' (silk thread).

5. The ancient name of Shiga prefecture is Ōmi.
6. This televised series about a country girl called Oshin who works in a spinning mill was shown in 1973.
7. Prime Minister at the time of the Ōmi strike (3rd cabinet).
8. *O-nigiri*: rice dumplings.

# 7 The Labour Conflicts of the Mitsui-Miike Coal Mines, 1959–60

*Kaoru Ōta*

**Kaoru Ōta**

1912 Born in Okayama prefecture on 1 January
1935 Graduated from the Faculty of Applied Chemistry of the Engineering Sciences Department of Ōsaka Imperial University; employed at the fertiliser plant of the Dainihon Tokkyo Hiryō Stock Company
1939 Left the company to join the Ube Nitrogen Factory of the Ube Kōsan Stock Company

Trade union functions

1946 Chairman of the Ube Nitrogen Factory Union
1949 President of the National Union Federation of the Ammonium Sulphate Industry; vice president of Zenka Dōmei (the National Union Federation of the Chemical Industry)
1950 Chairman of Gōka Rōren (the Japanese Federation of Synthetic Chemistry Workers' Unions) (until 1979)
1952 Vice chairman of Sōhyō (until 1958)
1958 Chairman of Sōhyō (until 1966)
1965 Received the Lenin Peace Award
Present Director of the Ōta Kaoru Institute

Publications

*Waga tatakai no kiroku* (Notes on Our Struggle), Akita Shoten, 1967
*Tenkanki no Nihon rōdō undō* (The Japanese Labour Movement in Times of Change), Heiwa Shobō, 1969
*Tatakai no naka de* (In the Midst of Battle), Aoki Shoten, 1971

*Yakunin o kiru* (Down with the Functionaries), Tōyō Keizai Shinpōsha, 1973
*Hibike rappa* (Trumpets Resound!), Nihon Keizai Shinbunsha, 1974
*Shuntō no shūen* (The End of the Spring Wage Offensive), Chūō Keizaisha, 1975
*Waga Miike tōsōki* (Notes on Our Miike Struggle), Rōdō Kyōiku Senta, 1978
*Kamitsu e no chōsen* (The Protest Against Overwork), Ningen no Kagakusha, 1978
*Yakunin o kiru II* (Down with the Functionaries, Part II), Tōyō Keizai Shinpōsha, 1984
*Kinben wa bitoku ka* (Is Diligence a Virtue?), Zenponsha, 1984

## I Editor's Overview

In 1960, the year in which the period of high economic growth reached its peak, a labour dispute occurred in the coal mines of the Mitsui company at Miike on the southern main island of Kyushu. This has been described as the greatest labour conflict of the Japanese post-war era. It coincided with the largest popular movement of the same era, the fight against AMPO. The Miike conflict was the last in a series of struggles of the management counter-offensive type and was characterised by attempts on the part of the managers to regain their entrepreneurial prerogatives by dismissing union officials. Faced with the ongoing decline of the coal mining industry, management planned adjustment measures which, as a precondition, required the destruction of the Miike union. At that time, the Miike union was regarded as the most powerful in Japan. In order to attain this goal, 2,000 persons were fired with the use of force, among them 300 union activists.

A labour conflict ensued which lasted 282 days and was later described as a 'confrontation between united capital and united labour'. During the dispute a second union was founded, and a number of incidents occurred which caught the attention of the public: there were brutal clashes between members of both unions, a member of the first union was stabbed to death by members of a group of armed thugs and so forth. The dispute ended in a bitter defeat for the union when its forces were depleted by the ebbing of the mass movement against AMPO, the withdrawal of Tanrō and the growing influence of the second union. As a result, the Japanese labour movement, which had overcome its stagnation after the red purges and had slowly gained strength, again suffered a severe blow. Since the end of this dispute, labour relations in Japan have remained firmly under management control.

## The 63-Day Strike

The company, Mitsui Mining, consisted of three mines on Kyushu (Miike, Tagawa and Yamano) and three on Hokkaidō (Sunagawa, Bibai and Ashibetsu); with 47,000 miners and 10,000 white-collar employees, it was the biggest mining company in Japan. In each of the coal mines, miners and employees established their own independent unions which were organised in two national organisations, Sankōren (the Mitsui Federation of Miners Unions) and Sansharen (the Mitsui Federation of White-collar Employees' Unions). The Miike union with 12,000 members formed the main force of Sankōren.

At first the union movement of the Mitsui coal mines followed a rather moderate course (except for the union of the Bibai mines which was a member of Zentan (the Industrial Union of Coal Miners), an organisation affiliated with Sanbetsu Kaigi). Moreover, the Miike union belonged to the right wing of the Japanese labour movement, which advocated a cooperative relationship between employers and employees. The Miike union first became active during the so-called 63-Day Strike in 1952. This conflict followed a decision by Sekitan Kōgyō Renmei (the Association of Coal Mining Companies) to cut wages. Tanrō organised a strike which lasted 63 days, but when the government announced a priority regulation based on the law regulating labour relations (abbreviated as the 'mediation law'), Tanrō was forced to accept a proposal mediated by the Central Labour Relations Commission and as a result suffered a severe defeat. During this dispute, Nihon Tankō Shufu Kyōgikai, abbreviated as Tanpukyō (the 'Collective Committee of Wives of Japanese Miners') was established, which was joined by 77,000 wives of coal miners throughout the country.

## The 113-Day Fight Without Heroes

In spite of the defeat in the 63-Day Strike, the Miike union intensified its activities. Supported by Itsurō Sakisaka, a professor of political economics of Kyushu University, it organised an education programme for the workers. In the Mitsui miners' residential areas, mutual aid groups, each consisting of five households, were formed for mutual assistance in everyday matters. Both measures had the aim of gathering strength for a massive conflict. On 7 August 1953, the company published its 'Guidelines for Rationalisation' which included the dismissal of 6,739 persons in the coal mining sector. This number was equivalent to 12 per cent of the workforce and included 2,771 workers at Miike alone. The fight against these rationalisation measures lasted 113 days until a settlement was reached on 27 December 1953. The management accepted the return of 1,841 persons who had refused to leave the company with severance pay. The conflict was called the '113-Day Fight Without Heroes' because the sacrifices and financial burden of the strike were equally shared by all union members. For the Sōhyō labour movement it marked a turning point which was characterised by the slogan 'From a fight led by officials to a struggle pursued by the masses'. The dispute also was the beginning of the strategy of 'struggles involving families and the neighbourhood' in which groups of Tanpukyō and neighbourhood groups of residential areas took an active role.

## The Miike labour conflict

On the face of it, the controversial aspect of this labour conflict was a wave of dismissals initiated by the management and against which the union offered resistance. But actually the main cause of the dispute was attempts by the management to assert its authority. Because of its victory in the fight without heroes, the union had gained confidence and began a 'workplace struggle' which concentrated on the two main issues of establishing a system of rotation and exercising production control. The system of rotation meant that the union controlled the periodical transfer of workers to other work areas in order to compensate for differences in wages due to assignment to certain lower-paid jobs. Production control here meant a system by which the workers could regulate their individual workload to adjust it to their own personal capacity for work. Both measures aimed at preserving the lives and improving the safety of the miners who had to do their job under very difficult conditions. The creation of an on-the-job organisation through which workers could determine their own workload and the adjustment of wages undoubtedly constituted a partial restriction of the management's prerogatives. Therefore management decided to fire those it saw as the active force behind the workplace struggle and intended to transform production into a sort of 'holy terrain' on to which no one had any right to trespass.

On 6 November 1959 Mitsui Mining informed the Miike union of its intention to fire 2,000 workers, among them 300 miners who were particularly active union members. The Central Labour Relations Commission on 12 November presented its first proposal for mediation which called for the maintenance of discipline in the workplace through cooperation between employees and employers, the implementation of production goals (which was tantamount to the abolition of production control and the system of rotation) and a personnel reduction through voluntary retirement from the company with severance pay. This so-called Nakayama proposal (named after the chairman of the Central Labour Relations Commission of that time, Ichirō Nakayama) was rejected both by the management and the union. On 11 December the company dismissed 1,297 persons, a move which was followed by lock-outs in all mines of the Miike mining area on 25 January 1960. Now the union called for an unlimited strike in all mines. At an extraordinary meeting of Tanrō it was decided that each member of the unions affiliated with Tanrō should contribute 600 yen in support of the Miike union's struggle.

However, the Miike union suffered from divisions in its own ranks. On 18 March Sansharen published a comment critical of the strategy of Tanrō and withdrew from this organisation, while within the Miike union itself a movement advocating the founding of a second union had grown and split off on 17 March. Then even Sankōren rejected a widening of the scope of the strike, and the Miike union became increasingly isolated. Consequently, on 26 March Tanrō decided to ask the Central Labour Relations Commission to try once again to mediate.

On the same day, management sent an order instructing 4,831 members of the second union to restart production. In this new situation, members of the second union began to attack pickets and committed other acts of violence while trying to enter the mines, and on both sides the number injured in such attacks grew. Then on 29 March a member of the Miike union, Kiyoshi Kubo, was stabbed to death by members of a gang of hired thugs. On the same day, the Central Commission, acting at the request of Tanrō, presented a second mediation proposal which called for the 'voluntary retirement of the affected workers' (the so-called Fujibayashi proposal). However, at a Tanrō congress from 9 to 16 April, no consensus could be reached on whether or not to accept the proposal. Sankōren pleaded for its acceptance, while Sōhyō firmly rejected it. Finally Tanrō decided to reject the proposal and Sōhyō declared its willingness to support each of the striking members with a payment of 50 yen per month. Throughout the country it organised 'associations for the protection of Miike'.

Now workers came from all over Japan to support the Miike miners. Each day a couple of thousand of them gathered for sit-ins and blockaded the pitheads, thereby preventing the transport of coal which was hauled by members of the second union. When the District Court of Fukuoka issued an injunction against these obstructions, a bitter fight for control of the pitheads ensued, involving 20,000 workers daily. On 19 July the authorities tried to enforce the injunction, and 20,000 pickets faced 10,000 policemen. A bloody battle was only narrowly averted by the Central Commission's announcement that it would try again to mediate. On 10 August it presented a third proposal, which in fact accepted the dismissals announced by the company and was even more disadvantageous to the union than the two earlier ones. But as the influence of the second union was steadily growing, and as even Tanrō was now prepared to go along with the proposal, the Miike union saw no alternative but to call off the strike and issue a declaration ordering its members to return to work. It had suffered a crushing defeat.

## II Lecture by Kaoru Ōta

In the previous sessions of this seminar, you have all heard lectures on labour conflicts given by various speakers. I myself have been the leader in more than thirty major strikes which each lasted more than a month. Even leading personalities of the labour movement normally have not led more than two or three big struggles. In this respect I, as one of the protagonists of the labour movement, differ from the other lecturers. On the basis of my own experiences I want to speak to you about the Japanese labour movement in general and about the labour disputes of Mitsui-Miike in particular.

## What are labour conflicts?

Let's begin by asking the question 'What are labour conflicts?' To give a somewhat simplified explanation, labour conflicts are activities with the aim of improving wages, working hours and conditions of the workers within a capitalist system. A capitalist will always try to keep wages as low as possible and to make his employees work long hours. If workers are not protected against such attempts, capitalists will reduce wages to such a low level that finally the workers will not be able to raise children any more. However, as this would mean that there would be no next generation of workers, the union law permits strikes as a preventive measure in order to ensure the reproduction of the workforce.

In recent times the Japanese population has stopped growing, hasn't it? This is because wages are no longer increased. People can afford to send only one child to high school, two children are already one too many. But in order to play it safe – it may happen after all that one child is killed, for instance in a road accident, which would create a gap – parents prefer to have two children. If the maximum number of children a family can afford is two and there are also people who do not want children at all, the population will slowly but steadily decrease. Because young people no longer want to have children, the average age of the population is rising. Young people prefer not to have children for economic reasons, because they cannot afford their high-school education. But again, if there isn't a certain number of children being born, the next generation of workers is missing, a factor which then will guarantee a certain level of wages.

Wages are usually determined according to the principle 'equal work – equal pay'. In Japan, however, wages are fixed according to the principle of seniority (wage according to length of employment). If for instance a West German, after having taken his O-levels, receives vocational training of three or four years, his wage will quickly increase, and the higher his qualification, the more money he gets. We can also see it this way: already after three or four years, his wages rise steeply, and if you draw a curve representing his wage in relation to the length of his working life, it will show rapid growth. But even in later years his income rises steadily, although not as rapidly, so that this curve will finally go down. If you compare this with the Japanese system of seniority wages, in which the wage level shows a steady but slow increase depending on length of employment, you will see that the total amount of money earned in a lifetime is higher in West Germany than in Japan. In other words, the Japanese system of seniority wages is a way of reducing lifetime earnings.

Strikes all concern such controversies as: 'You cannot lower wages any longer! If the pay doesn't go up, we won't sell our work to you anymore, and even if we refuse to sell it, this does not constitute a breach of the labour contract!' Because strikes are permitted by the law, they are a legal tool in the trading of the immaterial commodity, labour.

## Unions in Japan contrasted with unions abroad

However, even if you set out from this supposition, strikes in Japan are a controversial issue. Up to the level of department heads, all Japanese employees are union members, and this is why union splits occur every time a difficult struggle is in progress. There has hardly ever been a major labour conflict in this country which did not result in the division of the union involved. The reason for this tendency of unions to break apart is that Japanese unions have people among their ranks who simply do not regard themselves as union members. Those in somewhat senior positions, who in fact would like to belong to the management, immediately turn their coats if some manager comes along and tells them: 'Hey you, you'll become vice head of department soon, and later we'll make you department head!' There are always guys who think they can make a career out of licking the managers' boots, and because they tend to go over to the other side, you have a new union on your hands so fast that you never even see the vapour trail. If you see a Japanese union which has not gone through a split already, you start to think there must be something wrong with it.

Some days ago when I rode in a taxi I asked the driver, 'How much union dues do you have to pay?' He replied, '7,000 yen per month.' I went on: 'Say, your union is a yellow union, isn't it? So you might just as well leave it. Must be pretty annoying to be relieved of 7,000 yen every month.' 'You bet!' he said. 'So why don't you leave?' I asked him, and he answered: 'Because if you leave, the management won't like it a bit.' So this is what he said: if you leave the union, it's not the union that gets annoyed, it's the management! In Japan, management controls the workers with an institution which is called a union. Therefore you must not put Japanese unions on an equal footing with unions abroad.

To give you one example: in Italy, about 4.3 million employees are organised in the Italian Confederation of Labour, and about 2.5 million employees belong to unions which are affiliated with the Democrazia Cristiana (DC). These latter are unions which are just as conservative as those belonging to the LDP wing in Japan. If you deal with the capitalists, it's always better to be united, and therefore they thought of merging both federations into one organisation. As a condition for this merger, the unions of the Democrazia Cristiana demanded that anyone who belongs to the General Federation of Workers and at the same time is a member of a regional or the national parliament for the Communist or Socialist Party must give up his seat. They demanded this because of the strength of the Italian Communist Party: among the 4.3 million members of the Confederation of Labour there were approximately 1 million Communist Party members. Had the same thing happened in Japan, no one would have been forced to give up his seat in prefectural assemblies or the national parliament. In fact, more than half of all union officials chose their job exactly because they wanted to become members of parliament. In Italy, however, both members of the General Federation of Workers and of the DC wing gave up their seats and decided to serve the union movement, because they had become union officials in the first place in order to help the workers. In Japan, on the other hand, union officials who do their jobs only because they want to make a career are in the majority, and only a few of them lose any sleep over the workers' problems.

Therefore in Japan the Democratic Socialist Party and the Socialist Party receive contributions from the capitalists when elections are coming up. If a member of a foreign Communist or Socialist Party received money from the capitalists, he would be kicked out of the party. Social democracy in its essence has the goal of overcoming the inconsistencies of the capitalist system. It is simply absurd that those who want to overcome such inconsistencies from which the workers and the people as a whole suffer should accept money from the capitalists.

If you think about Japanese labour relations, you should never forget about these differences which emerge when you compare Japanese unions with their foreign counterparts.

## Strikes in Japan – strikes abroad

About ten years ago, the underground metro system in the United States suspended services for three weeks because of a strike. But no American got too excited. When after the Miike conflict I went to France, the taxi drivers had just gone on strike. In France, nobody got all worked up about it either. As it is the inalienable right of workers to go on strike in order to secure their livelihood, the people are prepared to accept a situation in which even the gas or the water supply is temporarily cut. Undoubtedly it causes some inconvenience if the public transport companies, the postal employees or other workers strike, but there is no other way to make the public aware of the importance of their work than stop it for a time and appeal for the sympathy of the people. If strikes as a means of defending one's own livelihood are widely accepted, you can speak of a firmly established sense of democracy.

If, however, in Japan a union has even a one-day strike, the papers carry screaming headlines and even people who do not really have to go to work suddenly want to go. It's just the same with my son. If I tell him, 'Today you don't really have to go to your company', he says, 'If I stay at home, I won't score with the management', and off he goes. Isn't it a complete nonsense? He might just as well take a day off. In foreign countries, people on such a day think, 'Hey, here we've got a good reason for staying at home.' Some contract workers of course have to go because they are paid by the day, but people with a fixed monthly income do not have to stay in a hotel[1] just because there is a strike, or do they? People who are so important that they have to spend their nights in hotels are very rare anyway.

In other countries a one-day strike would hardly be worth an extra article in the newspapers. In Japan it is good for a headline. If Kaoru Ōta was still chairman of Sōhyō and there was a strike, it would be one of unspecified duration! The Sōhyō officials of today do not want to do anything which lasts longer than 24 hours. And isn't it a fact that they seem to gain enough courage to call a strike only when the weekend is near or there are heavy snowfalls? The National Railway workers weren't much pleased when I told them, 'The unions of the National Railways – weaker than snow!' because they only do 24-hour strikes, but that's the truth after all. How can you bring the economy to a standstill with a strike of only one or two days? If you want to have higher wages but do not dare to organise a strike which might paralyse the Japanese economy, then you'll never succeed.

Taking these considerations into account, you may well ask yourselves whether Japan has experienced anything which by foreign standards could be called a strike at all. It would probably be more correct to say that there's hardly been such a strike so far. Well, that's about the size of it.

## The first labour disputes after Japan's surrender

After Japan's defeat in 1945, the Americans and the British thought that Japan, which after all had bombarded their fleets in Hawaii and Singapore and had advanced as far as Indonesia, was a powerful nation. During the occupation, the Allies therefore dismantled the big family corporations, the so-called *zaibatsu*, and the military cliques, the *gunbatsu*. They were determined to establish a democratic system. Because it is the civilian population which most of all suffers during a war, they were convinced that if politics in future depended on the will of the people, Japan would never start a war again. The occupation administration therefore wanted the workers to be in the vanguard of democratic development, and it favoured the founding of labour unions.

The national umbrella organisation Sōdōmei, which politically was close to the Socialist Party, received a lot of support in various ways from the occupation forces, because the unions affiliated with the Communist Party and belonging to the national centre Sanbetsu Kaigi were more influential than those of Sōdōmei. The mood among workers and other parts of the population during the war had shifted, turning against the violent oppression by the capitalists and the emperor system. After 1945, this changing mood gave rise to labour disputes with a political background. The Yomiuri and the Tōshiba conflicts were examples of such disputes during this era; they were different from the struggles which occur in normal times.

## The strikes of Tanrō and Densan in 1952

Shortly afterwards, labour disputes erupted in the coal mining and energy supply sectors. At that time, in the aftermath of the war, there was a serious rice shortage because the peasants, too, had been drafted for military service. The occupation authorities therefore concentrated their efforts on the development of coal mining, energy supply and the fertiliser industry; the latter was intended to increase rice production in order to accelerate the recovery of the Japanese industry. Coal mining companies, enterprises in the energy supply sector and fertiliser producers such as Ube Nitrogen where I myself was employed and which was part of the Ube Kōsan Stock Company, received subsidies on a large scale. Meanwhile, however, the rate of inflation had reached a high level, and Mr Dodge was sent over from America to introduce the so-called Dodge Line. With the implementation of this package of economic guidelines, all subsidies were cut. The management of the companies concerned reacted by claiming that because of the suspension of subsidies, wages could no longer be raised. This was the background of the 1952 strikes in the coal mining and energy supply industries.

The strike of Densan in fact was no real strike at all. Cutting the energy supply to households is no more serious a matter than if a child sulks a bit. Because the power supply of factories was not cut and production could go on without interruption, you cannot call the Densan action a strike. If they only switch off the power to family homes whose owners are not even involved in the dispute, but use electricity in their own homes for heating and cooking and taking a bath each day, then you cannot speak of a strike! At that time there was only one power producer in Japan, the Nihon Hassōden Stock Corporation, and therefore it was claimed that Densan was an industrial union. Later, however, the company was split up by the occupation administration and the government into nine regional units, i.e. independent companies. Because there were no big power plants on Shikoku, Kyūshū and Hokkaidō, the companies there incurred heavy losses, while those in Tokyo, in the Kansai and the Chūbu areas, made a profit. The union members of those profitable companies demanded higher bonus payments because, as they said, 'our company makes higher profits than the others'. Susumu Fujita (then chairman of Sōhyō) did not agree with these demands, but I told him: 'As long as only bonus payments are concerned, it doesn't matter so much if there is a wage differential. The wages and salaries aren't high enough to expect that the employees of these companies think about their colleagues in other firms. Therefore it's better to take what you can get.' But the union split over this issue, and Ryōsaku Sasaki, the former leader of the Democratic Socialist Party, created a second union.

Tanrō was also engaged in a dispute at that time. At first, the mine managers simply let the workers go on strike, and if they were confronted with a demand for higher wages, they used the subsidies paid by the government. But because those subsidies had been cut, the managers now claimed that further wage increases were impossible. However, living conditions of the coal miners were extremely poor, and therefore they decided to organise a nation-wide strike. In 1952, they launched a struggle which lasted 63 days. Because coal then accounted for about 80 per cent of the Japanese energy supply, train services had to be suspended and public baths were closed down, and this at a time when almost everybody still used the public baths. The strike thus created a social problem, and the Central Labour Relations Commission worked out an emergency regulation.

In my opinion, as long as there are still sufficient reserves of strength, a strike may go on as long as it takes to reach a solution, but in this instance Tanrō decided that after 63 days the workers were too exhausted to continue, and as a last resort they ordered the safety and maintenance personnel to leave the mines. For a labour movement engaged in a struggle, the withdrawal of these personnel was a fundamental mistake. It is the duty of any union to secure the employment of its members, and it is as clear as crystal that they need workplaces at which they are able to work. Withdrawing the safety and maintenance people meant that the mines would be flooded with water and production could not resume for a long time. Therefore 85 per cent of the unions affiliated with Tanrō rejected the withdrawal and decided to end the strike. In the end the settlement resulted in a 7 per cent wage increase and a non-recurring payment of 5,000 yen. Had the strike gone on, the chairman of the Central Labour Relations Commission, Ichirō Nakayama, would have agreed to a 10 per cent wage-hike.

## The labour dispute at the Ōmi-Kenshi Silk Mills of 1954

After this strike, the Japanese economy entered a more stable phase. Therefore one must differentiate between the earlier and the later strikes. The speaker before me was Mr Minoru Takita, who gave a lecture on the labour dispute of the Ōmi-Kenshi Silk Mills. Judged by international standards, this dispute cannot be called a major conflict. But during this strike Minoru Takita emerged as an outstanding union leader. I was then a member of the mediation committee of the Central Labour Relations Commission. While I, as chairman of Gōka Rōren (the Japanese Federation of Synthetic Chemistry Workers' Unions), was attending a congress of this industrial federation, representatives of the employers' associations and some corrupt committee members of Dōmei met and agreed to settle the dispute by paying only a small sum. Minoru Takita, however, immediately rejected this proposal. Suehiro Nishio and Komakichi Matsuoka who both belonged to the right wing of the Socialist Party then went to Minoru Takita and demanded that he put an end to the strike.

But what were the intentions of the Ōmi-Kenshi management? Well, they thought that the female workers of the Ōmi-Kenshi Silk Mills who mostly came from poor peasant families were obliged to bring home a little money for the *o-bon* festival,[2] and that therefore the whole strike would break down once *o-bon* drew nearer. The management in effect intended to get away by paying only a small sum and thus to put an end to the strike. But at this point in time Zensen Dōmei decided to support the female workers of Ōmi-Kenshi with a sum of a 100 million yen and pay each of them an '*o-bon* bonus'. The strike front thus remained intact, and by the end of August the Central Labour Relations Commission was again asked to submit a mediation proposal, whereupon the dispute could be concluded with a victory for the union. Being a committee member, I demanded a sum of 100 million yen as a payment for settling the strike, but

Ichirō Nakayama resisted: 'That's too much, you've got to go down a little.' So I answered, 'If that's so, I'll do as you say', and in the end the whole affair was settled at 95 million yen, which was a great victory for the workers.

Following the dispute, the left wing of the Sōhyō federation got together with elements who had been loyal to the company and tried to establish a second union. But I told them that they must not do this because it was important to maintain an organisation structured according to the industrial union principle, and I was able to prevent the split.

Minoru Takita also mentioned during his lecture that Dōmei had extended financial support during the Ōmi-Kenshi Silk Mill dispute, while Sōhyō on the other hand had not given any financial help during the Miike dispute, and after the strike the workers had been burdened with high debts. This is actually not the whole truth. The Ōmi-Kenshi Silk Mills employed only young female workers whose living costs were quite low. At Miike there were more than 10,000 employees, and the older ones mostly had families with on average four dependents, which is why their living costs amounted to a sizeable sum. If you compare the level of financial support, Ōmi-Kenshi received about 100 million yen, while Miike got 800 million. And at Miike even that was not enough. The scale of both conflicts was indeed very different.

Another important factor was that during both conflicts the capitalists of other companies did not prevent their workers from supporting the strike. In the case of the Ōmi-Kenshi Silk Mills the managers did not interfere because Ōmi-Kenshi was a second-rank company paying only low wages. Because personnel costs at Ōmi-Kenshi were so low, the bigger spinning mills were unable to compete with it. Therefore they had no reason to prevent their own unions from supporting the Ōmi-Kenshi workers.

The Miike dispute was a similar case. Working conditions at the Miike mines were better than in all the other mines in the country, and the coal mines of Kita-Kyūshū would have been unable to compete with Miike and would have gone bankrupt if the Miike union had become a yellow union and cooperated in an effort to raise productivity. But the militant Miike workers actively tried to prevent such a high level of productivity in order not to force the other mines to raise their productivity, too. Therefore the Kita-Kyūshū mines were not forced to enter the rat-race for higher productivity and all the other mines were not put out of business. The chairman of the Central Labour Relations Commission, Ichirō Nakayama, once told me: 'Colleague Ōta, if your union was a weak one, the Kita-Kyūshū mines would have gone bankrupt long ago. Thank God that your union is so militant.' This was the reason why the managers of other mines did not prevent their workers from supporting the Miike union. Nonetheless, it is also true that workers organised in the Sōhyō federation and union officials who led the female workers of the Ōmi-Kenshi Silk Mills stood firmly behind us, chanting slogans such as 'Victory for the Miike Workers' and 'Victory for the Ōmi-Kenshi Workers!'

## The 92-day strike of Kaiin Kumiai in 1972

The most impressive labour conflict in post-war Japan was probably the strike by Kaiin Kumiai in 1972 which lasted 92 days. The seamen fought for a two-day vacation each time the oil tankers stopped at a Japanese port. Because the tankers cast anchor for just one day, the seamen were unable to meet their wives. The capitalists rejected their demand out of hand, and this led to a 92-day strike. A stay of more than one day in port was unacceptable to the capitalists because they argued that the construction of new supertankers was so costly that loan interest payments led to extremely high costs. Therefore losses incurred by putting the tankers out of service for even a single day were unbearable. The shipowners wanted to use the tankers full-time. The wives of the seamen were furious. They were extremely frustrated because after a one-month voyage their men could not return to their homes even for a single day when they got back to Japan. In this struggle the families of the strikers were involved also. In the end the seamen were granted an additional paid holiday. You may think that it is somewhat extreme to call a 92-day strike for just one additional day off, but if you think about the labour movement in general, you will recognise that this is actually one of its central issues.

To give you an example, the working hours of engine drivers of the National Railways are currently five and a half hours per day. If you continue driving a train for a longer time, your physical and emotional capabilities will be reduced, because the train, having accelerated, travels at high speed. Therefore a time limit of five and a half hours has been introduced as an international standard. Nevertheless, Japanese regulations differ from those abroad. If you drive an express train in France, Italy or Germany for five and a half hours, the schedule provides that on the next day you can return to your family. In Japan, however, if an engine driver takes his train from Tokyo to, say, Kagoshima, the conductors and other train attendants, not to mention the driver himself, will not return home for four consecutive days. In foreign countries such a schedule would be unimaginable. Someone driving an express train abroad will, if not on the same day, at least on the next get back to his family. You apparently are not able to recognise the importance of this matter, but that only means that you do not have a modern point of view yet! You have not asked yourselves yet, 'What is man?' so I have to say something about culture at this point. The only difference between human beings and animals is the fact that human beings have a cultural life! But we, the Japanese – aren't we somehow more like animals than humans?

In Tokyo, a taxi driver leaves his home at eight o'clock in the morning, and if business is good, he will have a monthly net income of 300,000 yen. Is there any other country in which a taxi driver has to work from early in the morning until late at night? Certainly not in Europe, and I don't think in South-East Asia either. The labour movement must think about such matters. It should be normal for everyone to work for eight hours, to have eight hours in which to do as one pleases – cultural activities, if you like – and to sleep for eight hours.

But among the Japanese, are there even 10 per cent who are able to live such a life? Hardly so. And that's strange for a country which is considered to be the second largest economy in the world. If it really is such a prosperous economy, its workers should be permitted to enjoy a correspondingly fulfilled cultural life. But among Japanese workers there is hardly anyone who can live in a way which would deserve to be described as a 'cultural life'. If you take that into account, you will agree with my opinion that the seamen's strike was a marvellous thing indeed.

## The Mitsui-Miike labour conflict – its causes

The labour dispute at Miike developed in a situation in which the supply of cheap crude oil from Arab countries became more and more efficient and coal from mines such as the Japanese, which were no longer economically viable, was no longer competitive. Nevertheless, the militant workers of the Miike mines decided not to go on working if their safety in the mines was not guaranteed. This was the main issue of controversy during the workplace struggle at Miike. The more coal you produce, the higher the danger of collapsing tunnels. In order to prevent the tunnels from caving in, wooden support beams are used – nowadays they use iron beams – and the miners declared that they would not enter the mines if places where the tunnels were in danger of caving in were not secured with additional beams. As a result of their protest, the average number of people dying in collapsing tunnels each year was reduced from thirteen to one. If you lead such a fight at the workplace, the safety of the workers will increase, but productivity surely will not. So the management decided to fire all of the activists who had led this workplace struggle.

To clarify: this struggle did not develop because the Miike union was the strongest miners' union. In the mines of Kita-Kyūshū, there were a number of unions more powerful than that of Miike, notably that of the Kineshima mine at Saga and that of the Nittan-Takamatsu mine, and others too. But if you pursue such a fight for better safety standards too energetically, the management inevitably oppose the workplace struggles with the argument that costs resulting from increased safety procedures would render coal production unprofitable. Thus even for strong unions there is a limit to how far they can go with a workplace struggle for better safety.

At Miike, the conditions in the mines were so favourable that you could win the coal not merely by manual hewing, but also using machines. When producing coal with machines, there must be thick layers of coal above and below the tunnel. But you can never be sure when the whole thing might cave in, so workers, particularly those with families, felt threatened by the hazardous working conditions. With the Miike union growing strong, however, their fears subsided. The activists of the workplace struggle therefore enjoyed the complete trust not only of the miners themselves, but also of their family dependants. Because the company now intended to fire just these activists, a dispute developed.

At that time I was chairman of Sōhyō. Because of the ongoing replacement of coal by crude oil, I did not really approve of strikes in mines with a low level of productivity. As it was evident that mines with such inferior conditions as those in Japan would inevitably lose out against the competition if more cheap crude oil was imported, I was more in favour of creating a new law more effective than the existing one on the re-employment of dismissed workers and redeploying the workforce of unprofitable mines. As chairman of Sōhyō, I communicated my views to the chairman of Tanrō, Mr Shigeru Hara.

## The mediation by the Central Labour Relations Commission (headed by Mr Nakayama) fails

As a serious labour conflict was imminent, the chairman of the Central Labour Relations Commission tried to mediate. His proposal called on the company to retract the individual dismissals by which the management sought to get rid of workplace activists and contained an appeal to the workers to opt for voluntary retirement. The Commission intended to find a compromise if the number of workers willing to retire was lower than the company wished. Ichirō Nakayama also confirmed that if his proposal was accepted, there would be no forced dismissals. However, I didn't know this because Mr Shigeru Hara from Tanrō failed to inform me in time. Had I known it, I would have gone along with the proposal. But Tanrō refused to accept it.

About half-way through the strike, I held an extraordinary meeting of Sōhyō; at this meeting we decided to extend financial support to the strikers, with about 100 yen to be paid by each Sōhyō-affiliated union member. During this meeting it was claimed that Miike had the strongest union in Japan and that many of its activists were also members of the Socialist Party of Japan; a defeat in this strike might well ruin the whole Japanese labour movement. If each Sōhyō member gave 100 yen in support of the strike, this would amount to a total of 400 million yen (each member of Sōhyō gave up his summer bonus of 100 yen and from August onwards contributed 50 yen per month). Tanrō chairman Hara reacted by saying: 'If we receive 400 million yen, we cannot lose!' But we all were too optimistic, including myself. A union must preserve the living conditions of workers, and if the funds for a strike run low, especially if there isn't enough money to buy food for the strikers, you are in deep trouble. The unions in Germany or in England have lots of money, but we do not.

## The founding of a second union

Because the Miike union had already gone on strike several times, their war chest was soon depleted. In 1952 it had led a strike of 63 days. Afterwards each new wave of rationalisations had been accompanied by a strike. In 1953 the company adopted plans for a rationalisation which also entailed a personnel reduction. The Miike union together with the miners of Sankōren organised the so-called '113-Day Strike Without Heroes'. But on the one hand there was no special fund for the workers, while on the other hand the cohesion of Sōhyō was too weak to provide any additional financial assistance to the striking workers. Therefore the union decided to reduce the scale of the struggle and called a strike only in the conveyor section.

The union members of Miike as well as their families put a great deal of trust in the active union officials who led the workplace struggle to secure the livelihood of the workers. But unfortunately the executive members of the Miike union did not have the same degree of trust in their followers. For instance, at a crisis meeting the people who later formed a second union asked the central committee of the Miike union to put an end to the strike, and although they wanted to have a secret ballot on this demand by all union members, the executive committee paid no attention to this motion, suppressed the proposal and rejected a secret ballot. Had I been in a position to decide in this matter, I would have taken a secret vote, because if you don't have the support of the majority of workers, you cannot go on with a strike. Had about two-thirds of the workers declared their support, the strike would have continued. But with less than half of them willing to go on, there would have been no option but to end the strike, because otherwise the union would break apart.

Because in Japan all employees are members of enterprise unions, you never know when a union will break apart. Thus the members' opinions should be heard as often as possible. At Miike they were not asked about their ideas. This was one of the critical issues. Had I been chairman of Tanrō, I would have ordered a secret ballot. The chairman of the newly established second union wanted to take a secret vote and went to the former Tanrō chairman, Noboru Agune, who himself came from Miike and later became a delegate to the Upper House for the Socialist Party. Noboru Agune agreed with him, but the leader of the Miike union, Shigeru Kaibara, and other left-wing members autocratically decided to continue the strike. Because the managers exerted pressure on the employees with their claims that the company would go bankrupt if the strike went on, a second union split off.

Already, well in advance of this event, influential Sōhyō organisers had informed me of the fact that the founding of a second union was imminent. When I went to the headquarters of Tanrō and told them that because of the imminent division of the union it would be better to come to an agreement on resuming production and reach a settlement which meant real protection of the miners' lives underground, they told me: 'There will be no second union because the Miike union is too strong, and you, Ōta, have lost your marbles.' Ten days later they had a second union on their hands. Although it now existed, there was still a chance of continuing the fight. In 1960, coal still accounted for 60 per cent of Japanese energy consumption. Had Tanrō called a strike in all mines throughout the country, it would have won.

Originally there had been a strategy for the Miike struggle according to which Miike should first start a strike against dismissals. Then Sankōren planned to join in, and in the end all miners' unions would begin strike action in the *shuntō* (spring) wage offensive. However, first Sankōren dropped out. Only the Miike union went on strike, but the others failed to join in, because Mitsui, Mitsubishi and Sumitomo competed with each other in the coal mining industry. It was believed that if only the Mitsui miners went on strike, Mitsui would be defeated in the competition with Mitsubishi and Sumitomo and might possibly go bankrupt.

During the spring wage offensive in 1960 the Central Labour Relations Commission acted as mediator in the wage struggle of Tanrō. Within two days it successfully concluded its mediation attempt. The mining company managers, the union officials and the representatives of the Central Commission had already come to an agreement before the wage offensive had started. Normally, in a struggle such as that of the miners it takes a month before the Central Commission achieves a successful mediation. But in 1960 it took only two days to find a compromise and end the general strike of all enterprise unions of the mining industry. Afterwards the chairman of the city council of Ōmuta, who was a member of the Socialist Party, began building up a second union. Within the Miike union, he secured the support of the union's local offices at Mikawa, Yotuyama and Miyaura, and outside the mines the harbour office, which supervised the loading and shipment of coal, as well as five section groups in the offices of the Mitsui Mining headquarters which decided to support him. The Ōmuta city council man was also the boss of the Yotuyama union local, and managed to boost membership of the second union from its initial 3,000 to 4,000. In the end, of 13,000 members of the Miike union, 10,000 were prepared to join the second union, and the Miike union was left with only 3,000 members.

## The incident in which Kiyoshi Kubo was stabbed to death

Both at Sōhyō headquarters and at Tanrō we arrived at the conclusion that the time was ripe to put an end to the strike. Shinzō Shimizu (later to become a professor at Shinshyū University) was an adviser to Sōhyō, and because he had also advised the activists in the Miike struggle, he flew to Kyushu on our behalf to persuade the strikers to break off their struggle. Furthermore, Mr Shigeru Hara, the chairman of Tanrō, took the 4.00 p.m. express train 'Sakura' to Ōmuta. But on that very same day at five o'clock in the afternoon, a member of the first union, Kiyoshi Kubo, was murdered by a group of armed thugs hired by the company. Because one of their colleagues had been murdered, even members of the second union were seething with rage and loudly protested against 'those damned fools of the management'. Of 10,000 workers who had originally opted for the second union, 7,000 now returned to the first. This turn of events certainly was brought about by mere chance, and had Kiyoshi Kubo not been murdered, management would have won a great victory. I, as chairman of Sōhyō, would then have been forced to step down, and whether there would have been such a massive resistance against AMPO, I cannot say . . .

Recently I read the novel *Saka no ue no kumo* (Clouds Above the Hills) by Ryōtarō Shiba. Shiba writes that during the sea battles in the Sea of Japan, victory was achieved only through a combination of many coincidences. Nevertheless, Japan did actually beat the Baltic Fleet of the Czar! If Japan had lost at that time, there probably would not be a country called Japan today. 'Lucky chances' thus do occur, but only as long as people are prepared to put up a real fight. If they do not do anything, there will be no coincidences either.

## Failure of the mediation by the Central Labour Relations Commission (headed by Mr Fujibayashi)

When they heard that Kiyoshi Kubo had been murdered, the workers really blew their tops. It was simply impossible to go on as if nothing had happened. Because there was no way to ignore the matter, Mr Shigeru Hara, the chairman of Tanrō, called me. He wanted me to talk to the members of the Central Labour Relations Commission and ask them not to submit another mediation proposal. Because the union would have lost face had Shigeru Hara failed, I called Ichirō Nakayama and Keizō Fujibayashi of the Central Commission. What I did not know was that in the meantime Tanrō had turned around and officially asked them to mediate.

So I went to a big and elegant restaurant at Yotsuya-Mitsuke called 'Fukuda-ya' where Ichirō Nakayama was already waiting for me. He said: 'Hey, Ōta, you've come because you've heard about the request by Tanrō for a mediation, haven't you?' Being the chairman of Sōhyō, I could not simply say that I did not have a clue, so I answered: 'Yes, I've come because I heard about that', and he resumed: 'Why shouldn't we make a mediation proposal when they've asked us to do so?' 'Hmm, you know, a worker has been murdered, and at this stage a mediation wouldn't get us anywhere', I replied. These words of mine made a bad impression with the Central Commission, a fact which they often made me feel aware of afterwards.

The managers were already sure the second union would carry the day and so none of them was interested in a mediation by the Central Labour Relations Commission. I believe that Ichirō Nakayama asked the company to take a cooperative line concerning mediation in order not to annoy the union by adding insult to injury, and as a quid pro quo he would make a proposal which would accept the planned individual dismissals. Then even the management relented and said it was prepared to go along with mediation, but just as the Central Commission wanted to present its proposal, Kiyoshi Kubo was murdered and the workers mounted the barricades. When Tanrō suddenly again refused to consider a mediated proposal, the various statements made began to contradict each other. Nakayama even went to meet people of the higher echelons of Mitsui Mining, up to the president of the Mitsui Bank, Kiichirō Satō, and pleaded with them not to force the union into a further loss of face, as it had already suffered a serious defeat.

## The meeting of Tanrō: the decision to continue the strike

The rage of the workers after the murder of Kiyashi Kubo had not abated, so I decided to go on with the strike. The chairmen of Nikkyso (the Japan Teachers' Union), Kokurō and other national union federations advised against continuing the struggle, because further financial support was not possible. It was not the workers who said they could not go on, it was the union officials! Because the workers did not come to me with demands for mediation, I decided to continue. Tanrō chairman Shigeru Hara and other officials, however, wanted an end of the dispute. Therefore an extraordinary meeting of Tanrō was convened at which the general secretary of Sōhyō headquarters, Akira Iwai, and I as Sōhyō's chairman, were also present. Because Shigeru Hara favoured an end of the struggle and I the opposite, we agreed to speak neither for nor against the strike. But because I never can hold back my tongue, I carefully prepared a manuscript for my opening speech in which I neither advocated nor rejected a continuation. I had never prepared a speech of mine by working out a manuscript beforehand, and I have never done it again. Because the conference was organised by Tanrō, Hara was the first to speak, and contrary to our agreement he clearly indicated his intention to call off the strike. When I took the floor, I threw away my manuscript and told the audience: 'Let's go on!!' The discussions went on for eight days until finally a decision to continue the strike was reached. Tanrō advocated a quick settlement, but now that we had gone so far, I was in favour of an unlimited strike.

## Interim order: the pickets must be called back

The second union now mobilised approximately 5,000 of its members who tried to break through the picket lines. (The first union still had 8,000 members.) Once they had got through, they entered the mines. They had arrived by boat from Ariake Bay, and our pickets had to give up. Therefore each day Sōhyō mobilised 20,000 people who came from all over Japan. The number of policemen was about 10,000. If you take all of those people together, regardless of whether they were policemen or union members, there were more people involved than during the Seinan uprising, when Takamori Saigō[3] entrenched himself on Kagoshima. It was Ichirō Nakayama who made this calculation. However, the courts stepped in and issued an interim order which ordered the pickets at the pitheads to retreat. Had a violent confrontation between the police and the strikers erupted at this stage, up to 3,000 persons on both sides might have lost their lives and countless others would have been injured. In the struggle headquarters we heard that the zeal of the strikers who manned the picket lines was difficult to control, but as far as I know they must have been trembling with fear. Later some of them told me that they had been scared stiff. Because the Head of the National Police Forces finally declared there would be a catastrophe if nothing was done, the Central Labour Relations Commission again went in and tried to mediate.

But now the events converged with the fight against the Security Treaty. In this struggle against AMPO – just as the Miike struggle reached its climax – a couple of hundred thousand workers demonstrated in front of the parliament in Tokyo. Prime Minister Nobusuke Kishi, who was utterly surprised by this mass movement called the police, and then pushed the vote on the Treaty through parliament. Immediately afterwards his cabinet had to resign, because the people were outraged by Kishi's action which they regarded as an offence against parliamentary democracy. Hayato Ikeda became the new Prime Minister, and he chose a more conciliatory approach. His advisers from the top business associations and the police came to a joint evaluation of the situation, and they were convinced that mediation was inevitable. I was coming to believe that everything I did turned out wrong. But because Sōhyō would never again have been able to issue a mobilisation order if only one of the workers were to be injured or even killed, I thought it better not to risk any more sacrifices, now that a defeat seemed unavoidable.

At Miike, I was responsible for 20,000 workers who came from all industrial areas. I simply could not risk putting even one of them in danger of being injured. After all, a union has to protect the lives of the workers. Well, if a confrontation with the police leads to an outbreak of revolution, you must not be too pusillanimous, but otherwise you have to obey the rule: only go as far as will not endanger someone's life. Therefore I had no choice but to agree to mediation. When all of the other officials from Sōhyō and elsewhere told me 'Now it's enough!', I ordered the Miike union to suspend the strike.

The picket-line leader was a guy called Fujio Wakamatsu. He was a man like a bear, with a chest as strong as a barrel. When the police units had advanced to a distance of only 1 kilometre, he may have thought, 'Ōta will stop them.' But as he told me later, when the police suddenly turned their backs and marched off, he only thought, 'Phew, I got lucky again! Had the police units advanced any further and had it come to a confrontation, they might have given me a jail sentence of more than ten years for committing a breach of the public peace.'

## Rishokusha Koyō Hō (The Law on Re-Employment of Dismissed Employees)[4]

The Miike labour dispute thus ended in a failure, and the union was forced to agree to a very disadvantageous arbitration. When Tanrō gave up, it had to consent to a mediated proposal which sanctioned the dismissal of all of the individuals the company wanted to get rid of. Even Ichirō Nakayama was unable to persuade the company to take a more conciliatory course with regard to the Miike workers. But I did not learn about these aspects until some time later.

The impact of the Miike struggle, which ended in such a debacle for the Japanese labour movement and also for the political development of Japan, becomes clearer if you take the following facts into account. Until that time there had been no institution in Japan which looked after those who lost their jobs in a structural recession. When, for instance, coal was replaced by crude oil or the rearing of silkworms became unprofitable because Chinese and Korean silk was cheaper, the people who were put out of business by such structural changes of industry were completely without protection. In such a situation, you can strike as long as it pleases you, but you will not halt the change. There is no such thing as a capitalist who produces goods which do not yield a profit. In such a case offering resistance is useless. But at this time the government suddenly came to the conviction that, as in England where mines with low productivity were being closed, Japan, too, should have a system of unemployment benefits and a fund for those who were dismissed.

Because I knew that more than half of all Japanese mines would go bankrupt because of low productivity and increasing imports of crude oil, I had made a proposal in the Consulting Committee on Employment Matters – an advisory body established by the government – to pass a law which made it possible to provide several years of retraining for dismissed employees and then to obtain new jobs for them. The capitalists as well as the government had rejected my proposal, but because of the Miike labour dispute, each fired employee cost the company 6 million yen.

## Enthusiastic struggle against the Security Treaty

The Miike labour conflict also had a political dimension. In 1960 there was a mandatory revision of AMPO. Already one year earlier, the Socialist Party, the Communist Party and Sōhyō had jointly begun organising an opposition movement against AMPO. Although rallies were held each month, only about 10,000 people showed up. On the other hand, the Miike struggle rapidly intensified. Workers and other employees from all over Japan gathered in Miike, went back home, travelled to Miike again, and so on. Altogether more than 100,000 people actively supported the Miike workers. All of these people witnessed the Miike struggle with their own eyes and experienced the cruelty of what is referred to as 'the logic of capital'.

While the fighting spirits of the workers rose, the struggle against AMPO gained momentum, too. In modern industrial nations wage workers form the majority of the population. Hence a movement of progressive forces will become an influential factor only if the labour movement is involved also. A struggle led only by politically progressive forces will never succeed. If fears over employment and living conditions are mounting, workers become militant. And this is what happened at this time: because the labour movement received such a strong impetus, the fight against AMPO also intensified. The scale of this struggle widened to such an extent that the industrial federations of the unions of private railway and bus companies as well as Kokurō decided to go on strike, and even though there were huge demonstrations on the Ginza, nobody complained about them. Dismayed by this extensive mobilisation of ordinary workers, Prime Minister Nobusuke Kishi spoke of a terrible state of affairs and forced AMPO through parliament. However, soon afterwards he had to step down and was replaced by Hayato Ikeda and his new cabinet.

## The enterprise as a 'community of fate'

For the progressive forces of Japan as well as for the labour movement, the Miike struggle was of great importance, as also were the labour conflicts of the *Yomiuri* newspaper, the Densan struggle in the power supply sector, the labour dispute of the Ōmi-Kenshi Silk Mills and the fight of the seamen. The Ōmi-Kenshi dispute was of special relevance because it put an end to the blatant violation of the human rights of the employees, the traditional 'sad story of factory girls'[5] which still continued after the war. And the struggle of the seamen's union assumed a similar importance because its participants also fought for humane living conditions. The Miike struggle is of historic relevance in the sense that it became the nucleus of a nationwide campaign to protect the lives of wage-dependent workers, helped to establish an epoch-making social security system and promoted the fight against the Security Treaty in which workers from all over Japan took part.

In spite of these successes, the current labour movement shows a tendency towards the political right and has reached an impasse. This development is mainly caused by the fact that Japanese enterprises have become 'communities of fate'. That's because both before and since the Pacific War Japan has never experienced a shortage of labour. Only at one stage during the period of high economic growth were there not enough young workers, but the starting wages paid to new company employees were used as a lever, and throughout Japan the wages of employees who belonged to either Zenkoku Kinzoku (the Industrial Union of Metal Workers) or Denki Rōren (the Federation of Unions of Electrical Machinery and Instruments) rose. Initially this was the case for the wages only of new employees, while those of older workers remained the same, because there were plenty of them. So in Japan there has never been a real shortage of labour. Moreover, before the war and under the Emperor system labour unions were banned. Both factors combined were the cause for the continuing low level of wages in Japan. If there is a surplus of workers, it is better to be hired by one of the big companies. And because wages rise according to the seniority principle, a worker will receive less money if he changes his employer. I, for example, graduated from university in 1935 and began working for a company. When in 1939 I gave up my job after a quarrel with one of the managers, the wage of my former student colleagues who were of the same age as myself was 110 yen. In my new company, I only received 100 yen. Although I worked in a factory producing sulphuric acid and as an engineer was familiar with advanced technology, I received 10 per cent less than they did. It is precisely because of such conditions that Japanese enterprises have become 'communities of fate'.

## The weakness of enterprise unions

It is often said that Japanese employees are group oriented, while Americans are individualistic. However, Japanese workers do not feel a tie to the Japanese nation as a whole, but only to their companies. If competition among companies is as bitter as it is today, workers start to fear that their own company might lose against its competitors if they go on strike, and therefore they do not dare to do such a thing.

In Europe and the United States, unions are organised horizontally, i.e. they are industrial unions. If a company plans to introduce new machines as a rationalisation measure, the workers are able to oppose such plans because it could lead to the dismissal of highly qualified colleagues. But in Japan, the enterprise unions do not offer any resistance at all. For instance, a short while ago the *Yomiuri* and the *Asahi* newspapers completely scrapped the work done by typesetters. Because electronic word processing systems were introduced and the former printing process was abolished, all typesetters were transferred to other occupations. In other countries, for instance at the *Washington Post* and the *New York Times*, employees fought against the abolition of the typesetters' occupation over a period of more than a year. At *The Times* in London, half of the typesetters were permitted to remain, while the other half were made redundant by computer-controlled typesetting machines. Nevertheless the workers went on strike. This is how workers abroad offer resistance. Japanese workers would not dare to act like their foreign colleagues.

To give you one more example: about ten years ago when the Japanese shipbuilding industry overtook its English counterpart and became the strongest in the world, Italian, French and English dock workers made serious accusations against the Japanese labour movement. Formerly, iron sheets used in shipbuilding were joined by rivets. When this method was replaced by welding, the English riveters opposed it, and being members of an industrial union with a national organisation, they brought the whole shipbuilding industry to a halt. But in Japan, the riveters were workers employed by subcontractors, and they could not offer the same degree of resistance. Just recently when there was an accident at the Ariake mine of Mitsu-Miike,[6] half of the victims were seasonal workers employed by subcontractors. Such subcontractor employees can be fired by their companies at any time. Thus the Japanese shipbuilding industry was able to switch over to the welding technology without delay, overtake the English and become the No. 1 in the world. Here we find the main reason for Japan's rise to the status of an economic superpower on a global level. Well, South Korea is catching up and will eventually overtake the Japanese shipbuilding industry. Welding operations in automobile construction can be done by robots, but in shipbuilding this is not possible. Moreover, the wages of Korean workers are far lower than those of the Japanese, and Koreans, too, are willing to work long hours.

In Japan, Company B will lose in the competition against Company A if it does not introduce the same new technology Company A has just introduced. Hence new technologies spread very fast. Japanese unions are in no position to prevent companies from using them. If a worker opposes a new technology, he will simply be fired. There is nothing which could prevent Japanese companies from making use of the latest technological innovations. In Western Europe, unions strongly oppose new technologies, and their introduction has been considerably slowed. This difference between Japan and Europe leads to a difference in productivity. The rise of Japan to become a global economic power therefore cannot be attributed to the great performance of Japanese managers, but only to a lack in strength of the Japanese workers and their unions.

Now you will ask why it should be necessary to put up a fight against technological innovations. Well, of course the pride of people who for ten or fifteen years have worked as highly qualified turners, typesetters or welders suffers when they suddenly have to work on assembly lines. Just imagine: a profession you have been working in for a very long time is suddenly eradicated. This must be a blow to your pride! To a worker, his qualification means everything. If it is suddenly of no value, the meaning of his life is gone.

## Is diligence a virtue?

The Japanese tend to believe that because we have neither oil nor much coal or iron ore, the nation would perish if everyone did not work as hard as he can. This notion and a feeling of inferiority with regard to white Americans and Europeans, make the Japanese think they have to work like crazy. By promoting this variety of nationalism and by portraying the company as a community of fate, the yellow unions have widened their influence in the Japanese labour movement.

The proportion of labour costs in the production of a car in Japan is one third of that in the United States. This is because in the Japanese automobile industry more than half of all parts are manufactured by workers employed by subcontractors. The average monthly wage of these workers is 100,000 to 150,000 yen. Since this is not enough to live on, people have to work overtime. Because there are so many competing parts manufacturers, workers are immediately fired if they accidentally produce defective parts. To a worker, this pressure to produce only perfect parts is extremely stressful. To make only absolutely perfect parts, he must use all of his knowledge and abilities. But paying close attention to his work at all times puts a lot of stress on his nerves. Physically hard labour has all but disappeared in Japan, but mental work, with its corresponding mental fatigue and occupational diseases such as nervous disorders has increased, or hasn't it? Just imagine doing such a job each and every day! People are simply alienated from themselves. So on the way home they drink a glass of beer or sing songs in karaoke bars, because only then they can become normal human beings again. That's the situation of Japanese workers and white-collar employees. It's got nothing to do with the often praised 'diligence of the Japanese'. Having been a production worker myself, and as a long-time active member of the union movement, I know this from my own experience. They all work so hard only because they fear unemployment, and they all suffer from the stress of their living conditions.

To my mind, this leads to a disadvantage for the European and American workers who know what a culturally fulfilled way of life means; they are handicapped by their Japanese colleagues who do not. What will the effects of this disadvantage be? After all, video recorders and high-quality cameras are bought by American and European workers with their high wages. But if their wages do not increase and they lose their jobs because of the unfair Japanese competition, who is going to buy all the stuff? I believe that here we will find a limit to Japanese economic development. Moreover, there can be no doubt that countries such as Korea or Taiwan will catch up with Japan, and even though the Japanese may work as hard as they can, the Chinese and the Vietnamese are excellent workers, too. Imagine what would happen if they also started working like hell! Then the Japanese can stand on their heads if they like, but it will not do them any good!

The Japanese yellow unions thus contribute to the destruction of culture in the world. They accept that highly trained workers have to work long hours at low wages, that their qualifications remain unused and their personal pride is hurt. As a result, Japan enjoys a competitive advantage on the world markets. As unions have the task of securing a dignified life for their members, they must insist that if a change occurs in the professional fields of their members, this change does not happen overnight. If management wants to implement such changes at short notice and unions tolerate such measures, one may well ask whether they can really be described as unions. The union leaders may gather as often as they like and speak about a united labour front, but to ordinary workers their speeches are completely irrelevant. Plus 1 multiplied by 100 is 100, but minus 1 multiplied by 100 is minus 100, that's how it is. This is the truth about what today is commonly referred to as the 'united labour front'!

When I used to think about how to organise our spring wage offensive,[7] I always arrived at the conclusion: let's send the strong guys, the workers from the strong unions to the front, then combine our forces and find a solution which benefits all of us. This is what we called a wage offensive. But because among the unions of today there are too many who simply remain standing in the background, no one thrusts forward any more. If the results of such behaviour concerned only Japan, it would not be all that bad, but because these practices create problems for workers all over the world and cause unemployment among them, they simply cannot be tolerated any longer.

## The end

If you look at opinion polls in the newspapers, more than 70 per cent of the Japanese population are against a change of the constitution. This is proof of the common sense of the people. Our people have clearly grasped that the economy has grown so strong because Japan has not spent any money on preparing for war. Currently, world-wide military expenditures are in the range of $700 billion. This is two and a half times the amount of the annual national budget of Japan. If you spend that much money on unprofitable goods, the world cannot become a prosperous place.

Because of a structural crisis of the capitalist system, world-wide unemployment figures are on the rise. In the United States 8.5 million people are out of work, and 6 million of them can be counted among the long-term unemployed. The number of people out of job in Western Europe has passed the 10 million mark and the figure will rise further by a couple of million. Altogether, in the industrialised nations about 40 million people are unemployed. Because the population of all of these countries taken together is about 800 million and the average family consists of three persons, a figure of 40 million unemployed means that one in eight workers is out of work. The inconsistencies of the capitalist system are plainly visible.

But although workers are confronted with such a difficult situation, there is no sense of solidarity among them. The world labour movement is divided into the International Confederation of Free Trade Unions of the Western world and the World Federation of Trade Unions of the Soviet Union and the Eastern bloc countries. However, within the International Confederation of Free Trade Unions there are many who believe that it does not matter how long the hours are that the Japanese have to work and how low their wages are, but that as long as Japan remains an anti-communist country, everything will be all right. Because of this point of view, the Japanese anti-communist yellow unions have been allowed to become a stumbling block for workers in Europe and the United States.

The most important goal today must be to create real international solidarity among the workers, regardless of ideological differences, in order to overcome the world-wide problem of unemployment and to achieve an improvement in working conditions.

## Notes

1. When a strike affects the commuter system, many Japanese employees do not go home after work but rather spend the night in a hotel.
2. *O-bon*: Buddhist Festival of the Dead (14–16 August).
3. In 1877, the samurai Takamori Saigō on Satsuma (now known as Kagoshima) led an uprising against the central authorities in resistance to the reforms at the beginning of the Meiji era.
4. Kaoru Ōta simplifies the name of this law. Its full name was: Temporary Special Law on Dismissed Employees of the Coal Mining Industry (*tankō rishokusha rinji sochi hō*). However, this law of 15 October 1959, which covered only the re-employment of coal miners, became the basis for the later Law on Employment Policies of 1966.
5. These words refer to the deeply moving social report *The Sad Story of Factory Girls* (Jokō aishi) by Wakizō Hosoi (1925), in which he describes the situation of female workers in the Japanese cotton industry.
6. On 18 January 1984, a faulty conveyor caused a fire in one of the tunnels of the Ariake mine in Fukuoka prefecture; eighty-three workers died of carbon monoxide poisoning. A later investigation

reveals that safety procedures were inadequate and fire warning systems had been out of operation.
7. Ōta and Iwai began the union strategy of spring wage offensives in 1955.

# 8 The Labour Conflicts of the All-Japan Seamen's Union, up to 1972

*Kazukiyo Doi*

**Kazukiyo Doi**

1925 Born in Saga prefecture on 10 March
1943 Finished training as a ship's engineer at the Merchant Navy Training School; employed by the Tōyō Shipping Company; served on board ship as engineer
1953 Left the Tōyō Shipping Company

## Trade union functions

1953 Member of the executive committee of Kaiin Kumiai (the All-Japan Seamen's Union); worked in the local union office at Shimonoseki (Kyushu) and in the Main Fishing Department of the union office at Yaizu; later served as head of the local union office at Shimonoseki
1963 Member of the central executive committee of Kaiin Kumiai
1971 Deputy chairman of Kaiin Kumiai
1980 Chairman of Kaiin Kumiai
1988 Resigned as Chairman of Kaiin Kumiai; serving as adviser since then

## Current functions

Chairman of Kaiin Kumiai; vice chairman of Dōmei; Chairman of Gyōsen Dōmei; member of the board of directors of Zenmin Rōkyō; chairman of the Asian and Pacific Regional Organisation of the International Confederation of Free Trade Unions; member of the Seamen's Central Labour Relations Commission; member of the Commission on Rationalisations in Shipping and Shipbuilding; member of the Commission on the

Social Security System; member of the Commission on the Promotion of the Coastal Fishing Industry

## Publications

'Nenkin kyakusen wo kenzō shiyo – keizai hatten wo sasaeta o-toshiyori ni yume wo' (Let's Create a Pension Passenger Boat – A Dream of the Elderly Who Helped Economic Development Along), *Asahi Shinbun*, 12 September 1983
'Kommei kara no dasshutsu – mittsu no jissen' (Escape from Confusion – Three Practical Ways), *Keiei to Rōdō*, May 1984
'Rōdō undō no rekishi wo fumae minshuteki rōdō sensen no kakuritsu wo' (Securing a Democratic Labour Front Based on the History of the Labour Movement), *Keiei to Rōdō*, October 1984
'Chūkyū ishiki wo buchikowase – rōdō undō no saisei to shakai no kasseika e' (Down with Middle-Class Consciousness – Toward a Regeneration of the Labour Movement and a Revival of Society), *Keiei to Rōdō*, April 1985
'Rōdō kumiai to fukushi katsudō' (Labour Movement and Social Welfare), *Keiei to Rōdō*, December 1985

## I Editor's Overview

Kaiin Kumiai (the All-Japan Seamen's Union) comprises 160,000 members and is the only Japanese union organised according to the industrial union principle. It was first established in 1921 (according to the Japanese way of counting, the year Taishō 10) and its outstanding position can in part be attributed to the fact that its tradition goes back to pre-war times.

Except for a short period immediately after the war, the union has generally advocated a moderate course of cooperation between employers and employees, and it occupies a central position on the right wing of the Japanese labour movement. Nevertheless, it has also been very tenacious in its attempts to improve working conditions of seamen with due consideration being given to the special aspects of their trade, and it has not refrained from organising long-term strikes.

This is especially true of the 92-day strike in 1972 which was led under the motto 'Struggle to Recover Humanity'. This exemplary labour dispute resulted from urgent demands put forward by the seamen and their families who faced a serious deterioration of working conditions because of technological innovations and rationalisation measures. Since then, Kaiin Kumiai has successfully concentrated on following a line of internal democracy corresponding to the needs of its members, and the revival of this movement has received much public attention.

## 'Fight Against 43,000 Dismissals' (1946)

During the war, seamen had the status of non-combatants. Nevertheless, the war took a dreadful toll among them: among crews alone there were 30,000 dead and 40,000 injured. As soon as the war was over, the seamen faced dismissals and deprivation caused by the high rate of inflation. Immediately after Japan's surrender they formed a movement with the aim of rebuilding their union. On 5 October 1945, a meeting was held at which the All-Japan Seamen's Union was founded. Two pre-war unions, Nihon Kaiin Kumiai (the Union of Japanese Seamen) in which the ordinary crew members had been organised, and Kaiin Kyōkai (the Association of Naval Officers), were merged into the new union.

When in the summer of the following year the Shipowners' Association announced plans for a staff reduction of 43,000 men, a labour dispute arose. During the struggle, the union split into two factions, one around the union chairman Hidekichi Koizumi (conservative) and another headed by the chairman of the struggle council, Matsujirō Tanaka (progressive). Led by the left wing, the struggle was continued in close cooperation with Sanbetsu Kaigi and with Kokutetsu Sōrengo which at the same time was confronted with plans to fire 75,000 of its members. On 10 September the scale of the dispute was widened to a strike covering the whole industry, and ten days later the union managed to achieve the complete retraction of the rationalisation plans and a victorious end to the dispute. However, after the strike the group around union chairman Hidekichi Koizumi enforced the expulsion of forty-eight leaders of the strike and established a conservative leadership of Kaiin Kumiai.

In the following period, Kaiin Kumiai and Zensen Dōmei were the leading protagonists in a movement which published the 'Declaration of the Four Industrial Federations' in 1952, which criticised Sōhyō for having allowed the labour disputes of the energy supply sector (Densan) and the coal mining industry

(Tanrō) to degenerate into purely political struggles. It again played a prominent role during the founding of Zenrō Kaigi (founded in 1954, the predecessor of Dōmei) and firmly established itself as a key member of the conservative labour movement.

## The 36-day strike (1965–6)

This labour conflict led to the establishment of a system within Kaiin Kumiai which determined the role of union officials as mere representatives subject to the members' directives. In the spring of 1965 during negotiations on the revision of the labour contract, the union postponed a final settlement of the wage issue until November and agreed to a compromise which included a provisional increase of 5 per cent of the base wage plus a non-recurring payment of 3,000 yen. At an extraordinary union conference in October, the unions decided to demand a further wage increase of 5,700 yen and entered into negotiations with the shipowners' organisation. Since the shipowners adamantly refused to give in, the union began the first wave of a strike on 27 November. The strike proceeded in four waves totalling 36 days until a final settlement was reached on 31 January of the following year. Finally, despite a mediation proposal by the Central Labour Relations Commission which demanded a provisional allowance of 2,800 yen for seamen serving on international lines and of 1,800 yen for those working on domestic lines, both sides agreed on a wage increase of only 650 yen.

Following the strike, dissatisfaction grew among the union members who were not content with such a meagre result in view of the expenditure of a protracted 36-day strike. Their criticism concentrated on the way the strike had been organised and on the union's leadership. Represented by Seiji Horitsugi (a member of the executive committee) a movement developed which called for the resignation of the union's deputy chairman, Haruo Wada, and the head of the steamship division, Kaneko, who had been the responsible leaders of the strike. Within two to three months, about 10,000 members gave their signatures in support of the call for these resignations, which far surpassed the number of 5,000 required by the union's statutes.

The support this movement enjoyed among the union members was a consequence of rationalisation measures carried out by the management during the period of high economic growth and the ensuing increased workload. The growing demand for low-priced transport of raw materials such as crude oil and steel in the 1960s led to a continuing wave of technological advances in shipping and in turn to the introduction of larger and larger vessels, specialised vessels, high-speed ships with stronger engines, and to increased automation and so forth. Concomitantly with these changes crew sizes were reduced, sailors had to perform additional and unfamiliar jobs, time at berth was shortened and shuttle services introduced. The burden caused by these innovations rested largely on the seamen and their families, who grew more and more dissatisfied with a union leadership which did not offer any resistance against such an intensification of labour.

The movement led to the resignation of the union's chairman Kumazō Nakachi, his deputy Haruo Wada and the division head Kaneko, and at a union conference in October Yutaka Nabasama was elected chairman, an election which marked a shift of power from the pre-war group to the post-war generation.

## The 92-day 'Struggle to Recover Humanity' (1972)

During the spring wage negotiations of 1971, Kaiin Kumiai accepted a final offer by the shipowners of a 14.4 per cent wage-hike and provisionally sealed the agreement on 9 April. However, the Steamship Department Committee was not satisfied with this settlement and refused to give its consent. Union members who were again confronted with continuing rationalisation measures and an increase of their workload considered the effort made by their leaders insufficient. As previously during the 36-day strike, the union members once again expressed their wish for internal democratisation of their organisation, and the opinions of ordinary workers now carried greater weight with the union leadership.

Their objections led to the resignation of the union leadership at an extraordinary union conference on 30 June, and a new leadership under chairman Koji Murakami and his deputy Kazukiyo Doi was elected. During the 31st regular general meeting which was called by the new executive, it was decided to abandon the union's traditionally cooperative course of action with regard to productivity increases and rationalisation measures, an approach which went back to pre-war times, and to adopt a line which better reflected the voices of the union's rank and file members. As a first step in this direction, the complaints put forward by the workers and their families who were pressed hard by technological innovations and rationalisation were included in a list of demands. The union called this a 'Struggle to Recover Humanity' and on 20 December entered into negotiations with the shipowners. The union carried on a 92-day strike until finally on 14 July 1972 an agreement was reached.

This strike, which in its scale was unprecedented in the history of Japanese shipping, was closely watched not only by Dōmei, but by all four national labour organisations, and Sōhyō, Chūritsu Rōren (the Federation of Independent Unions of Japan) and Shinsanbetsu (the National Federation of Industrial Organisations) declared their unreserved support. Dock workers, transport workers and other unions of related industries showed their solidarity. As a result, the Ministry of Transport submitted a mediation proposal which favoured the union's demands, and it became possible to reach a settlement.

### Results

Of the ten largest shipping companies in the world, seven are Japanese. In this dispute Kaiin Kumiai managed to achieve a victory against the opposition of the global shipping companies and showed the might of a labour organisation structured according to the industrial union principle. Since this dispute, Kaiin Kumiai has successfully continued its effort to establish a democratic labour organisation which reflects the demands of its rank and file members.

## II Lecture by Kazukiyo Doi

Amongst today's Japanese workers, there is a widespread notion of belonging to the middle classes, and in every house you find a television, a refrigerator and a private car. Their apartments may be quite small, and their families lead very crowded lives, but the Japanese generally feel that they are part of a middle-class society.

The young people of today do not know the life of earlier times when there was barely enough to live on. You get the impression that they actually enjoy leaving their food uneaten in restaurants. It is not really unjustified to claim that the Japanese are spoiled by their affluence or that they lead wasteful lives. To my mind, anyway, the young people of today enjoy a carefree life.

Is there still anybody who considers how it became possible to have such a life? It did not after all come out of the clear blue sky. Only because there were working men and women who produced goods, sold them and contributed to the rebuilding of the economy, Japan today has become an affluent country. Of course, Japanese workers also benefit from this prosperity, but the situation of today where everyone has a sufficient income has not been achieved without struggles. I would like you to think about who has created today's living conditions. I believe that few grasp the significance of the role the labour unions have played in the process.

Moreover, I believe that the Japanese people underestimate the importance of the role played by the Japanese merchant navy. Is it not a fact that in their daily lives they pay as much attention to shipping as to the air they breathe? If I get the chance I often talk about how the Japanese economy and the life of the Japanese would look if there were not a merchant navy.

Take for instance the noodle soup all of you are used to eating. The only real domestic ingredient in this soup is water, and in fact one could claim that you are not eating a Japanese noodle soup at all because its main ingredients have been imported from abroad. Likewise nearly all the necessary things for making *tōfu*[1] or *nattō*[2] are brought into the country from abroad, and only a very minor proportion of them are actually produced in Japan – to such a great extent does Japan depend on food imports from foreign countries. At the moment, Japan's self-sufficiency ratio of foodstuffs lies at about 30 per cent, perhaps even lower. But it is not only food; the raw materials required for producing clothes, for construction and for furnishing are mainly supplied from foreign countries. If you try to find goods which Japan has no need to import, you end up only with water, air, rice and fish. All the rest, be they iron and non-ferrous metals, foodstuffs, and so on, are mainly imported from abroad.

It seems as if surprisingly few people are aware of the fact that these basic materials are transported by ship. Anyone will recognise that a certain product is foreign, but hardly anybody will go so far as to think about the process of its distribution, i.e.

that it has been transported by ship. So if you were now to ask me, 'If there weren't any ships, would Japan be starving?' I'd reply, 'Yes!' The highly developed Japanese economy of today, and our standard of living, depend on our importing raw materials from abroad, processing them and exporting the finished goods. In this process, ships have a very significant role.

Anyone can understand this much. But if I were to ask you whether you have thought about the people manning these ships, hardly anyone of you will be able to reply in the affirmative. But because goods will be moved only if there are men who handle the ships, the seamen have a very important task to fulfil with regard to the Japanese economy and the living standard of the Japanese people. If I thus talk about the relevance of the unions, the merchant navy and the seamen, you will no doubt be able to understand the significance of Kaiin Kumiai for the Japan of today. This is the subject I want to speak about here.

## The seamen of the Meiji period (1866–1912)

Speaking of ships, in earlier times there were mainly dugout canoes and sailing boats, and in Japan until the beginning of the Meiji period sailing vessels and rowing-boats were used for transporting goods and people. However, after the onset of the industrial revolution in the eighteenth-century steamships were developed and engines began to replace sails as a means of propelling ships. With the beginning of the Meiji era, the first steamships were introduced into Japan. At first these Western-style steamships were commanded by Englishmen, while Japanese were employed only as crew members. But because it was unsatisfactory to have Westerners indefinitely occupying all important posts on the ships, the Japanese government and the shipowners trained seamen who then qualified as naval officers. Japanese were soon also able to command ships as captains and engineers and take them on international voyages. In 1894 the Sino-Japanese war broke out, and in 1904 there was a war between Russia and Japan. During this time the international maritime traffic between Japan and foreign countries intensified and when the Russian-Japanese war broke out, Japan possessed a shipping capacity of approximately 1 million tons and the crews were mostly made up of Japanese.

But in the period between the beginning of the Meiji era and the outbreak of the Russian-Japanese war, the qualifications of Japanese seamen were poor. Their working conditions too were not good. Since ancient times the seamen had done a very dangerous job which was characterised by the saying 'one plank away from hell'. They operated their ships in a stormy and difficult natural environment, and even if they served on a cargo-ship of 10,000 tons, their voyage was hazardous because of the state of the engines and the poor materials which were used for shipbuilding. Disasters often happened. Whenever a ship sank, many crew members lost their lives, and if these crew members all came from the same area, they left their wives behind and whole villages became known as 'widow ghettos'. The seamen thus did their work under life-threatening conditions, and it was easy for them to fall into the frame of mind 'life is here today but gone tomorrow'. Thus they often spent all of their pay in one evening on gambling and amusement.

The shipowners, who were aware of the situation of the seamen, exploited them with the attitude: 'Who cares about those guys?' Moreover, captains and engineers at that time were mostly Englishmen and had introduced the English-style class system on ships without any changes. The officers treated the ordinary crew members like slaves. Not only was their pay miserably low, but during the Sino-Japanese war and the Russian-Japanese war they were exploited for the transport of soldiers, weapons, ammunition and military goods to such an extent that even on the brink of death they had to work like madmen. But although in times of war the number of ships grew rapidly, most of them were no longer needed once the war was over, and the seamen lost their jobs. This situation occurred again and again throughout the Meiji period.

To my mind it was only natural that the Japanese seamen would develop a feeling of intense hatred towards the way they were treated. During the first decade of this century, the various groups of seamen such as engineers or telegraph operators therefore began to get together and talk among themselves, saying: 'This can't go on any longer. Even though we are workers, it is only natural for us to demand a human life.' They talked about what to do in order to receive better treatment and to raise their social status. However, at that time they were no match for the employers.

In 1911, the Japanese seamen for the first time launched a

labour conflict. At that time Nihon Sen'im Dōshikai (the Association of Japanese Seamen), a group which centred around the stokers of the Japan Mail Ship Company and was led by the chief stokers (a post comparable to that of a foreman in a factory), prevented twenty-two ships in Yokohama harbour from leaving port for three days. They entered into negotiations with their employers and were able to achieve an improvement of the seamen's working conditions. This was the first strike involving Japanese seamen.

## The establishment of the Union of Japanese Seamen (Taishō period)

Because this strike had been a success, seamen of other companies were encouraged to demand better treatment. In 1914 the First World War broke out; again the number of ships rapidly increased and many seamen were hired. But when the war was over, they again lost their jobs. After the Great Kantō Earthquake of 1923, shipowners reduced the seamen's pay because of the economic downturn. Then between 1928 and 1930 the worldwide economic depression occurred. In 1931 the Manchurian conflict began and the war with China developed, widening in 1941 into the Pacific War. In these times haunted by war, earthquakes and other catastrophes, it was always the workers who were fired and driven into poverty and despair. But in such times the labour movement developed. Also the movement of the workers at sea advanced rapidly. During the Meiji era workers had been forced to endure cruel working conditions, but during the Taishō and the pre-war Shōwa period they had gathered strength and were now able to express their demands and contribute to the solution of their problems by negotiating with the shipowners and the government.

The establishment of the Union of Japanese Seamen, which organised the ordinary crew members, occurred about sixty years ago on 7 May 1921. Earlier there existed only Kaiin Kurabu (the Club of Seamen), founded in 1896, which admitted only naval officers (in 1909 renamed Kaiin Kyōkai); this club, however, cannot be regarded as part of the labour movement. The first time the Club of Seamen resorted to measures resembling a labour dispute was in 1915. Nevertheless, the officers did not think of themselves as workers. Today, officers and crew members alike belong to Kaiin Kumiai but in pre-war times they were divided into Kaiin Kyōkai and the Union of Japanese Seamen. The Union of Japanese Seamen was founded in 1921, while Kaiin Kyōkai began to develop union-like activities in 1920.

It must be added, however, that although the Union of Japanese Seamen was founded in 1921, the labour movement was outlawed in those days. It was suppressed by Chian Iji Hō (1925, the Law on Preserving Public Peace and Order), and Chian Keisatsu Hō (1900, the Police Law on Preserving Public Peace and Order). If the labour movement started to offer any resistance against the government or the management, its members were threatened with prison sentences. If in those days workers said, 'Let's go on strike', their action was considered more or less an act of sabotage, as strikes were against the law. Because there was no law on labour unions, there was no legal protection for organisations representing the workers' interests.

## The development of the seamen's movement (early Shōwa period)

In 1928 the Union of Japanese Seamen presented a list of demands to the Shipowners' Association, which included such matters as assistance allowances for shipwrecked seamen – for instance the so-called condolence money paid to the families of those who had died at sea, or compensation for personal property of crew members lost in wrecks. This led to the first contract Japan had ever seen between employers and employees. In view of the fact that such an agreement was reached against the background of a hostile social environment, it marked a great success. In this era when no labour union law existed, even the unions on shore had not yet been able to sign any contract with the employers.

To explain this point in more detail: in 1926 the Association of Shipowners, the Union of Japanese Seamen and Kaiin Kyōkai established the Joint Merchant Shipping Council. To this Joint Council the Union of Japanese Seamen presented its demands concerning assistance allowances for shipwrecked seamen, and as a result of the ensuing deliberations, the Council accepted the demands as justified, whereupon a labour agreement was closed with the Association of Shipowners.

The signing of a labour contract in those days when no labour law yet existed was an extremely important precedent not only for the seamen's union, but likewise for the unions on land. This is an exceptionally interesting issue. The fact that despite the absence of a labour law employers and employees recognised each other's position and signed a labour contract automatically meant a recognition of the labour union's existence by the employers. But even the government accepted the contract, because the Joint Council was a body authorised by the government. Therefore the agreement between employers and employees was also recognised by the government, which was an epoch-making event unprecedented in Japanese history.

In June 1928 in the face of a strike on board 380 ships, another agreement was reached within the Joint Council concerning minimum wages for ordinary crew members. And by the end of that year a further contract was signed, which covered severance payments for employees leaving their companies and other matters. These were events which, to my mind, ought to be recorded in red ink in the annals of the Japanese labour movement.

By the way, in 1928 the total number of organised workers in Japan was about 400,000. Of these 120,000 belonged to Nihon Kaiin Kumiai and a further 20,000 to Kaiin Kyōkai. Thus the number of organised maritime workers was about 140,000, or 35 per cent of the Japanese organised workforce.

Unfortunately, however, the time in which the labour movement, albeit illegally, was able to achieve some of its goals ended in 1938. Afterwards the Japanese political system was perverted by militarism, and a time began in which the free discussion of demands concerning workers' rights and their living conditions was banned and the opposition of the people against those in power was broken. Those who tried to offer resistance were arrested by the police and thrown into prison. Under these circumstances the labour movement was also totally paralysed. In order to mobilise all forces for the war effort, Kokumin Sōdōinrei (the National Mobilisation Act) was passed and Dai Nippon Sangyō Hōkokukai, abbreviated as Sanpō (the Japanese Association for Service to the State through Industry) was established. From then on the Union of Japanese Seamen and Kaiin Kyōkai were unable to pursue any kind of union activities. The seamen, too, had to cooperate in the war effort, and in July 1940 Kaiin Kumiai, and in November of the same year Kaiin Kyōkai, were dissolved. Both were incorporated into the war-time Nihon Kaiin Hōkokudan (Organisation of the Merchant Navy for Service to the State).

From then on the Japanese merchant navy was controlled by the state and the Merchant Navy Committee exercised tight control. Not only were ships requisitioned from all shipping companies, but the seamen were conscripted too, a situation which lasted until the end of the war. The movement of maritime workers was thus extinguished. Most of the unions on land had already been dissolved, and the last flame preserved by the seamen's movement was finally blown out in 1940.

## New start of the seamen's movement after the war – the barrack ships dispute (1945)

After the end of the war in 1945, General MacArthur announced that the most important measure in reconstructing the country was building up a democratic system. At the same time he decreed a ban on all weapons, including warships, and in order to prevent Japan from acquiring big ships capable of invading foreign countries again, an upper limit of 5,000 tons was imposed on the size of Japanese ships, and the total tonnage of the Japanese navy was restricted to 1.5 million tons. Of course, voyages of Japanese ships to foreign ports were banned too, and the Japanese merchant navy was completely paralysed.

Immediately before the war Japan had possessed a merchant shipping capacity of 2,700 ships with a total of 6.3 million tons, a figure which during the war had grown to 8 million tons. By the end of the war, the merchant navy had been reduced to 900 ships with altogether 1.5 million tons. Ships of a total tonnage of 8 million tons had been sunk during the war and a further 2.5 million tons rendered unserviceable. More than 30,000 seamen had been killed, or had died of diseases or were missing in action. This figure amounted to about 43 per cent of all crew members (if the crews of fishing vessels are included, 60,000 had died altogether). If you compare these figures with those for the military forces, the army had suffered casualties of 25 per cent while the Japanese Navy had lost 16 per cent of its members. Although the seamen had the status of non-combatants, the ratio of victims among them was more than twice as high as among the soldiers who were combatants! These figures reflect the bitter price the seamen had to pay for the war.

Because of these heavy losses, a number of problems arose directly after the war. Around 6.5 million Japanese had been left behind in South-East Asia, Oceania and other regions, and these people had to be brought back to Japan. Because there were no aeroplanes, they had to be transported by ship, but there were no longer any ships in Japan. So the Supreme Command of the American Forces provided 209 vessels of the Liberty and the LST class which, manned by Japanese seamen, undertook the repatriation. According to initial plans the whole programme would take four years to complete, but because of the zeal of the Japanese seamen, it was able to be concluded within two years.

When the programme was initiated, there were no seamen left in the Tokyo area. Because their obligation to perform support duties had ended with the war, the seamen had returned to their home towns. So 5,000 seamen had to be recruited without delay. But as everyone was busy securing the survival of his family and, after all, the times were gone when someone simply recruited you and off you went, they had to be called in by a direct order from MacArthur. In those days an order from MacArthur carried about as much weight as an order from the emperor during the war, and the seamen who had returned to their home towns set out for Yokohama. Well, now they were in Yokohama, but there were neither food nor shelter for those 5,000 men. So two ships of the Liberty and one of the LST class which had been provided by the US forces were converted to 'hotels' to give the seamen a place where they could sleep. (Because these ships were quite run-down and seedy, they were called barrack ships.)

But food supplies were insufficient, and the seamen had to sleep on straw mats spread out on the steel planks. Dissatisfaction grew among the men who lived there, packed together like sardines. After all, they had the important task of repatriating those who had been left behind, but the way they were treated was simply unacceptable. So they sent demands to the government for an improvement in their treatment, but the government did not deign to react. A dispute thus developed which was called 'the strike on the barrack ships'. Finally, within a month a solution was found and the treatment became better, whereupon the repatriation programme was carried out smoothly.

At that time nearly the whole population was on the brink of starvation, and if you spoke of food you meant things like radish leaves, sweet potatoes and scraps of soya. In 1947 hunger demonstrations occurred in front of the Imperial Palace and a general strike was scheduled for 1 February. It was a period during which the whole energy of the people was directed at securing their bare survival.

## The 36-day strike (1965–6)

I will now speak to you about the 1950s, a period in which Japan's economy and society underwent fundamental changes. These changes were caused by the Korean War which led to a boom in demand for Japanese industry while all over the world problems such as the high rate of inflation which had been caused by the Second World War diminished. Now began a time in which the living standard of the population rose as a result of a revival of industrial activity caused by an economic upswing. In 1955 the movement to raise productivity was introduced to Japan from the United States; Nihon Seisansei Honbu (the Japan Productivity Centre) was established and a transfer of American technology under the guidance of leading Tokyo business circles took place. In the provinces, the local Chambers of Commerce and Industry (Shōkō Kaigisho) were the main driving forces of this movement. With the beginning of the 1960s, the technological revolution reached its full impact, and electronics were rapidly introduced to all areas of industrial production as well as to the office.

The same happened in maritime traffic. Because of the increasing use of electronic devices in the 1950s, the engines buried deep down in the ship's hull were now operated and controlled from outside, and by using radar equipment it was possible to detect the shapes of islands and other ships from a great distance. This is what was called the automation of shipping operation. Thanks to these technological advances, a ship which formerly had required a crew of fifty seamen now could be operated by forty, and a crew of forty could be reduced to thirty-five.

It cannot be claimed, however, that the rationalisation of ship operation made possible by technological innovations meant an increase in safety for the seamen in the true sense of the word. In order to ride the wave of high economic growth, shipping companies rapidly introduced new equipment designed to replace human labour and thereby reduce costs. But if managers carry out a rationalisation by introducing new machinery, what consequences must be expected? The result of such measures is unemployment, investment in new equipment will be used to cut back on the workers' wages, and the mental and physical stress on workers grows. A further consequence is pollution. Gases containing sulphuric acid and other harmful substances are released into the air, and factory sewage and other residues run off into rivers and the sea. There the substances sink and become sludge, and passing through fish they find their way into the human body where they cause diseases and death. In order to reduce operational costs, during the period of high economic growth many harmful substances were released into the air and dumped in the ground, the rivers or the sea, and nobody cared about the consequences this might have. The workers had to fear for their health and lives, and they became angry. This was the background of many labour conflicts between the mid-1950s and the mid-1960s.

Kaiin Kumiai organised a 36-day strike from late 1965 to 1966. Because of a continuing slump in shipping, the union had refrained from making exaggerated wage demands. There was a contract with the shipowners which called for a periodic wage rise and wages were increased annually according to this system. Moreover, once every two or three years we demanded an increase of the basic wage scale (called base-up). This adjustment we demanded first in 1963 and then again in 1965. In spring of that year our demands concerned only the improvement of working conditions, while with regard to wages we accepted a provisional rise of 3 per cent or 5,000 yen. This, however, did not mean a wage increase in real terms. So we came up with a demand for a real wage rise in November 1965. The shipowners, however, argued that the wage rise agreed to in the summer was enough, and a further demand for higher wages in the autumn would violate the agreement. They showed a surprising degree of distrust in the union and opposed our demands with an unexpectedly inflexible attitude.

For example, during the regular conference of the All-Japan Seamen's Union in November 1965 they circulated a pamphlet slandering the union and, worse still, they rejected out of hand a list of demands sent to the coastal shipping companies without giving it as much as a glance. The shipowners wanted to put the union's stamina to the test this time and were not prepared to make any compromise whatsoever. And they did not limit their action to mere words: the coastal shipping companies jointly invested 24 billion yen in anti-union measures and clearly aimed to destroy the union once and for all. By contrast, the total amount of money the union demanded was no more than 20 billion yen per year. The financial resources accumulated to beat down the strike thus exceeded the total sum of the union's demands.

This led to a strike which lasted 36 days; it began in November 1965 and went on until a settlement was reached the following year. On the face of it the strike focused on a wage rise, but indirectly it was a sign of the seamen's dissatisfaction over the way rationalisation affected their living conditions and it expressed their opposition to an increased workload and growing unemployment, that is, to the many disadvantages rationalisation measures had brought to their lives and their work.

## The resignation of the union leadership (1971)

Nevertheless, rationalisation in the shipping industry continued unabated. On land, matters were not much different. The *Bolivar Maru* was a big cargo vessel built in 1965; it had a tonnage of 54,000 tons, a length of 223 metres, was 31.7 metres wide and had a draught of 17.3 metres. On 5 January 1969 when everybody on shore was still resting after the New Year's festivities, this ship broke into two pieces off Nojimazaki in Chiba prefecture and sank. Of the 123 crew members on board, 31 were reported missing. In 1970, again shortly after New Year, another ship of the same class, the 60,000 tons *California Maru*, broke apart in the same area and also sank. Both ships had carried union members among their crews, and the union urged the government, shipowners and shipbuilders to investigate their responsibility for these disasters. We were convinced that shipyards had been pressed by the shipping companies to build cheaper vessels and, in order to reduce costs, to use excessively thin steel plates. In our opinion, important structural parts had not been reinforced and the ships had other serious faults. The bereaved families started legal proceedings and demanded compensation, and they were supported by the union in their fight. The proceedings went on for thirteen years until in 1982 an out-of-court settlement was reached in which nearly all demands of the dependents were met and the case concluded successfully.

But the fact which came to light in the disasters of the *Bolivar Maru* and the *California Maru* was that during the period of rapid economic growth extremely hazardous vessels of experimental design had been built, manufactured with thin steel plates and, for the purpose of cost reduction, welded together in a slipshod manner. In their pursuit of profit, the shipowners had used the seamen as guinea pigs. On the occasion of both accidents, Kaiin Kumiai proclaimed a Fight for Safety during a union conference. It put together an inspection team and began investigating the safety of all big cargo vessels built after 1965. As had been expected, all ships were found to have serious flaws. There were some shipowners who, when they heard about the inspection team, secretly tried to reinforce the weak spots of their ships. Not only ocean-going ships were found to be flawed, but in many cases fishing vessels also.

This was the way the union expressed its doubts about the policy of high growth pursued by the government and the companies. This policy, which came in the guise of an improvement in efficiency, in reality meant an increase of workload in the name of higher productivity. If high-growth policies lead to pollution, what is the sense of it all? Economic growth should facilitate the creation of a society in which people can lead healthy and culturally fulfilled lives, but actually many of them were disabled for life by pollution, others were driven to insanity and some died at sea in the disasters of the *Bolivar Maru* and the *California Maru*. In the face of these facts, it is only natural to question the meaning of rapid economic growth.

This is why in 1971 Kaiin Kumiai brought its opinion to the attention of the government and the companies, claiming that the campaign to raise productivity created serious problems. However, there were also union members who strongly supported the productivity campaign, while others recognised the difficulties it would lead to, and as a consequence there were internal differences within our union. But as cooperation in the campaign to raise productivity brought no benefit whatsoever to the workers, in the end their dissatisfaction could no longer be disregarded, and the union issued the above mentioned statement criticising the management and the government.

Because of the intensifying discontent among the workers, the

1971 spring wage round, which was accompanied by a strike on ships of the coastal shipping companies, was concluded with an agreement on a definitive wage increase. However, when this agreement, which carried the preliminary signatures of both sides, was submitted to the relevant union body for decision (the Steamship Department Committee), it was turned down, which created a serious problem. To my mind this was a sign of the mounting discontent of the workers. The union leadership interpreted this rejection as a no-confidence vote, took responsibility, and resigned. Because of these resignations, an extraordinary union conference was convened and a new leadership elected.

Actually, there had already been, for some time, critical voices among union members who accused the leaders of trying to create a type of union in which they assumed a quasi-professional role. For instance, during the 1966 dispute workers had demanded the resignation of some of the union officials because they regarded their leadership during the 36-day strike as bureaucratic and too oriented towards achieving an easy compromise. This problem in the end had been solved by a court ruling which brought about a mediation between the two parties concerned, but the case had underlined the fact that between the rank and file members and the union leadership there were many issues of controversy.

## The 'Struggle to Recover Humanity' (1972)

These events led us to the struggle for a new labour contract in 1972. In this year, apart from getting a wage increase, our main objective was to show the dissatisfaction of the union members with the conditions under which they had to do their work. When we started to address this issue, a number of matters of discontent emerged. In spite of the many previous strikes, there had accumulated over the years a considerable number of complaints which had never been suitably dealt with. Therefore we decided that on no account would we allow this state of affairs to continue and expressed our preparedness to go on strike, even if it took a hundred days to find a settlement. With this resolve we presented our demands to the shipowners and entered into negotiations. This struggle really took on large proportions: we organised a strike which lasted 92 days until a settlement was reached. Even in foreign countries strikes of such a scale are rare.

Kaiin Kumiai does not only include crews of the merchant navy. Seamen on fishing trawlers and harbour tugboats also belong to us. Seamen on international and domestic lines are organised in the Department of Merchant Navy Crews, while the Fishery Department not only comprises the crews of ocean-going trawlers and coastal fishing vessels, but also employees of the fish-processing industry. Domestic shipping also includes long-distance and short-distance car ferries as well as passenger boats, and finally there are the crews on tugboats and harbour transport vessels. All of these different sectors are united by our union. If you compare this situation with foreign unions, the difference is that most of the unions abroad are so-called craft or trade unions. Different professions are organised in different unions. For instance, plumbers have a union to which only plumbers belong, or painters are members of a union which restricts its membership to painters. In contrast to them, Kaiin Kumiai is an industrial union with subdivisions comprising all occupational groups whose work has any connection with the sea, and all ranks from the lowest deck hand to the sea captains.

This union now launched an all-out strike which brought Japanese shipping to a virtual standstill. However, even for a union as strong as ours such a strike is a very difficult affair. During a strike, no wages are paid to the workers, and if the strike goes on for a month, the members are left without income for that time. Thus the union must pay the living expenses of its members. Of course, it cannot pay their full wages and salaries, but it must at least guarantee an income high enough to secure their livelihood. So a strike is a very expensive matter. Accordingly, the way a labour dispute is organised is of extreme importance, and Kaiin Kumiai had planned its tactics in great detail. Nevertheless, the costs of the strike amounted to 2 billion yen (the 36-day strike of 1965 had cost 500 million yen).

We called this dispute the 'Struggle to Recover Humanity'. A characteristic demand was the one for a guaranteed number of days at berth. During the period of rapid economic growth, seamen who had brought a cargo vessel back home from abroad had to embark on a new voyage to foreign ports on the same day, without having even one day of rest in port. During their voyages, seamen cannot get together with their families. Only on their return are they able to meet their families again. If the ship stays in the port for three or four days, they can either return to their home towns or their families can travel to their port of call and they can enjoy their reunion in peace. But in the period of high economic growth (and actually things are not so much different today) a ship which arrived at a port in the evening was unloaded and reloaded during the night and at noon of the following day set out on the next voyage. The seamen therefore did not get any rest at all. They had no chance of seeing their wives and children, not even if they entered a Japanese port. The greater part of their lives they spent working at sea – such working conditions can only be described as inhuman. The union therefore demanded that shipowners let a ship stay in port for at least two days. For if you have two days in port, you can send for your family and take your children for a walk in a nearby park. As a consequence of our demand for a two-day stop-over the shipowners agreed to a one-day stay in port and to reimburse the travel costs of family members twice a year. However, to a seaman the difference between a one-day and a two-day stop-over is still a serious matter.

## The outcome of the strike

At present, the union has obtained working conditions for its members which guarantee that a crew member on an international line will spend nine months at sea and then have a vacation of three months. The seamen thus can take three months off in one year – compared to workers on land, this is not really much. Workers on land today have a five-day week with two days off, and they also have paid holidays. And if they must pay a visit to their children's school or kindergarten or if their wives are ill, they can take additional leave from the company. If you add up all of those different kinds of leave, you arrive at a total of 130 to 140 days per year. But the seamen have no more than ninety days. They have to work in a harsh natural environment and under difficult working conditions for nine months without a chance of seeing their wives and families, and only then can they take three consecutive months off. And yet the government, shipowners and transport companies on land claim that the seamen have too much leave.

The objections of the shipping companies go like this: because the seamen are on board for nine months and then have a three-month vacation, we have to hire relief seamen for these three months. Such a reserve is essential. On the other hand, the number of ships with a Japanese crew is steadily declining, and many shipping companies use foreign crews in their stead. If a shipowner mans his ships with South Koreans, Taiwanese, Filipinos, Indians or Bangladeshi, wage costs amount to a mere third or quarter of those for ships operated by Japanese seamen. Therefore, since the 1950s shipowners have increasingly come to the conclusion that it is advantageous to use foreign ships, provided these ships have the same tonnage. In 1971/2 (i.e. at the time of the 'Struggle to Recover Humanity') Japanese shipping companies already used foreign vessels. Only for ships whose operation requires specialised skills or those which serve on important lines with a fixed schedule where punctuality is essential can they not do without Japanese seamen. At present 700 million tons per annum of goods imported to and exported from Japan are transported by ship. Of these, more than 30 per cent are carried by foreign ships and the remaining 70 per cent by the Japanese merchant navy. Of all-Japanese merchant ships, 55 per cent are exclusively manned by Japanese, while the other 45 per cent have foreigners among their crews.

The number of Japanese ships is decreasing, but the union fights with all its energy to secure the employment of its members. The pay of a single seaman may be low, but taken together wage costs are huge. Shipowners say that for economic reasons they cannot accept these costs any longer and thus oppose the demands put forward by the union. They want to reduce the number of days off in order to increase the utilisation ratio of the workforce.

To my mind, in terms of performance Japanese seamen rank among the top in the world, but working conditions, employment problems and the workplace environment make extraordinary demands on them. This is why in 1972 we fought for seemingly insignificant improvements such as a time in port of at least one day in order to give the seamen a chance of seeing their families. We, as members of the Japanese ocean transport and fishing industry, are very much aware of the significance of our role in the development of the Japanese economy and the people's standard of living, and in spite of severe conditions we are investing all our strength in doing an outstanding job. Despite this, the

Japanese government and the managers do not always recognise the value of our labour. They only look at matters from a viewpoint of economic rationality. This is what creates dissatisfaction among us, and in order to be able also to guarantee a human life for seamen in future, we will not cease to fight to preserve and improve their existing working conditions.

## The future of the labour movement

In three or four years, all of you will become active members of our society. It is often claimed that today's workers, and not only the young ones, have lost their fighting spirit. Although this may be so, you should never forget that in a society where there are employers and employees, the employers will always have a stronger position. But regarding the employers as one's enemies in a conflict simply because one is weak is not right either, because employers are nothing without employees and vice versa. And as this is so, there is an unbreakable bond between them. Therefore there is no other way but that of a mutually beneficial coexistence, which requires a capacity for mutual understanding on a basis of equality and for taking into account the other side's interests as well. As long as the present social system continues to exist, I think this is the only natural attitude.

In today's society of highly educated people there is a transition from the old-style blue-collar workers to white-collar employees. Hence many old-fashioned practices of the traditional labour movement are no longer suitable. It is now necessary to establish a modern labour movement better adapted to the demands of the present era with its fast technological change. And a new type of union must be developed which is open to the ideas and demands of young people.

You will all become active participants in social life in due course, and I sincerely hope that you will contribute to the modernisation of today's labour unions. If under the present capitalist-liberal system unions are unable to freely communicate their opinion to the government, if they do not offer resistance against a dictatorial use of power and resist and prevent such developments, employees and the weaker groups within our society are heading for hard times indeed.

Of course, some of you will be directly involved with the labour movement, while others will not. Anyway, the important matter is that all of you think about how to lead a life which is useful to society. In this society characterised by constant change, how can young people lead such a useful life? In my opinion, no matter whether you join a company or become a public official, the most essential thing is that you find such a way of leading a socially useful life.

## Notes

1. *Tōfu*: soya bean curd.
2. *Nattō*: fermented soya beans.

# Appendix: Chronology of Events, 1896–1972

The following chronology lists events in the history of the labour movement which are outlined in this book. Also listed are the circumstances which made up the political background of these events.

## Before 1945

| | |
|---|---|
| 15 January 1896 | Establishment of Kaiin Kurabu (the Club of Seamen, organisation of naval officers); 1909 renamed Kaiin Kyokai ('Association of Naval Officers'). |
| 7 May 1921 | Establishment of the Union of Japanese Seamen (organisation of ordinary crew members). |
| July 1940 | Dissolution of trade unions. |
| 23 November 1940 | Establishment of Sanpō (Dai Nippon Sangyo Hōkokukai, the Association for Service to the State Through Industry). |
| 12 August 1942 | Outbreak of the Pacific War. |

## 1945

| | |
|---|---|
| 26 July | Publication of the Potsdam Declaration. |
| 15 August | The Emperor announces the end of the war. |
| 16 August | In Yokohama, seamen publish a manifesto calling for the establishment of a union. |
| 30 August | The Supreme Commander of Allied Powers, General MacArthur, arrives at Atsugi. |
| 11 September | General Headquarters (GHQ) orders the arrest of thirty-nine war criminals. |
| 18 September | Chinese forced labourers at the Mitsubishi Bibai coal mines revolt. |

| | |
|---|---|
| 19 September | GHQ issues guidelines for press publications (press code). |
| 25 September | Founding of the World Federation of Trade Unions. |
| 30 September | Sanpō is disbanded. |
| 2 October | Korean forced labourers at the Yūbari coal mines on Hokkaidō revolt. |
| 5 October | Establishment of Kaiin Kumiai (the All-Japan Seamen's Union). |
| 10 October | 3,000 political prisoners are released. |
| 11 October | MacArthur announces a five-point plan for reforms which among other points calls for the establishment and promotion of trade unions. |
| 15 October | Chian Iji Hō (The Law on Preserving of Public Peace and Order) and Chian Keisatsu Hō (the Police Law on Preservation of Public Peace and Order) are repealed. |
| 18 October | The Democracy Study Group of the *Yomiuri* newspaper is founded and works out a five-point list of demands. |
| 23 October | During a plenary meeting of Yomiuri employees, the five-point list of demands is adopted (First Yomiuri Dispute). |
| 24 October | Founding of the United Nations Organisation. |
| 25 October | At the *Yomiuri* newspaper the struggle for production control begins. |
| 2 December | GHQ declares that the managing director of the *Yomiuri* newspaper, Matsutarō Shōriki, is a suspected war criminal. |
| 5 December | Establishment of the Employees' Union at the Tōhō film studios. |
| 11 December | The union of the Keisei railway line fights for control over train services (until 29 December). |
| 12 December | End of the First Yomiuri Dispute; in a lead article, the newspaper is declared 'henceforth to be an organ of the people'. |
| 14 December | The union of the Tōshiba Horikawachō factory is founded. |
| 22 December | The Trade Union Law is passed. |
| 28 December | At a conference of the three Allied foreign |

ministers of the United States, Great Britain and the Soviet Union, the establishment of the Far Eastern Commission (FEC) and the Allied Council for Japan (ACJ) is announced.

**1946**

| | |
|---|---|
| 1 January | Start of the *People's Yomiuri*. |
| 1 January | The Emperor renounces his divine status. |
| 4 January | GHQ conducts a purge of militarist elements in the public service. |
| 11 January | Hitoshi Yamakawa proclaims the formation of a people's front. |
| 12 January | The five factory unions of the Tōshiba company in the Kawasaki area demand a five-fold increase in wages and establish production control (First Tōshiba Dispute). |
| 29 January | The First Tōshiba Dispute ends in an unqualified victory for the union. |
| 5 February | In Fulton, USA, Winston Churchill makes his speech on the 'Iron Curtain'. |
| 9 February | Establishment of Shinbun Tan'itsu. |
| 17 February | Establishment of the Tōhō Employees' Union. |
| 25 February | Establishment of Kokutetsu Sōrengō (the Union Federation of the National Railways). |
| 1 March | The Trade Union Law comes into effect. |
| 20 March | The Tōhō Employees' Union presents a list of demands aimed at improving working conditions and establishes production control (First Tōhō Dispute). |
| 6 April | End of the First Tōhō Dispute. |
| 10 April | First general elections after the war under the new electoral law. |
| 28 April | Nichieien is founded. |
| 1 May | First May Day festivities since the end of the war (first time in eleven years). |
| 3 May | First session of the Military Tribunal for the Far East. |
| 19 May | Big demonstration against the insufficient food supply (Food May Day). |
| 20 May | MacArthur declares that demonstrations are |

| | |
|---|---|
| | taking on excessive proportions. |
| 4 June | GHQ issues a warning against the editors of the *Yomiuri* newspaper because of a violation of the press code. |
| 12 June | The management of the *Yomiuri* newspaper orders the dismissal of chief editor Tōmin Suzuki and five other editors (Second Yomiuri Dispute). |
| 13 June | The government publishes a 'Declaration on the Maintenance of Social Order'. |
| 24 July | The National Railways announce plans for dismissal of 75,000 employees (Dispute of 15 September). |
| 30 July | Founding of the Second Union of the *Yomiuri* newspaper. |
| 1–3 August | Founding conference of Sōdōmei (the Japanese Federation of Trade Unions). |
| 19–21 August | Founding conference of Sanbetsu Kaigi (the Congress of Industrial Unions of Japan). |
| 21 August | The struggle of the seamen against 43,000 dismissals begins. |
| 5 September | Conference of Kokutetsu Sōrengō at Ujiyamada. |
| 10 September | The strike of Kaiin Kumiai develops into a strike of the whole shipping industry. |
| 14 September | End of the strike of the railway employees. |
| 14 September | The Tōshiba Union Federation in the Kantō area presents a three-point list of demands (October Struggle of Tōshiba). |
| 20 September | End of the strike of the seamen. |
| 29 September | Kokutetsu Sōrengō holds its Third Extraordinary Conference at Togura; the 'Fight for the Right to a Minimal Livelihood' begins. |
| 30 September | 'Walter incident' at Tōshiba. |
| | 1 October The October Struggle of Sanbetsu Kaigi begins (participation of the Tōshiba unions, Zentan – the Japan Coal Miners' Union and others). |
| 5 October | The industry-wide strike of the employees of newspapers, news agencies and the broadcasting service fails; only the broadcasting |

| | |
|---|---|
| | employees continue. |
| 5 October | Nichieien announces a strike of the entire industry for October (Second Tōhō Dispute). |
| 7 October | The Union of Electrical Power Workers (Densan) joins the October Struggle. |
| 13 October | Rōchō Hō (The Law on the Regulation of Labour Relations) is passed. |
| 16 October | End of the Second Yomiuri Dispute. |
| 3 November | Proclamation of the Japanese Constitution. |
| 12 November | 'Irvin incident' at Tōshiba. |
| 21 November | The Tōshiba unions end the October Struggle. |
| 26 November | Formation of the Joint Struggle Council of the Employees of the Public Sector (Zenkankō). |
| 3 December | End of the October Struggle at Tōhō. |
| 17 December | People's Congress demanding the 'Guarantee of a Minimal Livelihood' and the overthrow of the Yoshida cabinet. |
| 22 December | Densan ends the October Struggle (establishment of the Densan-gata wage system). |

**1947**

| | |
|---|---|
| 1 January | Prime Minister Shigeru Yoshida in his New Year speech denounces striking workers as 'lawless scum'. |
| | January the three Tōshiba Union Federations demand a minimum wage (Fourth Tōshiba Dispute and Fight Against a Wage System based on Independent Economic Viability); afterwards an impasse is reached until the dispute merges with the fight against the adjustment measures of the company in 1949. |
| 15 January | Establishment of the All-Japan Union Council for Joint Action in Labour Disputes (Zentō). |
| 18 January | Zentō announces a general strike for 1 February. |
| 31 January | MacArthur bans the planned general strike. |
| 31 January | The chairman of Zenkankō, Yashirō Ii calls off the general strike in an NHK broadcast. |
| 12 February | The Truman Doctrine is promulgated. |

| | |
|---|---|
| 8 March | The company Shin-Tōhō is founded. |
| 6 May | Founding of Densan (formation of a union according to the industrial union principle). |
| 1 June | The Katayama cabinet is formed (coalition of three parties, the Prime Minister belongs to the Socialist Party). |
| 5 June | Establishment of Kokutetsu Rōdō Kumiai or Kokurō (the National Railway Workers' Union). |
| 5 June | The Marshall Plan is announced. |
| 20 October | Formation of the Anti-communist League within Kokurō. |
| 30 October | The Tanrō (Japan Coal Miners' Union) is established. |

**1948**

| | |
|---|---|
| 6 January | US Secretary of the Army, Kenneth C. Royal, in a speech announces plans for 'transforming Japan into a fortress against communism in Asia'. |
| 23 January | The Tōhō management demands a revision of the labour contract. |
| 5 February | Zentei (The Japan Postal Workers' Union) decides on its strategy for the March labour disputes (regional struggles). |
| 10 February | The Katayama cabinet resigns. |
| 8 April | 270 employees of the Tōhō film studios are fired. |
| 12 April | Establishment of Nikkeiren (the Japanese Federation of Employers' Associations). |
| 22 July | Memorandum by MacArthur in which he advises that public employees are to be deprived of of their right to strike and have their right to collective bargaining restricted. |
| 25 July | The Head of the Labour Division of GHQ, James S. Killen, announces his resignation as a protest against MacArthur's memorandum. |
| 30 July | Zentei delares a 'state of emergency' for its organisation because of MacArthur's memorandum. |
| 31 July | The National Railway Workers' Union |

declares a 'state of emergency' for its organisation because of MacArthur's memorandum.

31 July — Cabinet Decree No. 201 is passed.

15 August — The Republic of Korea is proclaimed.

19 August — Enforcement of an interim order at Tōhō (strikers are evicted from the studios, 'the only thing which was lacking were the warships').

9 September — The Democratic People's Republic of Korea is proclaimed.

11 September — GHQ announces three principles concerning the structure of wages.

19 October — End of the Third Tōhō Dispute.

12 December — Kōrō Hō (the Law on Labour Relations in Public Enterprises) is passed.

16 December — The Chinese People's Liberation Army enters Beijing.

18 December — GHQ submits to the Japanese government nine principles concerning economic reconstruction.

**1949**

19 January — The unions of the United States, Great Britain and the Netherlands leave the World Federation of Trade Unions.

8 February — Mochikabu-kaisha Seiri Iinkai (The Commission for the Dismantling of Industrial Holdings) submits to Tōshiba a draft decree based on Kado Kaizairyoku Shūchū Haijo Hō (the Law on Economic Deconcentration).

10 February — The fight against plans for an adjustment of the company begins at Tōshiba (Fifth Tōshiba Dispute).

7 March — The Dodge Line is announced.

22 May — Revison of Rōdokumiai Hō (the Trade Union Law) and Rōchō Hō (the Law on Regulating Labour Relations).

30 May — Teiin Hō (The Law on Personnel Levels in the Administrative Organs) is passed.

1 June — Kōrō Hō (The Law on Labour Relations in Public Enterprises) comes into effect; the National Railways and the two monopoly

| | |
|---|---|
| | enterprises (tobacco and salt) are transformed into public enterprises. |
| 9 June | Start of the Jinmin Densha (People's City Railway). |
| 1 July | Plans for the dismissal of 95,000 employees of National Railways are announced. |
| 4 July | In the first wave of dismissals, National Railways fire 30,700 employees. |
| 5 July | Shimoyama incident. |
| | In the second wave of dismissals, the National Railways fire 63,000 employees. |
| 15 July | Mitaka incident. |
| 18 July | Dismissal of fourteen left-wing members of the struggle committee of Kokurō. |
| 23 July | Publication of the 'Decree No. 0' by Kokurō (the fired members of the Struggle Committee are expelled from the union). |
| 17 August | Matsukawa incident. |
| 7 September | Proclamation of the Federal Republic of Germany. |
| 1 October | Proclamation of the People's Republic of China. |
| 7 October | Proclamation of the German Democratic Republic. |
| 14 October | Kokurō is revived under the leadership of the Mindō wing. |
| 4 November | At Tōshiba, a second union is founded. |
| 16 November | End of the Fifth Tōshiba Dispute. |
| 23 November | Accompanied by the head of the GHQ Labour Division, Amis, five representatives of the Japanese union movement travel to Europe to attend the founding conference of the International Confederation of Free Trade Unions. |
| 28 November–5 December | Founding conference of the International Confederation of Free Trade Unions. |

**1950**

| | |
|---|---|
| 10 January | US Secretary of State Acheson announces plans for enlarging American military bases in Japan and on Okinawa. |

| | |
|---|---|
| 16 January | The Socialist Party is split into a right and a left wing. |
| 31 January | US President Truman orders the building of the hydrogen bomb. |
| 14 February | The Soviet Union and the People's Republic of China sign a treaty of friendship, cooperation and mutual assistance. |
| 17 May | Tōhō announces plans for a consolidation of the company involving the dismissal of 35 per cent (1,315 employees) of its entire staff (Fourth Tōhō Dispute). |
| 6 June | MacArthur announces the expulsion from the public service of twenty-four leading officials of the Communist Party of Japan. |
| 25 June | Outbreak of the Korean War. |
| 11–12 July | Founding conferences of Sōhyō. |
| 24 July | Newspapers, news agencies and the broadcasting service start a purge of left-wing elements (red purge). |
| 10 August | The formation of a Police Reserve Force is announced (predecessor of the Japanese Self-Defence Forces). |
| 13 October | 10,000 persons suspected of being war criminals are re-admitted to public office. |
| 28 December | End of the Fourth Tōhō Dispute. |

## 1951

| | |
|---|---|
| 1 January | MacArthur stresses the need to rearm Japan. |
| ? March | Nichieien is dissolved. |
| 10 March | At its 2nd Conference, Sōhyō adopts the 'Four Principles for Peace' (this step marks the organisation's development 'from a chicken to a gander'). |
| 28 April | Sōdōmei is dissolved. |
| 1 June | A 'Group for the Revival of Sōdōmei' holds a conference with the purpose of re-establishing Sōdōmei. |
| 20 June | 69,000 previously banned persons are re-admitted to public office (first re-admission). |
| 6 August | 13,900 previously banned persons are re- |

| | |
|---|---|
| | admitted to public office (second re-admission). |
| 4 September | Start of a conference in San Francisco whose purpose is the signing of a Peace Treaty with Japan. |
| 8 September | AMPO is signed. |

**1952**

| | |
|---|---|
| 20 January | Conference of the right-wing Socialist Party. |
| 28 January | Conference of the left-wing Socialist Party. |
| 1 February | Strike against staff reduction and for wage increases at the Ube Kōsan company. |
| 14 April | Strike of Densan. |
| 1 May | 'Bloody May Day' incident. |
| 14 July | The Subversive Activities Prevention Act is passed. |
| 11 September | Establishment of Tanpukyō. |
| 16 December | End of the 63-day strike in the coal mining industry. |
| 18 December | The strike of Densan fails. |
| 23 December | Zensen Dōmei, Kaiin Kumiai and other unions publish the 'Declaration of the Four Industrial Federations' in which Sōhyō is criticised. |

**1953**

| | |
|---|---|
| 5 August | The Law on Limiting the Right to Strike (official title: Law on Limiting the Types of Labour Disputes in Electric Power Supply and the Mining Companies) is passed. |
| 7 August | Mitsui Mining Co. announces a staff reduction of 6,739 employees as an adjustment measure ('113-Day Fight Without Heroes'). |
| 27 November | End of the Miike strike. |

**1954**

| | |
|---|---|
| 22 April | Founding of Zenrō Kaigi with Minoru Takita as its chairman. |

| | |
|---|---|
| 3 June | Start of the labour dispute at the Ōmi-Kenshi Silk Mills. |
| 1 July | Founding of the Japanese Self-Defence Forces (Army, Navy and Air Force). |
| 12 July | At the 5th Sōhyō Conference, Minoru Takano and Kaoru Ōta compete for the post of general secretary; Minoru Takano is re-elected for a fourth term in office. |
| 16 September | End of the Ōmi-Kenshi labour dispute. |

**1955**

| | |
|---|---|
| 22 January | Sōhyō joint spring wage offensive with eight industrial federations (beginning of the spring wage offensives). |
| 14 February | Founding of Nihon Seisansei Honbu (the Japan Productivity Centre). |
| 26 July | 6th Sōhyō Conference: Akira Iwai is elected general secretary; start of the Ōta-Iwai line. |
| 13 October | The right-wing and the left-wing Socialist Parties reunite. |
| 15 November | Unification of the conservative forces: founding of Liberal Democratic Party (LDP) |

**1958**

| | |
|---|---|
| 21 July | 7th Sōhyō Conference: Kaoru Ōta is elected general secretary. |
| 15 September | Joint struggle of Nikkyōso (the Japan Teachers Union) against an evaluation system introduced by the education authorities. |
| 8 October | Sōhyō announces its intention to prevent a revision of the Police Service Act. |

**1959**

| | |
|---|---|
| 19 January | Mitsui Mining Co. presents plans to the employees' union for the adjustment and reconstruction of the company. |
| 28 August | Mitsui Mining Co. announces a staff reduction of 4,580 employees in all company mines |

| | |
|---|---|
| | (among them 2,200 redundancies at the Miike mines). |
| 6 November | Mitsui Mining Co. informs the Miike union of its intention to fire 2,000 individually selected employees, among them 300 union activists. |
| 11 December | Mitsui Mining Co. fires 1,297 employees who had rejected voluntary retirement from the company. |

**1960**

| | |
|---|---|
| 6 January | In negotiations on the revision of AMPO, an agreement is reached. |
| 19 January | The revised AMPO is signed in Washington. |
| 24 January | Founding conference of the Democratic Socialist Party. |
| 25 January | Lock-out at Mitsui Mining Co.; the Miike union embarks on a strike of unspecified duration. |
| 17 March | Founding of the second Miike union. |
| 29 March | The miner Kiyoshi Kubo is murdered at Miike. |
| 1 April | 14th united action for the prevention of AMPO; three industrial federations and forty-three unions call a 24-hour strike. |
| 15 April | 15th united action for the prevention of AMPO; a petition carrying 70,000 signatures is handed to parliament; clashes between riot police and students. |
| 17 May | Sōhyō organises a mass meeting at the pitheads of the Miike mines in which 100,000 people participate. |
| 20 May | The Liberal Democratic Party forces AMPO through parliament. |
| 10 June | 'Hagerty incident'. |
| 15 June | The female student Michiko Kanba is killed in a clash between riot police and students. |
| 19 June | AMPO comes into effect. |
| 20 June | 19th united action for the prevention of AMPO; 111 unions and a total of 5.4 million people take part in mass demonstrations. |
| 20 July | The Central Labour Relations Commission |

| | |
|---|---|
| | starts mediating in the Miike dispute; a clash between riot police and the union is avoided. |
| 10 August | Third mediation proposal by the Central Labour Relations Commission under its chairman Fujibayashi. |
| 1 November | The Miike union announces the strike to be over and calls on its members to resume work. |

**1965**

| | |
|---|---|
| 27 November | Kaiin Kumiai presents its demand for a wage-hike (36-day strike). |

**1966**

| | |
|---|---|
| 31 January | The strike of Kaiin Kumiai is concluded with an agreement. |
| 15 April | Within Kaiin Kumiai, a movement demanding the resignation of part of the leadership emerges. |

**1971**

| | |
|---|---|
| 12 April | The Steamship Department Commission of Kaiin Kumiai refuses to accept an already negotiated wage agreement. |
| 30 June | Extraordinary conference of Kaiin Kumiai; election of a new union leadership. |

**1972**

| | |
|---|---|
| 10 January | Founding of the Union of Naval Radiotelegraphy Officers. |
| 11 April | Kaiin Kumiai starts strike action (92-day 'Fight for the Recovery of Humanity'). |
| 14 July | The strike of Kaiin Kumiai is concluded with an agreement. |

## Translation of Japanese organisational and statutory names

| Full Japanese name | Japanese abbreviation | Full English name | English acronym |
|---|---|---|---|
| Chian Iji Hō | | Law on Preserving Public Peace and Order | |
| Chian Keisatsu Hō | | Police Law on Preserving Public Peace and Order | |
| Chūō Keizai Saiken Iinkai | | Central Commission for Economic Reconstruction and Consolidation | CCERC |
| Chūō Rōdō Iinkai | Chūrōi | Central Labour Relations Commission | CLRC |
| Chūritsu Rōren | | Federation of Independent Unions of Japan | FIUJ |
| Dai Nippon Sangyō Hōkoku Kai | Sanpō | Association for Service to the State through Industry | ASSI |
| Denki Rōren | | Federation of Unions of Electrical Machinery and Instruments | FUEMI |
| Densan | | Industrial Union of Electrical Power Workers | IUEPW |
| Dōmei | | Japanese Confederation of Labour | JCL |
| Gōka Rōren | | Japanese Federation of Synthetic Chemistry Workers' Unions | JFSCWU |
| Jeitai | | Japanese Self-Defence Force | JSDF |
| Jichirō | | All-Japan Prefectural and Municipal Workers' Union | AJPMWU |
| Jinmin Densha | | People's City Railway | |
| Kado Keizartoku Shūchū Haijo Hō | | Law on Economic Deconcentration | |
| Kaiin Kumiai | | Japan Seamen's Union | JSU |
| Kaiin Kyōkai | | Association of Naval Officers | ANO |
| Kansai Rengōkai (of Tōshiba) | | Kansai Union Federation | KSUF-T |
| Kantō Rengōkai (of Tōshiba) | | Kantō Union Federation | KTUF-T |
| Kinzokurōkyō | IMF-JC | Japan Council of International Metal Workers' Federation | IMF-JC |
| Kokutetsu Rōdō Kumiai | Kokurō | National Railway Workers' Union | NRWU |
| Kokutetsu Sōrengō | | Union Federation of the National Railways | UFNR |
| Kōkyō Kigyōtai-tō Rōdōkumiai Kyōgikai | Kōrōkyō | Union Council of Public Companies and State Owned Enterprises | UCPCSOE |
| Kōmuin Hō | | Law on Public Servants | |
| Kōrō Hō | | Law on Labour Relations in Public Enterprises | |

| | | | |
|---|---|---|---|
| Kōrōi | | Committee of the Public Sector Labour Relations | CPSLR |
| Mochikabu-kaisha Seiri Iinkai | | Commission for the Dismantling of Industrial Holdings | CDIH |
| NHK Rōdōkumiai | Nipporō | Employees Union of the Japan Broadcasting Association | EUJBA |
| Nihon Eiga Engoki Rōdō Kumiai | Nichieien | Industrial Union of Japanese Film and Theatre Workers | IUJFTW |
| Nihon Kaiin Kumiai | | Union of Japanese Seamen | UJS |
| Nihon Keieisha Danta Renmei | Nikkeiren | Japanese Federation of Employers' Associations | JFEA |
| Nihon Rōdōkumiai Kaigi | Nichirō Kaigi | Japanese Congress of Unions | JCU |
| Nihon Rōdōkumiai Sōrengōkai | Rengō | Japanese Trade Union Confederation | JTUC |
| Nihon Sen'in Dōshikai | | Association of Japanese Seamen | AJS |
| Nihon Tankō Shufu Kyōgikai | Tanpukyō | Collective Committee of Wives of Japanese Miners | CCWJM |
| Nihon Kyōshokuin Kumiai | Nikkyōso | Japan Teachers' Union | JTU |
| Rishokusha Koyō Hō | | Law on Redeployment of Dismissed Employees | |
| Rōchō Hō | | Law on Regulation of Labour Relations | |
| Sanbetsu Kaigi | | All-Japan Congress of Industrial Unions | AJCIU |
| Sankōren (of Mitsui) | | Mitsui Miners Union | MMU |
| Sanrengōkai | | Tōshiba Consultation of the Three Local Unions (Kanto, Kansai, Tohoku) | TCTLU |
| Sansharen (of Mitsui) | | Mitsui White-collar Employees Union | MWEU |
| Seisaku Suishin Rōso Kaigi | | Union Council for the Promotion of Political Measures | UCPPM |
| Sekitan Kōgyō Renmei | | Association of Coal Mining Companies | ACMC |
| Senshu Kyōkai | | Shipowners' Association | SA |
| Shinbun Tan'itsu | | Industrial Union of Newspaper, News Agency and Broadcasting Employees | |
| Shinsanbetsu | | National Federation of Industrial Unions | NFIU |
| Shōkō Kaigisho | | Chambers of Commerce and Industry | CCI |
| Sōdōmei | | Japanese Federation of Trade Unions | JFTU |
| Sōhyō | | General Council of Trade Unions of Japan | GCTUJ |
| *tan'i kumiai* | | single factory unions | |
| Tanrō | | Japanese Federation of Coal Miners Unions | JFCMU |
| *tansan* | | industrial federations of enterprise unions | |
| Teiin Hō | | Law on Personnel Levels in the Administrative Organs | |
| Tekkōrōren | | Japanese Federation of Steel Workers' Unions | JFSWU |
| Tetsurō | | National Railways Workers' Union - second union | NRWU |

| | | | |
|---|---|---|---|
| Tōhō Jūgyōin Kumiai | | Tohō Employees Union | TEU |
| Tōhō Rōdōkumiai | | Tōhō Enterprise Union | TEU |
| Tōhoku Rengōkai of Tōshiba | | Tōhoku Union Federation (Tōshiba) | TUF-T |
| Tōshiba Rōren | | Tōshiba Union Federation | TUF |
| Zen Nihon Jidōsha Kōtsū Rōdōkumiai | Zenjikō | National Federation of Automobile Transport Workers' Union | NFATWU |
| Zen'nōrin | | Union of Forest and Agricultural Workers | UFAW |
| Zen Kankōchō Kyōtō Iinkai | Zenkankō | Committee of Joint Struggle of Government and Public Corporations Workers Unions | CJSGPCWU |
| Zen Nihon Eiga Engoki Rōdōkumiai | Zen'eien | Federation of Cinema and Theatre Workers' Unions | FCTWU |
| Zen Nihon Jidōsha Sangyō Rōdōkumiai | Zenji | Industrial Union of Japanese Automobile Workers' | IUJAW |
| Zen Nihon Kaiin Kumiai | Kaiin Kumiai | All-Japan Seamen's Union | AJSU |
| Zenka Dōmei | | National Union Federation of the Chemical Industry | NUFCI |
| Zenkoku Kinzoku | | Industrial Union of Metal Workers | IUMW |
| Zenkoku Minkan Rōdōkumiai Kyōgikai | Zenmin Rōkyō | Japanese Private Sector Trade Union Council | JPSTUC |
| Zenkoku Minkan Rōdōkumiai Rengōkai | Zenmin Rōren | Japanese Private Sector Trade Union Confederation | JPSTUC |
| Zenkoku Rōdōkumiai Renraku Kyōgikai | Zenrōkyō | The Consultation of Trade Unions of Japan | CTUJ |
| Zenkoku Rōdōkumiai Sōrengō | Zenrōren | All-Japan Trade Union Confederation | AJTUC |
| Zenkoku Rōdōkumiai Kyodetōsō Iinkai | Zentō | National Committee for Joint Strike Action | NCJSA |
| Zennitsū | | Union of the National Transport Company | |
| Zenrō Kaigi | | All-Japan Labour Union Congress | AJLUC |
| Zensen Dōmei | | Japanese Federation of Textile Workers' Unions | JFTWU |
| Zentan | | Industrial Union of Coal Miners | IUCM |
| Zentei | | Japan Postal Workers Union | JPWU |

# Index